TRUTH IS A TOTAL DEFENSE:

MY FIFTY YEARS IN TELEVISION

TRUTH IS A TOTAL DEFENSE: MY FIFTY YEARS IN TELEVISION

BY STEVEN BOCHCO

DEDICATION

For my children, Melissa, Jesse, and Sean

CONTENTS

1

In the summer of 2010, my wife Dayna and I were driving north on Interstate 5 through California's Central Valley, bound for our home in Napa. It's roughly a six-hour car drive, and we'd always make a pit stop at the Harris Ranch, an enormous working ranch, hotel and restaurant complex about halfway between L.A. and Napa.

It was July 16th, a Friday, and hot. About an hour north of Harris Ranch, I started feeling a little queasy. I thought it was indigestion. But within minutes, what I thought was indigestion turned into chest pain, then hot burning pain on the left side of my neck, radiating down the inside of my left arm. I started to sweat. "Holy shit," I said to myself. "I'm having a heart attack and I'm in the middle of East Bumfuck, California. If I call 911, where will they take me?" So I kept driving, which was pretty stupid, I admit, but as the saying goes, denial is not a river in Egypt.

After about another hour of driving, during which I never said a word to Dayna, my symptoms began to abate, and by the time we got to Napa, I was feeling better, and I'd pretty much talked myself out of the idea that I'd had a heart attack.

But at the house, an hour later, the symptoms returned full-blown, and I told Dayna to get me to a hospital. I said the dreaded words out loud for the first time: "I think I'm having a heart attack." Dayna didn't believe it. I'm too fit, too healthy, etc. "Well, I'd rather be a live hypochondriac than a dead schmuck," I said, and off we went to St. Helena Hospital, which, it turns out, has a world class cardiac care unit. Napa Valley isn't exactly the sticks, and St. Helena Hospital is indicative of the wealth and philanthropy that characterizes Napa Valley's lucrative wine industry.

I walked in the door of the Emergency entrance and told the young woman in reception – which on a Friday evening at 5 pm was virtually empty – that I was having chest pains. Within ninety seconds I was on my back in an examining room, shirt off, hooked to an EKG machine. The on-call cardiac surgeon, Dr. James Lies (a helluva name for a doctor – but it's pronounced *Lease*), happened to be on the premises, and after looking at the EKG printout, declared what I already knew – I'd had a myocardial infarction, aka a heart attack. I was immediately wheeled into a cath lab, and the last thing I remembered was being told by the nurse that he was going to shave my groin.

I woke up an hour later, pain free and feeling fine. Dayna was there in the hospital room with me, and Dr. Lies told me I'd had a blockage in my left circumflex artery, and that after inserting a stent, the artery was once again functioning normally. I was kept in the hospital for two nights, primarily as a precaution against bleeding from the femoral artery, which was the entry point in the groin for the catheter that Dr. Lies snaked up into my heart.

I was released from the hospital's care on Sunday morning, and we drove home to Los Angeles on Monday. It was, all in all, no more than a lousy weekend.

But that's the point: I'd had a heart attack, and basically all it did was ruin my weekend. Who knows if, twenty-five years ago, I would have even survived?

When my father was diagnosed with prostate cancer in the early nineteen seventies, I watched him struggle with impending death. As his cancer spread over the next two years, and it became clear to all of us that he wasn't going to survive, he shut down emotionally and was practically non-responsive to my pleas that he share what he was going through with me. He was too angry and scared and, when he finally died, I felt as if both of us had missed out on an important opportunity. His was an opportunity to unburden himself of fears, regrets, and a lifetime of grievances. Mine was an opportunity to bond with him, tell him how much I loved him, and hold his hand (literally and figuratively) during this painful and frightening time.

What I learned from my father's death was that dying is your last act of parenting – an opportunity to include your children in the end-of-life process, and teach them by example that dying can be done with dignity, courage, love, and gratitude. I promised myself that I would include my kids in the journey in ways that my own dad couldn't.

Of all the ways I had imagined myself dying in the course of my lifetime, I never thought for one moment that a heart attack would ever do me in. I had always imagined dying a more linger-ing, "romantic" death, not unlike my father's, and that I would die at home, surrounded by my loving wife and children. Cue the vio-lins. But a heart attack? No. That's too fast. Death by heart attack wouldn't even give me a moment to reflect on my own passing. And what about all that beautiful stuff about including my kids in the journey?

The moral of the story is that life will fuck you up at every turn. You don't get to choose how you die, and generally you're too busy living in the moment to choose how you live.

2

Four years later, on the morning of June 16, 2014, I was taking my usual three to four mile morning walk, and at the end of it I felt a little fatigued. I'd been experiencing that same fatigue after my walks for several weeks, but usually within ten minutes or so, the feeling was gone. Nevertheless, it felt odd to me, and I decided to have it checked out. I thought it might be a common side effect of the statin meds I was on. A simple blood test would reveal if that were the case, so the next morning I went over to my doctor's office for a blood draw.

My doctor and close friend, Bob Koblin, called me three hours later. "Where are you?" he asked me.

"I'm in my office," I said. "Why?"

"I'd rather not have this conversation over the phone. Can you come over?"

As I hung up the phone I could feel the blood draining from my face. I walked out to my car, and my first thought was, "I have leukemia." My grandmother had died of it when I was a child, and I guess that, at some unconscious level, I thought it was in my genetic tide pool. My second thought was, "I'm a dead man."

During the twenty-minute ride over to Bob's office, I tried to calm myself. I knew he'd never ask me to come to him like that if it wasn't serious, but I tried to avoid signing my own death warrant prematurely.

When I arrived at Bob's office, he got right to it. My blood panel was totally screwy. He wasn't sure why, but he obviously knew – or suspected – it was something serious. Now I was truly terrified. Bob loaded me into his car and personally drove me over to a prominent hematologist in Beverly Hills, Barry Rosenbloom, who took another blood test that confirmed the earlier one. Barry's first instinct was that I had a relatively mild form of lymphoma that was treatable, long term – *long term*: music to my ears – with medication. The best-case scenario was that something else would kill me before the lymphoma. Barry also wanted to give me a bone marrow test on the spot, to confirm his initial suspicion. If you've never had one, it's kind of scary. The pain wasn't as bad as I thought it would be – Barry injected me with a numbing agent first – but in order to withdraw the marrow, a needle is inserted deep into your hip bone, and you can hear the crunching of the bone as the needle goes into it. Bob Koblin held my hand throughout the entire procedure, a gesture of friendship I will always be grateful for.

The preliminary diagnosis, based on the bone marrow analysis, was that whatever I had was not a simple lymphoma, but a more advanced form of leukemia. Needless to say, I was scared shitless.

When we got back to Bob's office, I asked him to call Dayna and explain to her what was going on. I didn't trust myself to keep my composure as I told my wife I might have a fatal disease. Unlike the previously described heart attack four years earlier, this situation wasn't going to yield to a quick, surgical intervention. I was heading into a long tunnel, and I could only hope that the light at the other end wasn't a train.

And, in fact, the news over the next several days went from bad to worse. The lab at Cedar Sinai Hospital had diagnosed my disease not as lymphoma, but as full-blown leukemia. My marrow sample was sent to several other labs, where the diagnosis was refined and confirmed. I had a leukemia that was so rare, there'd only been a couple of hundred cases diagnosed. For those of you keeping score, it's called Blastic Plasmacytoid Dendritic Cell Neoplasm. I don't know what the hell it means, either.

Treatment for this leukemia would ultimately require lengthy hospitalization, three rounds of chemotherapy, and finally, for dessert, a bone marrow transplant.

To this point, I hadn't told anyone what was going on, but now I knew I needed to share my situation with my family and closest friends, so I emailed this letter to about fifty people:

Sent by: Steven Bochco
Date: June 23, 2014
Subject: Shit happens

Dearest Friends,

I'm writing to all of you collectively because it's going to be too big a pain in the ass to have this conversation individually with each of you.

I've been diagnosed with a rare form of leukemia, or as it's known in the ghetto, blood cancer. It's so rare (a couple of hundred cases they know of) they don't even know technically whether it's leukemia or just lymphoma. It's got a fancy name I can't spell or pronounce. And who gives a shit, anyway. The bad news is, it's going to be a nasty three to six months upcoming for me. It'll start with a cycle of chemo. I will lose my hair. (Can't wait to see that!) I will look like shit and feel like shit. Then, when the cancer is in remission, they'll put me in the hospital for a couple of weeks, where more chemo will kill my bone marrow cells. This is the scary time, since without an effective immune system, I'm vulnerable to infection. So, no tongue kissing with any of you for a while. I will then undergo a bone marrow transplant. Should that go according to plan, my new marrow will commence growing blood cells, and I should get stronger over the course of some weeks, though I'll have to be on anti-rejection drugs for awhile. This is also a vulnerable time, so the above cautionary re swappage of bodily fluids remains in place. The good news is, I won't have to be on these drugs indefinitely and, again, if all goes according to plan, this treatment won't simply put me in remission, but will actually affect a total cure. Hopefully, by end of year I should be totally back on my feet, feeling strong, working out, combing my hair, and whipping my skippy.

I wanted you all to know this from me directly, and not through the grape vine, because there may be times when I feel shitty, or vulnerable, or embarrassed, and won't want to see people, or can't really see people. But please know that when this is all behind me, and I am healthy and cured and planning to live to be a hundred, I am going to have a great big celebratory party and tongue kiss everyone!

I'm not much for prayer or religion, but I will be strengthened by all your good wishes and hopes for a successful result.

Much love,

Steven

Then I emailed my only sibling, my sister, Joanna.

From: Steven Bochco
Date: June 24, 2014 at 3:06 PM Pacific Daylight Time
Subject: Shit happens

Hi Joanna,
Hope you're all well and happy.
Right now, I'm neither.
I need to fill you in. Whatever our family bullshit has been over the years, it is family, and you need to know what's going on: I've been diagnosed with a pretty rare and complicated form of leukemia. I'm still in the middle of various tests, I've got Cedars, UCLA, and City of Hope involved (they're all tops in the field), but here's what I know at the moment: My leukemia is called blastic plasmacytoid dendritic cell neoplasm, with a surrounding cell complication (they think) called myelo dysplastic syndrome that might involve a separate but simultaneous treatment, which further complicates matters. The goal is to get all of it into remission so that they can then perform a bone marrow transplant. That's the riskiest part of the deal, apparently, because they have to completely destroy my existing bone marrow (aka my immune system) in order to transplant the new one. During this time, I will be profoundly susceptible to all kinds of dangerous

infections, which is why, during that four to six week period of time, I'm kept pretty much in isolation. Every doc I've talked to says that City Of Hope is the best place to be, and I'm meeting with those docs next week. In the meantime, I'm having more tests performed, a Cat Scan tomorrow, more blood evaluations, etc., and by the time I meet with the honcho at City Of Hope, they should have some sort of consensus on my treatment protocol. It's going to be a long and nasty four to six months, and if I survive all of that, there's a nervous year or so beyond that, but once that year is passed, the chances are that I will actually be cured. That's the light at the end of a long tunnel. There's certainly a chance I won't survive. Don't know what it is statistically, and don't want to. Of course, nobody gets out alive, but I was expecting a somewhat longer run than this.

Anyway, I'm sorry to be bringing you this difficult and frightening news. I don't have anything more definitive at the moment, but I will know more next week, and I promise to keep you in my loop.

Shoot up some positive vibes for me. I'm going to need them.

Love,
Steven

My sister Joanna was a transcendental meditation teacher, had been to India many times, had studied for years under, and for all I know on top of, some famous gurus, and professed to be a profoundly spiritual person. She also advertised herself on Facebook as a life coach, whatever the hell that is. Her husband, Alan Rachins, was an actor who had played the character of Douglas Brackman in L.A. LAW. Here was her reply:

Date: Tuesday, June 24, 2014 at 10:34:58 PM Pacific Daylight Time
From: Joanna Rachins
To: Steven Bochco
Subject: Shit happens

My dearest Steven,

These are my pearls so far: Take that "control" thing you have and make it work for you by attacking this situation internally as well as externally. Whatever you have to go through, internally choose to go through it, rather than becoming the victim of it. You will survive this.

Fear and love are two sides of a coin. Choose love whenever you can. The energy of love is healing and light. The energy of fear drags you down. We're all human and fear is fear, but when you can, when you have the choice, stay in love. Work it. Find it. Create it. Even pretend it. You will survive this.

Drop extraneous baggage and anyone who produces it. On an energetic level, it bunches up and gets stuck in the body. That has physical ramifications. You will survive this.

This is an inner journey as well as a physical one. You are a great soul. I don't mean your professional or even personal greatness. I mean on a soul level. All the component parts that go to make up Steven, the you you know yourself to be inside, this soul has true greatness in its DNA.

I know you. I love you with all my heart, unconditionally. You will survive this.

Until later. J

> Remember that line: *"I love you with all my heart, unconditionally."*
> And then, the next day, this follow up email from her:

"Oh, and the most important of all: stay in the moment. Don't let the mind take you...........just deal with each moment and what it brings. Your mind will want to take you to all the "realistic" scary places. Try to resist. Just one step at a time. Put one foot in front of the other. YOU WILL SURVIVE. Xoxo"

There are probably half a dozen excellent cancer hospitals in America, but I wanted to stay in Los Angeles, which pretty much narrowed the field to UCLA and City Of Hope. I interviewed a doctor at UCLA who was extremely knowledgeable, but had the bedside manner of a jackhammer. He was thin, small and twitchy, and he spoke so fast I couldn't keep up with him. When I asked him to slow it down to civilian speed, he said, "Oh. Sure." And kept on spitting out words like an AK-47. There was no way I was going to be trapped in a hospital room for months with this guy as my doctor.

A day or two later, I went to meet Dr. Stephen Forman at City Of Hope. I'd been told by those who knew him that he "walked on water." I quickly found out why. Aside from the fact that he was one of the top hematologist/oncologists in the business, he was also a profoundly empathetic man who I instantly felt at ease with. If I had to get on this particular flight, I wanted Steve Forman to be my pilot.

The next time I saw Dr. Forman, he asked me if I had any siblings. I told him I had an older sister. "Good," he said. "We should have her tested right away because there's a one in four chance that she'll be a perfect marrow match." So I sent her the following email:

Hi Joanna,
At some point in the process they may suggest testing you as a possible marrow donor. Are you up for that? The test is no biggie. But if you're a good match, it does involve a hospital procedure, to harvest bone marrow, should you be willing. And your ass would be pretty sore for a few days. There's a worldwide donor bank that would probably yield a pretty good match, so it's not a life determining decision. But the question will come up, I suspect, so I thought I'd mention it now.
Xoxo
Steven

I didn't hear back from Joanna for several days, so I sent her another email:

Hi, Joanna,
I was curious if you got this email (below) I sent you last Wednesday, or if it somehow fell through the cracks in your computer. Let me know. Thanks.
Xoxo
S.

This is the email reply that I received:

Dearest Steven,

Your email did not fall through the cracks. I couldn't get back to you right away because this is a momentous decision and I really had to grapple with it.

Your question sent me to Google. I did a lot of research, including consultations with my health practitioners, and even a shrink.

This is a huge thing you are asking and I had to reflect on it so as to be sure I am making a decision, wrenching as it is, that supports my body as well.

Of all the ways I could be there for you, all the parts of myself I could offer, I cannot offer you what you ask. I have spent many years healing my body from the toxic effects of emotional and physical abuse. I must now honor this body that I've worked so hard to heal, in the way that is the most beneficial for me and my family.

I offer you my love and support and all of the knowledge, experience, resources, and wisdom I have accumulated from my own journey, to support you with yours........if this is of any value to you.

Love,

J

Needless to say, I was shocked. Where was all that "*I love you with all my heart, unconditionally*" crap? I couldn't imagine my only sibling turning down a request, even if it was only a one in four chance, to save my life. I replied to her email:

I am stunned by your response, as are all my doctors, family and friends. (This is only the second time my doctors have heard of a response such as yours in all their years of doing this work. The other one was a brother who demanded to be paid for his marrow, which the recipient couldn't afford.) Nevertheless, I accept your decision and wish you peace with it. Hopefully, there is another marrow donor somewhere out there who is not afraid to help a stranger overcome a life threatening disease. I enter the hospital next week for an intensive double course of chemo, and then — assuming we can find a donor — a third round of chemo and bone marrow transplant.

Please don't respond any further. I need to focus my energy, and the energy of the people who support and truly love me, toward my survival, and you are obviously not part of that program.
S.

I haven't spoken to my sister since. I doubt I ever will again.

3

In the early winter of 1964, I was in my second year as a playwriting major at Carnegie Tech (now Carnegie Mellon), in Pittsburgh. A Hollywood producer named Sam Goldwyn, Jr., son of legendary Sam Goldwyn, had produced a less than memorable film called The Young Lovers, starring Peter Fonda and a young actress named Sharon Hugueny. Sam was literally hand carrying the film from campus to campus promoting it, and after every screening he'd participate in a Q&A with those students in attendance. I had already begun to fantasize about a writing career in film, so I was, to say the least, an eager attendee.

After the screening and during the Q&A, I raised my hand and asked Mr. Goldwyn why it was that Hollywood relied so heavily on source material like novels and plays, rather than original material written expressly for the screen. Mr. Goldwyn explained that it wasn't for lack of trying, but source material far outnumbered original material written for the screen. Don't ask me where I got the balls to do this, but I reached under my seat, grabbed a manila envelope and thrust it toward him, and said, "Here's a piece of original material. Mine."

Mr. Goldwyn sheepishly refused my offering, explaining that, for legal reasons, he couldn't accept unsolicited material; that it had to be submitted through a bona fide agent or manager. Thank God he didn't accept my offer, because the envelope was empty!

Flash forward five months, and I'm in Los Angeles with my girl-friend, Gaby Levin, sleeping on my sister's couch for the summer. I had met Gaby when we were both freshman playwriting students at Carnegie Tech. Gaby had very quickly hooked up with a somewhat older drama student named Steve Cohen, who I nicknamed Fatty. I couldn't understand what a beautiful young woman like Gaby saw in a fat, balding guy like Steve Cohen, but hey – there's no accounting for taste. In any event, Gaby and I became very close friends, and towards the end of our first year in school, Fatty Cohen knocked her up and essentially left her on her own to deal with the pregnancy. School was just about finished for the year, and Gaby, who'd arranged on her own to have an abortion, had nowhere to stay, so I brought her to stay with me in my apartment, my roommate, Leonard Auerbach, having already left for the summer. I pretty much nursed her through the whole ordeal, and by the time she'd recovered, we had evolved from being good friends to being lovers.

We spent that summer in New York, Gaby living with her father, Herman, an enormously successful Broadway producer whose claim to fame, among others, being that he produced My Fair Lady, and me living at home and working as a shipping clerk at a record company owned by friends of my parents.

At the beginning of our sophomore year, Gaby dropped out of school and got a job as a salesgirl at a downtown Pittsburgh department store – you can imagine how pleased her mother was – and that's pretty much how we spent the year – Gaby working, and me going to school and shuttling between my apartment and hers. It was my first (semi) live-in relationship, and I think both of us felt, for the first time in our lives, like adults who could take care of ourselves.

At the end of the school year, we went to Los Angeles. My sister had invited me to bunk in with her for the summer. She was a young, pretty actress in those days, living in Hollywood at the time, and my plan was to find a job – any job – hopefully in the film industry. Gaby, meanwhile, was going to live at home with her folks. Her mother Evelyn and stepfather Lou, who was a very successful entertainment attorney, representing, among others luminaries, Stanley Kubrick, lived in Bel-Air. I had grown up in a family that was always scrabbling for a buck, and these people – Gaby's father, mother, and stepfather – from my perspective, were loaded. We weren't going to hold a bake sale for any of them.

On my first day in Los Angeles, I took a chance and called Sam Goldwyn, Jr.'s office. I told his assistant over the telephone that I was one of the students that saw The Young Lovers during Mr. Goldwyn's campus tour, and was wondering if I could talk to him. Amazingly, she put me through to him, and I said, " I don't know if you remember me, but I'm the idiot who tried to hand you that envelope at Carnegie Tech." I doubt he remembered me, but he laughed anyway, told me that of course he remembered me, and when I told him I was looking for a summer job, he invited me over to meet with him.

The next day, I met Mr. Goldwyn at his office at the Goldwyn Studios in Hollywood, so named after his father. He had a two--office suite with an adjoining space for his assistant. I told Mr. Goldwyn that I was bunking on my sister's couch for the summer, and was looking for a job. He said he was running a small office, just him and his assistant, and couldn't really afford another hire. I told him that I was looking for experience, and that I'd happily work for free. I guess he was impressed with my eagerness, because he told me he'd give me fifty dollars a week out of petty cash, in return for which I could occupy the empty office and read books and scripts and synopsize them for him. Unbelievable. Just like that, I had landed my first real job in Hollywood!

Over the course of the next two months, I must've read and synopsized a hundred scripts and novels, and at the end of the summer, Sam asked me if I'd stay on permanently. I was extremely flattered and excited by the offer, but told him I needed to return to Carnegie and complete my education. He wondered if I could transfer my credits to UCLA and finish school there, but UCLA didn't offer a degree in Fine Arts, so none of my credits were transferable. But I was so excited by the offer, I decided to withdraw from Carnegie and pursue the opportunity that Sam was offering me.

Based on this golden (Goldwyn?) opportunity, Gaby and I decided to get married, much to her, and my parents' chagrin.

Nevertheless, we were adamant, and we were married at her folks' home in Bel-Air. At all of twenty, I was so young that my father had to sign for me so I could get a marriage license. Pathetic.

We found a small apartment in Hollywood, settled in, and I commenced my new, "real" job at Sam Goldwyn Jr.'s company for somewhere in the neighborhood of a hundred and twenty-five bucks a week. I was happy as a pig in shit, but eventually, the sameness of the job, day to day, began to wear on me, and my desire to finish school continued to gnaw at my conscience. I finally called the Head Of Drama at Carnegie Tech, a wonderful man named Earle Gister, and I told him I wanted to come back to school, but that I couldn't afford the tuition. He said, "Don't worry about the tuition. Come back and I'll give you a scholarship." So I quit my job (Sam was incredibly gracious), Gaby and I loaded up our '64 Mustang – a wedding gift from her father, Herman – and we drove across country to Pittsburgh in time for me to enroll for the second semester of my junior year. I had spent my first year of college at NYU – a miserable time for me – and when I'd transferred to Carnegie, I was able to bring with me about a semester's worth of credits, so I was actually now in sync with the rest of my class.

Gaby set up housekeeping for us a short walk from the campus, and I felt enormously relieved to be back at school. Earle Gister, true to his word, had given me an MCA Writing Fellowship, which paid my tuition for the remainder of the school year.

MCA – Music Corporation of America – had been one of the largest talent agencies in Hollywood, headed by Jules Stein and the legendary Lew Wasserman. In 1962, during an ongoing battle with the Justice Department over its monopolistic practices, MCA bought Universal Studios and divested itself of the talent agency, and quickly became the biggest, most powerful studio in Hollywood.

In those days, Universal (MCA), along with the William Morris Agency, gave out about a dozen scholarships to various universities around the country, and it was one of these scholarships that Earle was able to give me. And, as it turned out, Gaby's step-father, Lou, had some very close relationships with the higher ups at Universal by virtue of all the clients he represented, and so when summer rolled around, and I was looking for another job, Gaby and I went back to Los Angeles (this was now 1965), where Lou arranged for me to meet with an executive at Universal named Jennings Lang. Jennings was a former MCA agent, and when the agency disbanded, he became a highly placed executive at Universal. His claim to fame (or infamy) had been that in 1951, when he was still an agent, he was shot by a well-known producer of the era, Walter Wanger, who accused Jennings of carrying on an affair with his wife, the movie star, Joan Bennet, who Jennings represented. The story goes that Walter Wanger shot Jennings in the nuts and that, thereafter, Jennings was known around town as Jenning.

Be that as it may, Jennings in turn sent me to see a fellow named Mike Ludmer, who was the head of the feature story department. In those days, all the studios had story departments, manned by a group of readers whose sole job was to read and synopsize every script, novel and play that came across any executive's desk – which is, in fact, exactly the job I had held with Sam Goldwyn, Jr. for over eight months. Mike, knowing he was being asked to essentially "give the kid a job," offered to place me in the maintenance pool. I asked him what that was, and he told me the maintenance pool delivered typewriters, desks, chairs, etc. to the dozens of offices scattered all over the lot. I told Mike I didn't want that job.

"Are you kidding?" he said. "We have guys in the maintenance pool and the mailroom with Masters degrees, hoping to work their way up the ladder, and you're telling me you don't want that job?" I said I wasn't going to learn anything schlepping typewriters around the lot. I was happy to work for free, but I wanted a job that was going to teach me something. Mike just stared at me for a few moments, with a who-is-this-kid look on his face, and then he said, "Okay. How much do you need?" I said it didn't matter, that I'd work for nothing. "I'll give you eighty bucks a week," he said. "You'll work for me."

Universal had a summer program for its scholarship recipients: two weeks in L.A., all expenses paid, an office on the lot, and complete access to all the writers, producers and directors at the studio.

Mike assigned me to coordinate the program and essentially be the liason between these young scholarship recipients and the studio. In addition to that chore, I was to continue doing for Mike what I'd done for Sam: read books and screenplays and synopsize them for him.

August 5th, 1965, was the day the Watts riots broke out in Los Angeles. The apartment Gaby and I lived in on Melrose Avenue east of Vine Street was (at least as far as we were concerned) pretty close to the area of the worst rioting, and at her parents' urging, we abandoned our place and found a little apartment on Wilshire Boulevard in Westwood, right near the UCLA campus, that we were able to rent on a month-to-month basis. While Watts was erupting, we were settling into a comfortable space on the West side of Los Angeles, far enough away from the rioting that it felt like something that was happening in another world. Except it wasn't another world – it was Los Angeles, California, in the United States of America in 1965, and it was the first time that our generation – preoccupied as we were with the rapidly expanding war in Vietnam – came face to face with the issue of rancid race relations in our own back yard.

At the end of the summer, as we were getting ready to return to Pittsburgh, Mike invited me to come back to Universal when I graduated the following May, and he would give me a permanent job. Are you kidding me?

Holy shit! I spent my last year of college with a job waiting for me in Hollywood! Needless to say, I was the envy of my peers. I could hardly believe my good luck, and were it not for my relationship with Lou Blau, Gaby's stepfather, I'd never have gotten my break.

A quick word about nepotism. I'm all for it. Film and television is a tough business. There are a thousand qualified young people for every job opening. If you can get someone – a parent, a relative, a friend – to help you get a foot in the door, why not? But however you get that foot in, you're still going to have to go through the door yourself, and once you're in, you've got to stay in on the merits. In my fifty years in television, I've never seen anyone succeed on anything but.

My last year of school was a blur of activities, and two weeks before school ended, Gaby left Pittsburgh for L.A. to find us an apartment. One of my best friends in college, and to this day, was the actor, Michael Tucker (of L.A. LAW fame), and he was going to spend the summer with us in L.A. and try to find work as an actor. We didn't even stick around for graduation – we took our last final exam, jumped in the car, and drove fifty-two straight hours from Pittsburgh to Los Angeles. I think we arrived on a Friday, and the following Monday morning I reported to work at Universal.

I regret to this day that I didn't stick around for graduation. I was the first person in my family to ever get a college degree, and I should have been sensitive enough to realize what a thrill my graduation ceremony would have been for my parents. But I was so anxious to begin my professional life that I couldn't wait the extra week. I have regretted that impatience and insensitivity my entire life.

By the time I attended graduation ceremonies at Carnegie Mellon in 2006, my dad had long since died, and my mother was too fragile to make the trip. I was in Pittsburgh to receive an honorary doctorate, and it was a thrilling experience – not the doctorate itself, though I was flattered – but rather, the pomp and ceremony of it. Since I had skipped my own graduation, this one made me feel as if it were my own – a special feeling I'll never forget.

4

May, 1966. I had just graduated college and I had a job waiting for me at Universal. When I arrived at Universal on my first day of work, I sat down with Mike Ludmer to discuss salary, and he offered me a hundred and twenty-five dollars a week. I told him that I was married, I had gas to pay for, rent, food, etc. and that I needed two hundred a week. We settled at a hundred and eighty. I was elated. At the age of twenty-two, I was making more money than my father!

All my parents ever fought about was money. My mother wanted to spend it, and my father couldn't make it. It was a toxic brew of frustration, rage, and unmet expectations. By the time I was eight or nine, I figured out how to avoid the horrible, self-destructive merry-go-round of financial misery: get a job! And I did, starting at around age eight. My mother had a little business with a friend of hers, manufacturing costume jewelry. My mom would design the stuff, and together she and her friend would market and sell it to wholesalers and retailers, alike. So, after school, I'd take the bus down to their little shop on 38th Street in the heart of the Garment District, and I'd deliver their cargo to their wholesale buyers. I don't remember what they paid me – I was eight years old – but I immediately understood the bargain: I will do whatever the job requires, in exchange for which I will get money. And money was freedom. I understood that, from my earliest childhood, being witness to the terrible fights my parents had.

Between the ages of eight and eighteen, here are the jobs I held, either during summer, or after school, or both: Delivery boy. Freight elevator operator. Shipping clerk. I worked in a coat factory one summer – horrible. In ninety-degree weather, they were shipping winter coats. I worked in a music copying company, operating the printing machine. It was an Ozalid Streamliner, a monster of a machine occupying four fifths of a tiny room, which operated on a combination of light, heat, and ammonia. If you subjected anybody to that job today, kid or adult, you'd be put in jail for every workplace violation on the books. But I was paid a buck and a quarter an hour, and I worked twenty hours a week, after school and on weekends, and I was making twenty-five to thirty bucks a week as a teenager. I was able to avoid asking my parents for an allowance. By the time I was twenty, I'd been working most of my life, and work – as a concept – didn't intimidate me in the least. I loved the independence that making my own money gave me. And I knew, from the earliest age, that there was no job I wouldn't – or couldn't – do, in order to make a decent living. I didn't know much about the complications of adult, married life, but I knew that whatever beefs I would have with my future wife (wives), they weren't going to be about money.

I ran the same MCA scholarship program that I'd run the summer before, along with my reading and synopsizing. One day, I walked into Mike's office, beside myself with excitement. I had just read Ken Kesey's extraordinary novel, Sometimes A Great Notion. I told Mike he had to read the book, that it would make a great movie. About a week later, Mike found me and said, "You might want to come down to my office later this morning, because I'm having a meeting with Ken Kesey." Ken was the first true celebrity writer I had ever met. It was the sixties, the revolution was *on*, baby, and Ken Kesey was one of my generation's true heroes, the author of One Flew Over The Cuckoo's Nest in addition to Sometimes A Great Notion, and famous for his psychedelic bus and his friends and family, known as the Merry Band of Pranksters.

Universal subsequently bought the book rights to Sometimes A Great Notion, and made the movie, starring Paul Newman. I naively thought that because I had brought the book to Mike's attention, I would somehow get to write the screenplay. Yeah, good luck with that. The truth is, I wouldn't have had a clue at that time how to adapt such a huge, complex work to the screen. My eyes, as it were, were bigger than my stomach.

Over the course of the next year, I got to meet all the great producers, writers and directors at Universal. I met the famous director, Mervyn LeRoy (who produced The Wizard Of Oz and directed several great classics: Thirty Seconds Over Tokyo, Little Caesar, I Am A Fugitive From A Chain Gang, to mention just a few). There was also a famous film producer of the era, Ross Hunter, who produced most of the Rock Hudson/Doris day movies, in addition to an enormous hit at the time, Airport, and he took a particular shine to me. Ross used to jump up on his desk and do imitations of Carol Channing. It was crazy, and I was having the time of my life.

While my career was solidifying at Universal, it's fair to say that my marriage to Gaby was fraying so badly that, finally, in 1968, the fabric no longer held at the center, and we split up. Aside from the fact that we were both too young to be married, the drug culture of the sixties had pretty well captured Gaby, and the fact that I didn't partake drove a wedge between us that was probably the last straw. That, and the fact that (at least according to her), she was having an affair with a writer named Barry Pritchard. (Hey, Barry? How've you been? It's been what – fifty years? Wherever you are – if you're alive – go fuck yourself.)

It wasn't a difficult divorce. Between us, we didn't have a pot to piss in, and her stepfather handled the legal end of things, gratis.

I moved out of the apartment and found a place in West Hollywood, above Sunset Boulevard, across the street from the Tiffany Theater, where a satirical comedy troupe originally out of San Francisco, called The Committee, was performing nightly. I didn't know it at the time, but one of The Committee's performers, Barbara Bosson, was the woman I was going to spend the next twenty-nine years of my life with.

After Gaby and I had split, friends of mine from college, who were also living in Los Angeles, re-introduced me to Barbara. I remembered that we had met briefly in Pittsburgh several years earlier, while I was still married. She was studying at the Pittsburgh Playhouse, and we met at a party. As I recall, we enjoyed each other's company, but our paths never really crossed again. This time, we hit it off immediately and, as we were both single, we began to "date." I use quotation marks around the word, because Barbara worked every night across the street, so dating in the traditional sense of the word didn't really apply. Around eleven-thirty every night, I'd go across the street to the Tiffany Theater, and when the show was over, we'd go eat at various late-night diners in the neighborhood.

Before long, Barbara moved in with me, and a year later, she got pregnant with our first child, Melissa. We obtained the services of a baby sitter, and got married on Valentine's Day, 1970, the month after our daughter, Melissa, was born.

During this time, I was working as Story Editor on my first television series, Name Of The Game. As a story editor, my job was to meet with writers, help them shape their stories, and then – as necessary – rewrite their scripts. It was arduous duty. There were so many levels of approval that were needed – first, the studio, then the network – that by the time a writer got past the story stage and into the script phase, he might well have lost enthusiasm for the project. My boss, the executive producer, was a lovely man named George Eckstein. George's job as executive producer was wide ranging. He was tasked with overseeing virtually every aspect of production: casting, hiring directors, editing and post production, plus having to answer to studio and network concerns on an ongoing basis. When I became an executive producer/show runner years later, I was enormously hands on when it came to stories and scripts. My feeling was then, and still is, that "if it ain't on the page, it ain't on the stage." On Hill Street Blues, I created the position of co-executive producer, usually filled by someone who was not a writer, but a director instead, who could then relieve me of the responsibility of overseeing directors, along with all the other physical aspects of production. My experience was that actors and directors might make good material soar, but bad material would inevitably bring down the entire enterprise. Nevertheless, it's likely that in the course of a full season of television episodes, a few clunkers are going to find their way into the mix. You try to put as much lipstick on those pigs as you can, and move on to the next episode.

Everyday, after watching dailies (the work product from the previous day's filming), Dick Irving, who was the Universal executive in charge of our show, and who fancied himself a director, used to berate George mercilessly. "This film sucks! I can do better than that! We spent a fortune on this location. What kind of a fucking idiot lets the director film that scene in front of a brick wall?" – and on and on, for minutes at a time, in front of a dozen people sitting in a screening room. Poor George would go back to his office after these beatings and swallow a fistful of Valium.

In all fairness, Dick Irving turned out to be a good friend and mentor to me. I had written a movie of the week with a pal of mine, Bernie Kukoff, and Dick suggested that I produce it under his supervision. I turned him down. Startled, he asked me why. I told him that I didn't like being yelled at, and Dick was a screamer. He promised me he wouldn't yell at me. I told him that if he did, I'd fall down on the floor and start to cry. He laughed, and swore to me he'd never raise his voice to me, and he never did. The movie of the week was called Lt. Schuster's Wife, and it starred Lee Grant. She was, to use the vernacular of the time, a bitch on wheels, and was the first of many actors and actresses over the course of my career that altered my opinion of the species.

Speaking of actors: to that point, the wackiest experience I'd ever had with an actor was when Universal sent me to Las Vegas for ten days. They were making a special two-hour episode of Name Of The Game, with guest stars such as Sammy Davis, Jr. and Dianne Warwick, among others. Name Of The Game was itself a three-wheeler, by which I mean there were three separate shows under The Name Of The Game umbrella. One starred Tony Franciosa, another starred Robert Stack (that was the one I was working on for George Eckstein), and the third starred Gene Barry, with whom (it was said) every conflict could be resolved by giving him a new blazer. But of the three actors, Tony was by far the best, albeit the most volatile. He had a reputation for putting his hands on people, and I'd been told that at one point he'd cold-cocked an assistant director.

For some reason, Tony took a special liking to me. Universal had sent me there in the first place so I could be available for day-to-day rewrites, which I would do at night and then give to the production office so they could print them out and distribute them to the actors the following morning. I guess Tony particularly liked the scenes I was writing for him, because he'd come to my room almost every night to discuss the scenes he was to shoot the next day. Frequently, there'd be a knock on the door and some gopher would hand Tony a packet of pills. I assumed they weren't aspirins.

On nights when I didn't have to write, I would usually wind up in Sammy Davis, Jr.'s palatial suite at Caesar's Palace, where he would give impromptu concerts for the assembled cast and crew. It was pretty remarkable.

Some weeks later, back in Los Angeles, during another episode's production, Tony refused to come out of his trailer. It was about nine-thirty in the morning, and the entire production ground to a halt. Tony said he wouldn't come out until he'd seen his psychiatrist. So the assistant director called the psychiatrist, who arrived forty--five minutes later and closeted himself with Tony in Tony's trailer. About an hour later he came out and said to the assistant director, "If you can break for lunch now, when you come back, Tony will be ready to work." The assistant director thanked him, and as the psychiatrist was leaving, the assistant director stopped him.

"Doctor, we'll break for lunch now, but can you tell me what Tony's problem is?"

The doctor paused a moment, then said, "His problem? He's crazy, that's his problem."

I met Tony on several occasions, many years later, at various social events. He was charming, warm, and in every way that I could discern, a normal and well adjusted family man. I can only assume that his erratic behavior from years earlier was a function, to some degree, anyway, of drugs and/or alcohol. I met many more actors in subsequent years that struggled with the same problems, with behavior to match.

Several years later, and having developed a thicker skin, I worked on a project – The Invisible Man, starring David McAllum – which was executive produced by a man named Harve Bennett. I had written the pilot script and was the credited producer. We were all in the editing room one afternoon, and I offered up an editing suggestion. Harve jumped down my throat, screaming at me for having the temerity to offer an opinion. It was humiliating to me, and everyone else in the room was clearly embarrassed, as well. At the end of the day, I went to Harve's office and told him that as my boss, he could order me to do anything, yell at me, whatever – but that if he ever humiliated me like that in front of other people again, I'd knock him on his ass. Like most bullies, Harve immediately backed down and apologized, his lame excuse for his behavior being that in our business, you got shit on by the people above you, and you shit on the people below you. What a philosophy, huh?

I learned a lot in my twelve years at Universal, but among the most important lessons I learned was how NOT to behave. And in that category, Harve Bennett was a tenured professor.

Mike Ludmer knew I wanted to be a writer, and so by 1967--8, he had steered me to a producer named Harry Tatleman, an old-school, cigar chomping fat guy who delighted in calling me Stiff. Under Harry's tutelage, over the course of a couple of years, I worked on three or four projects. Universal used to take its unsold pilots, as well as hour-long episodes of its weekly anthology series, Chrysler Theater (not unlike other great anthology series of the time, like Studio One, Kraft Theatre, etc.), and turn them into two--hour movies that they would package and sell as movies overseas. It was my job, under Harry's supervision, to deconstruct these one--hour films, write an additional hour's worth of script, and reconstruct it. The additional material would then be filmed and edited into the existing hour. Voila! – a two-hour movie. I had no idea, until years later, how valuable these assignments would be.

The first project I worked on was a one-hour Chrysler Theater drama entitled A Slow Fade To Black. It presented a unique writing challenge in that none of the actors in the original show, including, among others, Rod Steiger and Robert Culp, were available. Consequently, I came up with a complicated back story for all the main characters as young people just starting out, and we cast young actors to portray the youthful Steiger, Culp, et al. It was a tremendous learning experience. I had no emotional stake in the material. It was purely an exercise in craft and structure, and I had a wonderful time doing it – sort of like unraveling a knitted scarf, and turning it into a sweater. When it was finished, I was invited to a screening. The title cards flashed by, one after another, and when it got to the writing credit, it read:

Written By Rod Serling and Steven Bochco.

There it was. My first professional writing credit, shared with one of the greatest writers in the history of television. I didn't know whether to be proud, or embarrassed. I think embarrassment carried the day.

In the late Spring of 1971, Dick Irving called me and told me to go meet with two guys who'd sold a series to NBC that was to be part of what the network called its Mystery Wheel: three rotating ninety--minute dramas, one of which was called McCloud, with Dennis Weaver, who played a New York City cop on horseback; another, McMillan and Wife, starring Rock Hudson and Susan St. James. Rock played the D.A. of San Francisco, and Susan played his wife, the daughter of a San Francisco detective, and they solved cases together. The third spoke of the wheel was a cop drama created by the two guys Dick Irving wanted me to meet with, Richard Levinson and William Link.

I told Dick I'd happily meet with them but that I'd never done a cop show before and, more importantly, had never done a mystery show. Dick said, "That doesn't matter – go meet the guys. They need a staff writer for next season. The show is called Columbo."

Bill and Dick were terrific – in their late thirties, they were about ten years older than me – and polar opposites of each other. Bill was short, almost Oriental looking, with a wispy beard and mustache, who smoked cigars, and Dick was tall and lean and always on his feet, pacing, smoking cigarettes, talking a mile a minute. When they wrote, Dick was always behind the desk at the typewriter, and Bill would sit in an easy chair puffing away. They told me that they'd made two previous Columbos – Prescription Murder, which aired in 1968, and Ransom For A Dead Man, which aired in 1971, and that NBC had finally picked it up to series as part of their Mystery Wheel. I repeated what I'd said to Dick Irving about being a complete novice in the mystery genre, but they waved that off, assuring me they'd help me with the plotting complexities. I liked them both very much and thought, what the hell – why not?

Over the next two years I wrote seven Columbos, and they changed my life (well, my career, at least).

The first year of Columbo was a wonderful experience. Under Bill and Dick's guidance, I grew as a writer, I began to get a handle on the mystery genre, and I had a box seat at the ferocious, almost daily, battles that they fought with Peter Falk.

Peter was a wonderful guy – at least to me. As a child, he'd lost an eye, and had worn a glass eye ever since. The other eye wasn't so hot, either. It tended to wander, so most people thought the wandering eye was the glass eye, and the glass eye was the good eye. Personally, I could never quite remember which was which, which made every conversation with Peter a little disorienting.

Peter would always stick his head into my office with that cock-eyed look of his, his cigar sticking out of his mouth, and ask me how I was doing. For a young writer working in a tiny office ten hours a day, being recognized by the star of the show was a tremendous boost. And with Peter, it was always genuine.

I was nominated for an Emmy for the first Columbo I wrote, directed by some young director on the lot named Steven Spielberg. Steven and I became pals during that time. We were both young, ambitious kids, and we'd often go to Art's Delicatessen in Studio

City for lunch and talk about our dreams for the future. It would've taken a larger crystal ball than I possessed at the time to accurately predict that Steven would become one of the world's greatest film directors, and that I would achieve the level of prominence in television that I did.

At the Emmys that year, though I lost (appropriately) to Bill and Dick for an episode they wrote, when Peter won the Emmy for his portrayal of Columbo, one of the first people he thanked was me. It put me on the map.

Almost until the day Peter died (sadly, of Alzheimer's), we would run into each other at the Riviera Country Club, where we both played golf – he played, I hacked – and he remained unfailingly sweet and friendly to me. But with Bill and Dick, it was a different matter. They were always fighting over scripts, stories, God knows what. Peter was, clearly, a control freak, and, at least in his mind, Columbo became *his* show, not Bill and Dick's. Their fights became so frequent and angry that Bill and Dick left the show after the first season. Peter had won; he'd driven them off. It was the first time, though certainly not the last, I'd ever seen an actor attempting to use his power to dominate the creative direction of a show.

Columbo was a hit for almost twenty years on NBC, first as a regular series, and then, in later years, as a series of special-event TV movies and, increasingly, over the years, Peter controlled almost every aspect of the show's production. Columbo was a good show. Arguably, a great show. But it would have been even better if Bill and Dick had remained at the helm.

Over the years, Dick Levinson became a very close friend. One year, I talked him into bringing his wife and daughter Chrissy (now a successful TV writer/producer in her own right) to the great Hawaiian resort, the Mauna Kea Beach Hotel, on the big island of Hawaii. Dick, who was the most frantic, impatient man I'd ever met – a classic type A personality – arrived at the hotel and, while I was sitting at the beach bar with my friend Gareth Wootton, indulging in an afternoon Mai Tai, we saw a threesome in the distance, heading our way. Gareth squinted, and said to me, "Is that man wearing wrinkled white tights?" It was Dick Levinson, with the whitest legs I'd ever seen on a human being. He arrived at the bar and, without any greeting at all, said to me, "They ought to bring the terminally ill to the Mauna Kea."

"Why's that, Dick?"

"Because every day seems like a year."

Dick took his family and left the next day.

In 1987, at the age of 52, Dick died of a heart attack. He'd been having chest pains for two years and refused to go to the doctor. The night before he died, he left a detailed letter to his wife Rosanna, which he left on his desk, instructing her as to where the spare keys to the house where, etc., and then went to bed. He woke up the next morning, took a shower, stepped out to dry himself, and keeled over. I'm still angry with him, as I suppose his family is. If he'd gone to the doctor any time during those two years, he'd probably have wound up getting by-pass surgery, and would be alive today.

5

After the first season of Columbo, and before commencement of production on the second season, Universal laid me off. Typically, Universal's standard contract included a guarantee of forty-eight weeks of employment so that during the production hiatus between seasons, they wouldn't have to carry the salaries of a bunch of low-level writers like me. Being laid off was financially tough. The only thing that was getting my family through this period of unemployment was the residual checks from summer re-runs of Columbo.

One day, Dick Irving called me and said, "I want you to go see Ned Tanen," who at the time was the head of Universal's low budget feature film division.

So I went to see Ned, and he said that they were making a movie with Douglas Trumbull, who was a special effects master who'd worked on Kubrick's "Space Odyssey: 2001."

Ned told me that they were supposed to start shooting on an abandoned aircraft carrier docked in San Pedro in four weeks, and they didn't have a script. Literally. They did not have a script! All they had was a twelve page outline called Silent Running, written by Michael Cimino and Derek Washburn, which didn't even contain a story. It was simply a concept. It was a provocative idea about these huge domes in outer space that contained the world's few remaining forests, as the world of the future had essentially lost the ability to sustain them.

I told Ned I'd love to take a whack at the script. A few days later I pitched my story idea to Ned, Doug Trumbull, and the film's producer, Mike Gruskoff, and they all said, "Yeah, that sounds great – do that!" I went home and wrote the screenplay of Silent Running in one week. My total compensation, per Writer's Guild weekly minimums in those days, was seven hundred and fifty dollars. Ned and Doug were so thrilled, they let me hang around for another week and paid me an additional seven-fifty. So my entire compensation for writing the screenplay of Silent Running was the princely sum of fifteen hundred dollars. Believe me, I wasn't complaining. Not yet, anyway.

The movie starred Bruce Dern, and for my money, all fifteen hundred bucks of it, he ruined the script. This was in 1971, and Bruce was, I suppose, sort of, like, far out, y'know, wow, deeply embedded in the hippie culture of the time, and he turned all the dialogue into a stew of hippie vernacular. I said to Mike Gruskoff, "What are you doing? You're taking a piece of material set way in the future, and you're letting this guy ruin its timelessness. It's ridiculous. In five years this is going to be a dated movie."

But who was going to listen me, some punk they'd paid fifteen hundred bucks to for the script?

The only good thing that came of the experience was that I resolved to stay out of the movie business. It was clear to me that the screenwriter on a movie is about as useful as tits on a bull. Once you've written it, you might as well leave town. Or, in this case, the planet. And I asked myself, "Where is the only place I might have a chance to control my own material?" And the answer was, television.

In all honesty, I can't say that I ever really had control over anything I wrote for television during the twelve years I was at Universal, because their system simply didn't allow for it. But my years there prepared me for when I would finally gain control of my work.

In 1972 I attended the Writers Guild of America, West awards show in Beverly Hills. I'd been nominated for a writing award for Columbo. During the ceremony, when the award was announced for the best two-hour movie written for television (The Neon

Ceiling, produced by a man named Bill Sackheim, who would become one of my most influential mentors), the winning writers, Carol Sobieski and Howard Rodman, took the stage. Carol said all the appropriately nice things, thanking the producers, the director, the cast, and all the usual suspects. Then it was Howard's turn to speak. Howard, a great writer and arguably one of the most important dramatists of what was referred to as The Golden Age of television, was a burly, bald, bullet-headed man who looked fearsome. And, true to his look, he didn't disappoint. He railed against the networks and the studio who'd made The Neon Ceiling. He railed against the Writers' Guild arbitration process. Apparently, he'd been the original writer on the project, and Carol had come on the project later, to rewrite the script. They wound up sharing credit, and Howard was furious that his script had been co-opted. Standing right there next to Carol Sobieski, he called her an autistic vandal. Those were his exact words. Autistic vandal. It was one of the most cringe-worthy moments I'd ever witnessed. I'd never seen someone vent publicly with so much hostility. It was all anyone spoke about for the rest of the evening.

Fast-forward a couple of months to late winter of 1972. Dick Irving called me and told me that there was a TV pilot script that had been written for ABC by Howard Rodman, and Rodman had refused to do another rewrite. Dick wanted me to effect the changes Howard wouldn't. Having seen Howard up close and personal, I was leery, but said I'd certainly read the script.

The script was called Cyborg, and it was a science fiction piece. It was one of the best scripts I'd ever read. I called Dick back and said I couldn't do the rewrite because I didn't know how to make it better. According to Dick, ABC wanted lots more action and excitement, and Universal wanted the sale. Nevertheless, I stuck to my guns, telling Dick I didn't want to contribute to "dumbing down" such a fine piece of work.

Ten minutes later, my phone rang. It was Howard Rodman. He thanked me profusely for my support of his script, but then he asked me to please do the rewrite ABC was asking for. He said that while he couldn't bring himself to do it, he wanted the show to succeed. He needed the money. Reluctantly, but with Howard's blessing, I did the rewrite.

The script was approved by ABC, and the pilot was produced by Universal. The network changed the title of the pilot script from Cyborg to The Six Million Dollar Man, ABC made three movies for television based on it that ran in 1973, and then turned it into a regular series that ran for five seasons, from 1974 to 1978. I hope Howard made a lot of money.

One of the first phone calls I received when Hill Street Blues went on the air in January of 1981 was from Howard Rodman. He said that Hill Street was the best television series he'd ever seen, and could I please send him a videotape of each week's episode so he could watch the show without commercials. I was enormously flattered, and sent him videotapes (remember those?) of every episode until he died in December of 1985.

In 1973, The Writer's Guild of America, West, called a strike that lasted sixteen weeks. It was financially devastating to me, as I'm sure it must have been to many writers. My wife and I had just bought a house we couldn't really afford in Santa Monica, and I spent the entirety of the escrow period walking a picket line in front of Goldwyn Studios (of all places), in Hollywood. On the first day of the strike, we were all milling around the sidewalk in front of the studio, getting our placards from our strike captains, when a gorgeous, chauffeured, green Mercedes Benz sedan pulled up to the curb. From the passenger seat alighted a nattily dressed man, who popped the trunk and, with his driver's help, removed a folding tray and a large, silver samovar filled with hot coffee. The man's name was Paul Henning, an Oscar-nominated writer and the creator of The Beverly Hillbillies, and we drank his coffee as he walked the picket line with us. It was pretty funny. He and I represented the absolute polar opposites of the financial spectrum, but there we both were, on that picket line, striking for an increase in the general financial welfare of all industry writers. As I became more successful over the years, I never forgot Mr. Henning's generosity toward his fellow writers and, in the fullness of time, and through several strikes, I have tried – literally – to follow in his footsteps.

The strike was particularly frustrating for me because I had been tapped to produce my first television series, a show called Griff, for ABC, starring Lorne Greene. A sixteen-week strike, aside from the obvious financial stress it put on me, also put me behind the eight ball because, when we went back to work, we had to get our shows ready to go on the air in eight weeks. Eight weeks? I was in a panic. I was going to have to pull a writing staff together, a production team, cast the remaining series regulars, come up with stories, write scripts, etc., all in eight weeks. This was a tough enough assignment for a seasoned producer, let alone a novice, which I was.

The executive producer of the series, a man named David Victor, had found fame as the producer of Marcus Welby, M.D., and had been in the business longer than I'd been alive. He had a vague Eastern European accent, wispy gray hair, dandruff on his shoulders, and one eye that wandered. I always wondered what it would be like to have dinner with him and Peter Falk at the same time. David was also a superb politician. He understood studio politics, played the game brilliantly, and, basically didn't work very hard.

At that time, the head of Universal Studios was a man named Frank Price.

Frank Price and I first crossed paths in 1967 when Mike Ludmer assigned me to help him out on a project. Frank was the Executive Producer of a new show that was going on the air in the fall. Apparently, after they'd edited the first six episodes or so, they were all about five to seven minutes short of airtime. My assignment was to write additional material for each episode that would be filmed and edited into the existing episodes.

I met Frank in a screening room, he explained the situation, and told me to watch all six episodes, after which we'd talk about the added material. I watched all six without a break and, when Frank came back, I told him I could absolutely do the job but – unsolicited, I might add – I said I thought the episodes were terrible and I doubted the show would survive its first season. Not exactly the way for a young writer to endear himself to the future head of TV at Universal. But I was young, brash, and what I said was pretty damn rude and thoughtless.

Anyway, I did the work, the episodes were re-edited, and the show went on the air as scheduled. The series was called Ironside, starring Raymond Burr, and it ran on NBC for eight years.

By 1973, Frank was president of Universal Television and was, arguably, the most powerful executive in the television business, as Universal was the primary supplier of programming to NBC, and provided, as well, most of ABC's Movie of The Weeks. And I think, based on our previous experience, he didn't much care for me. Our relationship didn't get any better during the strike that year. As previously noted, I was going to be producing my first series, Griff, and during the strike, Frank and David Victor, the executive producer, were casting the supporting roles without any communication with – or input from – me. Call me crazy, but as a producer, I thought I had a right to that input.

One of the actors in consideration was a perfectly nice and very handsome young actor named Ben Murphy, whose weasel of an agent, probably in an attempt to ingratiate himself with me on behalf of his client's interests, was courting my wife, Barbara, who, at the time, had no representation. I didn't know Ben, but I'd seen some of his work on television, and while I didn't think he was bad, I wasn't particularly a big fan. One day, during the strike, the agent called Barbara and, in the course of their conversation, told her that Universal had cast Ben Murphy in Griff. Barbara, knowing how I felt, inadvertently expressed some dismay on my behalf along the lines of "Oh, no."

The agent hung up on Barbara and immediately called Frank Price, threatening to pull Ben from the show because the producer – that would be me – didn't like his client. By the time the dust settled, the agent had squeezed some additional compensation for Ben, and I was – permanently – in Frank Price's doghouse.

When the strike was finally over after sixteen weeks, all the executive producers and producers were invited to a lunch hosted by

Frank, the purpose of which was to give us all a pep talk, as we had to be ready to go on the air with our shows in *eight weeks.*

David Victor, my executive producer, was sitting next to me at lunch. It was a serve-yourself buffet of roast beef, other cold cuts, potato salad, etc. While Frank was welcoming us back and exhorting us to meet our impossible delivery dates, David Victor was wolfing down his food as if he were going to the electric chair that night. At some point, I became aware of a gurgling sound to my right. I looked over, and David was choking. Red faced, eyes watering, and unable to breathe, he suddenly horked up an entire slice of un–chewed roast beef onto his plate. I quickly looked away, trying not to laugh – or puke – while keeping an eye on David peripherally. He looked from side to side and, assuming no one had seen this disgusting event, took his knife and fork, cut the offending slab of spittle-covered beef into smaller pieces, and ate them. Yummy.

Griff was a disaster. I was a brand new producer, I was getting no help or guidance from my executive producer, and the head of Universal Studios Television wasn't exactly my biggest fan. What was wrong with this picture? Just about everything.

And poor Lorne Greene. He was a lovely man. He'd starred in Bonanza, one of the most successful series in television history, and here he was, stuck in a crappy private eye show written and produced by a kid who didn't know what the hell he was doing. The best thing about the show was Lorne's hairpiece. It was a beauty. It must've been made from the hair of a yak's ass. It was perfect. I've never seen a better one, before or since.

Mercifully, Griff was cancelled after thirteen episodes.

The one positive and constant aspect of my Universal years was my friendship with Stephen J. Cannell. Improbably, Steve and I became best friends at the studio. I say improbably because I was a relatively poor Jewish kid from the upper Westside of New York, and Steve was a wealthy Gentile raised in Pasadena. But we shared a like sense of humor, and we'd both started at Universal at roughly the same time. By 1974, however, Steve had become a star, writing and producing one of the best and most popular series ever made,

The Rockford Files. Steve was a wonderful and prolific writer, and I would look forward to grabbing up every new Rockford script, hot off the press. Steve had found his voice in Rockford, and for all his success then and in the future, you could argue that his Rockford scripts were the best he ever wrote.

At the lowest point in my life, career-wise, Steve was a ceaseless cheerleader on my behalf. We'd go to lunch every Friday at El Torito, a popular Mexican restaurant in Burbank, and drink margaritas, talking about life and career. While Steve's star was rising, my star, such as it was, was plummeting, and he would always encourage me, reminding me of my good work on Columbo, and urging me to never quit on myself.

He asked me to create a show with him – I believe he thought that, with his help, my stock would rise at Universal, which was one of the most generous gestures anyone had ever made towards me. The show turned out to be Richie Brockelman, Private Eye, a 1977 series about a teenaged private eye, starring Dennis Dugan, which Frank Price didn't much care for and barely promoted to NBC. It was only because of Steve's influence that Frank grudgingly urged NBC to give us a six-episode order. Needless to say, it was six and out.

When Hill Street Blues burst on the scene in January of 1981, Steve Cannell, who'd been my biggest booster when I was at my professional and personal lowest, became my biggest fan and booster when Hill Street turned my career into a shooting star. In fact, Steve turned down a cop show pilot at ABC, telling their head of development that Hill Street Blues was the best cop show ever made, and he didn't want to compete with it.

Stephen and I remained dear and close friends until his death from melanoma in 2010, and there isn't a day that goes by when I don't think of him with love and gratitude.

In 1974-75, I toiled in relative obscurity as the story editor on McMillan and Wife. My producer was a wonderful man named Jon Epstein who, many years later, I gave one of my Emmys to – he had leukemia, he had always hoped to win one, and never did. I had the nameplate replaced with one that bore his name, and gave it to him at a huge party we held for Jon in the ballroom of The Beverly Wilshire Hotel. He died several months later.

McMillan and Wife starred Rock Hudson and Susan St. James, and there was no love lost between them, though they never really quarreled or held up production. They just didn't much care for each other. Certainly it was no secret in our business that Rock was gay, though in those days, it wasn't really public knowledge and the studios did an excellent job of keeping those kinds of pesky facts covered up. When Rock died of AIDS in 1985, the joke around town was, why did they bury Rock with his ass sticking up out of the ground? Answer: So his friends could drop by for a cold one. We've come a long way since then.

One day, Rock called me in my office. He was shooting a scene first up after lunch, and he didn't understand it. Could I come over to his trailer and explain it to him? Sure, I said, and hoofed over. I'd never been in his trailer before, and when I entered, there were four men, including Rock, and they were all crocheting pillows. It was, to say the least, a startling image.

Anyway, Rock proceeded to tell me that he was confused by the scene. I asked him what, exactly, didn't he understand about it? McMillan And Wife was a pretty straightforward mystery show, but it turned out that Rock never read the scripts. He'd simply read the scenes he was supposed to shoot next, and learn the lines. I had to tell him the entire story before he finally understood what the scene in question was about. No wonder Susan didn't much care for him. It's hard for an actor or actress to do their best when the person they're acting with doesn't understand the material, or has just learned their lines. It's disrespectful to both the material and the other performers. I don't remember exactly what they were paying Rock in 1974, but it was in the neighborhood of a quarter of a million dollars an episode. For that kind of money, most people would commit murder. Rock could have at least read the damn scripts.

Early in 1976, I had met Bill Sackheim for the first time. Bill's reputation as a writer and producer preceded him. He had been responsible for some of the best television movies ever made, including the previously mentioned Neon Ceiling. He also produced a riveting movie call The Law, starring Judd Hirsch and wonderfully written by David Rintels.

Bill was executive producing a new CBS series called Delvecchio, also starring Judd Hirsch, and he invited me to come aboard as one of two producers. I would be in charge of supervising the writing, and my co-producer, Mike Rhodes, would be in charge of physical production, with both of us reporting to Bill.

In 1976, TV dramas didn't have staff writers. There was a thriving free-lance marketplace, and most script assignments were farmed out to these writers, who in a good year, could wind up writing ten scripts for various shows.

Bill and I had many story meetings with multiple writers, and initially commissioned about four scripts. When a draft of our first script was delivered, I anxiously took it home to read, and was happily relieved. I thought it was quite good. The next morning, I had barely settled into my office when Bill called to ask me what I thought of the script. I told him I thought we'd made a good start; that it was well in the ballpark.

"It's a piece of shit," Bill said. "Come over to my office and I'll take you through it."

In his office, Bill proceeded to dissect the script with scalpel--like precision. He pointed out where the story didn't work. He indicated where characterizations had gone astray. He reinvented pieces of the story. Having essentially disassembled the script, he then proceeded to methodically re-construct it, and told me to re-write it.

I left his office mortified – not just at the fact that I had thought the script was pretty good, but at the fact that I simply didn't see all the ways that it *wasn't* good. I think I learned more about writing in those couple of hours than I ever had before.

The entire season was like a tutorial, with Bill being the tutor and I being the willing student. I wound up writing eight episodes of Delvecchio and re-writing the rest. It was the most intensive learning experience I ever had, and the first inkling of my sense that I had an original writer's voice inside of me.

By the end of Delvecchio's run (one season, twenty-two episodes made, twenty aired), Bill Sackheim and I had become fast friends, and would remain so until the day he died. And when the show got cancelled in the spring of 1977, I knew my time at Universal was coming to an end. I determined to leave when my contract expired in 1978.

6

After the short lived Richie Brockleman, I finally left Universal for MTM, the Mary Tyler Moore company, founded by her husband Grant Tinker, and her manager, Arthur Price.

The first series I created and produced for MTM was a show called Paris, starring James Earl Jones. It was a good try on my part, but I still hadn't developed the chops needed to run a successful television series, and my problems were magnified by the fact that James Earl and I held completely different takes on what the show was supposed to be. I wanted to do a series about a middle management cop with tons of responsibility and no real authority. I was also interested in the politics of the work place, especially as it pertained to a paramilitary organization like the cops. James, on the other hand, wanted a series in which he was a more traditional, heroic cop. Run and jump. Chase and capture. Assume the position, asshole! We clashed incessantly.

I remember once being summoned to his dressing room while he was having electrolysis performed on his face. While we argued about the script, the electrolysis technician swabbed Jimmy's face with alcohol, touched it with her electrolysis gun, and Jimmy's entire face exploded in flames. She patted the flames out quickly, but his face was beet red. Needless to say, it cut our conversation short.

At one point during the season, which felt like a crucifixion to me, I called Billy Sackheim (help!) and we met for lunch. I told him how miserable I was. My writing staff wasn't good enough, I feared I wasn't good enough, I was continually at odds with my star, and the show wasn't anywhere near my expectations.

Billy listened calmly as I unburdened myself. And when I was done whining, he said, "Here's what you need to do." I waited for his words of wisdom. "Work harder," he said.

"What?" I practically shouted. I pointed out, at higher volume than probably necessary, that I was working fourteen hours a day as it was. I left home in the dark, I returned home in the dark, my dog barked at me and my kids didn't know who the hell I was. How could I work any harder than I already was?

Billy said if I wanted to be a successful creator and show runner, I simply had to figure it out. I was furious at him. He just shrugged. "Work harder."

Paris was cancelled after thirteen episodes. But the next series I co-created and produced was Hill Street Blues. And I finally understood what Billy meant when he told me to work harder. He wasn't talking about the hours. He was talking about how to use those hours. It was one of the most important lessons of my professional life.

Let me wrap up my Universal years with one last observation: by and large, young people in our business, and I suppose in every business, think they're better than they really are, or at least further along in their development than they really are. I was probably guilty of that premature self-evaluation myself. I had to leave Universal, the place of my professional birth, in order to grow up. The culture of Universal being what it was in those days, I doubt I could have ever found my true voice as a writer had I stayed. But what amounted to a twelve-year apprenticeship was invaluable. I learned my craft. I forged life-long friendships. I learned the importance of loyalty, and the perils of self-centeredness. I was blessed with some wonderful mentors. I don't think I could have sustained the level of success I ultimately achieved for as long as I did, had it not been for those twelve complicated, frustrating years spent at Universal.

Speaking of long apprenticeships and great mentors, in 1983, at age forty, I'd taken up golf. I was now officially a geezer. Around

1985, just when I arrived on the 20th Century Fox lot, I started taking a weekly golf lesson from a teaching pro at Riviera, Maury Demot. Maury kept touting me on this kid she wanted me to meet, a golf rat named Mike Robin, who had just graduated from the University of Miami and was looking for an entry-level position in television. As a favor to Maury, I met with Mike and was very impressed with him. He'd studied film and television in school, and was more knowledgeable about the changing technologies of our business than I was. (A low bar.) I hired Mike as a PA, and he turned out to be a diamond in the rough. He was smart, anticipatory, and a relentlessly hard worker. And he made it look easy. In those days, the writers and I would work on Saturdays, and sometimes on Sundays, as well. Around lunchtime, Mike Robin would suddenly stick his head in the door. "I just happened to be in the neighborhood. You want me to grab you guys some lunch?"

Mike became an integral part of our L.A. Law family and, over the years, he rose up to become an associate producer, then a producer, then a director, and an executive producer. By the time Mike left my employ, after eleven years – virtually as long an apprenticeship as I'd served at Universal – he'd become an accomplished professional at every level of our business. Mike went on to form his own company, which became hugely successful, producing shows such as Nip/Tuck, The Closer, Major Crimes, and Longmire. I'm reminded of Mike because, generally, our business is so transitory. People come and go, as do shows. It's rare, in that environment, for close and lasting relationships to emerge, and not everyone gets the mentor they deserve. In Mike Robin, I was lucky to get the mentee I needed.

7

When I was working on the ill-fated Griff in 1973, the Universal executive in charge of the show was a young guy named Stu Erwin. Stu was a child of the industry, the son of a well-known TV actor of the same name, who'd starred in his own hit TV series from 1950 to 1955.

Stu and I became good friends, and when he left Universal to join Grant Tinker at MTM, by now a thriving independent production company, we stayed in touch.

A few words about Grant Tinker, who became one of the most important mentors I ever met in my professional life. I had originally met Grant, briefly, when he was an executive at NBC, before leaving to form MTM, which would become one of the most famous independent production companies in the history of television. Grant was a genuinely modest man who had the highest regard for writers. He would often take a group of us to lunch at Art's Deli, in Studio City. Can you imagine Frank Price doing that? I can't.

Years after I met him, and he'd already left MTM to become chairman and CEO of NBC, I had dinner with Grant and told him I'd always harbored a secret ambition to run a network. Grant became genuinely upset with me. "You have a typewriter," he said. "You're a writer. Why in God's name would you ever want to be anything else?" That was Grant. And, yet, he taught me more about executive skills, and how to run a company, than anyone I'd ever known.

Under the heading I'd Rather Be Lucky Than Good, Stu called me around September of 1977, just when I was at the lowest point in my career. I hated Universal, I felt completely stifled creatively, and on top of everything else, my dad was dying. I had told him a lie on his deathbed, that I'd signed a new seven-year contract at Universal. He had said to me, on more than one occasion, "Promise me you'll take care of your mother." The lie I told him was my way of reassuring him that my financial future – and therefore Mom's – was secure. In truth, I had decided to leave Universal and seek employment elsewhere when my contract expired in early 1978. I knew that Universal would give me a new contract, but I also knew that as long as Frank Price was running the joint, I'd never get a chance to really do my own shows. I'd be used primarily as a cork – someone to fill a hole as the need arose. No thank you. I'd been there twelve years. I'd started out as a kid fresh from school, but I was thirty-four now, I had a wife and two children, and it was past time to leave the nest.

And, as if I had won the lottery, Stu told me that he and Grant were looking to expand MTM's production output to include more hour shows, and were hoping I might come over and join them when my deal expired at Universal. I'm not the praying type, but their offer was nevertheless a prayer come true.

MTM, in 1977, had already had a string of enormously successful half-hour shows. The original Mary Tyler Moore Show ran for seven years (1970-77), The Bob Newhart Show ran for six years (1972-78), Rhoda ran for four seasons (1974-78), and MTM's first successful one-hour series, Lou Grant, was just beginning its successful five year run. The original Mary Tyler Moore Show had spawned five successful spin-offs. MTM was also developing a one-hour pilot created by one of my closest friends, Bruce Paltrow (father of Gwyneth and Jake, who was – and remains to this day – my son Jesse's best friend).

I couldn't have been happier to be leaving Universal for MTM, and my attorney, Frank Rohner, aka The Doberman – a nickname I'd given him because of his relentless negotiating style – negotiated a three-year, 250,000-dollar contract for me. And if my episodic fees (assuming I sold a series) exceeded my guarantee, MTM would pay me the difference. It wasn't a fortune, exactly, but good money by any standard, and certainly more than enough to guarantee I'd be able to keep the promise I'd made to my dad on his death bed.

When I first met Frank Rohner, I had no representation of any kind: no agent, lawyer, or manager. I was under a long-term contract to Universal and didn't feel I needed one. At the time, Frank was a partner in a well known entertainment law firm called Shearer, Fields, Rohner & Shearer, and was just leaving the firm to strike out on his own. He had about half a dozen clients, among them Harve (You Get Shit On By The People Above You And You Shit On The People Below You) Bennett. When I told Harve I didn't have an agent, he said I didn't need one, but that I should definitely have an attorney, and he set up a lunch for me to meet Frank. I liked him instantly, despite the fact that his politics were somewhere to the right of Atila The Hun. He told me all the reasons why he thought I needed an attorney, and I was struck by how right he was. He explained that he was more of a financial manager than an agent, and I needed that kind of supervision in my life. So I signed on with Frank, which turned out to be the smartest thing I've ever done in my professional life.

When my contract at Universal expired in the spring of 1978, I checked into MTM's studio (CBS Studio Center, in Studio City) that they co-owned with CBS. It was as if I'd died and gone to heaven. MTM was the polar opposite of Universal. Grant Tinker had created a warm, welcoming, writer-centric environment, and after twelve years at Universal, it was a revelation. Plus, Bruce Paltrow (Brucie to his pals) was there, so I didn't feel like a stranger. My office was in a small building upstairs from Brucie's offices, and his pilot, The White Shadow, had just been picked up to series by CBS. Brucie immediately asked me if I'd like to write an episode, and I happily agreed.

The first thing I did when I checked onto the studio lot was to go visit Grant Tinker on the fifth floor of the executive building. I remember he was wearing jeans, sneakers, and an open collared shirt and sweater. He couldn't have presented a more starkly different presence than my old boss, Frank Price, in his Universal-issue prick suit, and I was immediately put at ease by his warmth and friendliness. After we'd chatted for a while, I asked him what kind of shows he wanted me to think about developing. He said, "We didn't bring you here to do what we want, we brought you here to do what you want." He told me that as soon as I had an idea I wanted to develop, he'd take me over to whichever network we felt most comfortable with, and pitch it.

Wow. I couldn't believe what a wonderful place I'd had the good fortune to wind up at. With Brucie and his irrepressible humor as my guide, I commenced the next phase of my career. Of course, I didn't know it at the time, but the next seven years would change my life forever.

I'd heard that Brucie was tough on writers. He'd scribble his notes on the back of a writer's draft, things like: "I hate this! This is a piece of shit! The writing sucks!" Stuff like that. And, of course, when the poor writer would come in for his notes meeting, Brucie would pick up the script and the writer would see all those horrible comments written on the back. Funny, but cruel. Brucie's humor was wicked, and there was a mean streak to it, as well.

When I finished the first draft of my episode, I wrote a three--page bogus opening containing the worst writing I could possibly come up with – horrible, expository dialogue, terrible scene structure, impossible camera directions. It was awful.

I brought the script down to Brucie's office and said, "Here, I think this is really terrific." Brucie was very pleased, and said he'd read it that night. "No, no," I pleaded. " I really want to get your reaction. I'll sit here while you read it now." Is there anything more uncomfortable than someone sitting across from you, watching you read? Poor Brucie. We were such good friends, he couldn't say no. He opened up the first page and began to read. The color drained from his face. He flipped to the second page, and finally – about half way down – he realized what I'd done, and we both busted out laughing. Any potential discomfort there might be working with a close friend disappeared. Brucie read the script right then and there, he loved it, and we never changed a word of it.

Bruce Paltrow taught me how to have fun at work. We would play football in the parking lot. We'd go upstairs to the executive suites and harass the secretaries, and play practical jokes on the bosses. At Brucie's instigation, he and I once walked into Mel Blumenthal's office. Mel was the head of Business Affairs, and his desk was a simple table top – like a door without the knob – overloaded with paper work piled high. In the aggregate, the paper alone must have weighed two hundred pounds. Mel was on the phone. He had one of those earpieces so he could talk hands-free, and he was engaged in some serious and animated conversation. Bruce and I, without a word, grabbed either end of his desk, and shoved it – with Mel sitting behind it – up against the wall behind Mel's back, so that Mel was tightly pinned. There was no way to get out. Thusly trapped, Bruce and I left the building, with Mel still yakking on the phone. I have no idea how he finally extricated himself. Juvenile behavior, I grant you, but fun.

Mel was not a well-liked person at MTM, particularly so, after Grant left. He was a cold, calculating negotiator who seemed to take particular delight in driving the hardest bargain he could. A really good business affairs negotiator always leaves a little something on the table, a small price to pay for the good will it engenders. Mel would have none of that. The Hill Street Blues actors were always grousing about their low pay, but Mel and Arthur always took the position that if they raised one actor's pay, they'd have to raise them all, and by that time there were thirteen regulars. One December, late in Hill Street Blue's run, Bruce Weitz, another old friend from Carnegie, who played Mick Belker, gave Mel a graveyard plot for Christmas.

Mel and his boss, Arthur Price notwithstanding, the environment Grant created was infectious, and MTM was gaining a well--earned reputation for being a writer's company. There was no hierarchy. The entire company consisted of Grant, Arthur, Mel, Stu

Erwin, and Abbey Singer, the head of production. If you needed to talk about creative affairs, you went straight to Grant. If you needed to talk about production budget issues, you went to Arthur Price. And if you needed casting advice, you went to Lori Openden. That was it. We were there to have fun and create and produce our own shows, with minimal interference. Grant loved and respected writers, and every one of us wanted to please him with the very best we were capable of.

8

In my first year at MTM, I made three pilots and one Movie of The Week. Paris was a one-hour pilot for CBS, directed by Jackie Cooper and starring James Earl Jones; Every Stray Dog and Kid was a ten-minute presentation film for NBC, sort of a mini-pilot for a one-hour series, directed by Jimmy Burroughs; and Operating Room, also for NBC, a one-hour pilot directed and co-written by Bruce Paltrow. The Movie of The Week, for ABC, was called Vampire, starring a strange but compelling actor named Richard Lynch, who, in 1967 in Central Park, under the influence of drugs, set himself on fire, scarring himself terribly in the process.

Kevin Thomas, then the television critic for the Los Angeles Times, hated it. I was deep in the throes of writing and producing Paris when the movie aired on ABC. That Saturday morning, around 6:30 a.m., I was preparing to go into work – I had to write an entire episode of Paris over the weekend – and had completely forgotten that Vampire was going to be on that night. I made a pot of coffee and went out to the driveway to grab the newspaper.

On the front page of the Calendar section of The L.A. Times was the following headline: "VAMPIRE MOVIE A PAIN IN THE NECK." Uh oh. It got worse from there. In his review, Kevin Thomas called the movie execrable – a four-syllable word for shitty. In fact, several weeks later, reviewing another Movie of The Week directed by E.W. Swackhammer – who'd directed Vampire – Mr. Thomas referenced the director's work by reminding readers that Swackhammer had previously directed "the execrable Vampire." The week after that, in reviewing yet another movie, Mr. Thomas referred to the director of photography as having photographed the "lamentable" Vampire. This guy wouldn't let me up.

I had written Vampire with Michael Kozoll, who I'd become friends with several years earlier when he wrote several episodes of Delvecchio, the 1976 series starring Judd Hirsch, Charlie Haid, and Michael Conrad I wrote and produced for Bill Sackheim when I was still at Universal. It was the first realistic cop-show I'd ever worked on, and I became good friends with Joe Gunn, one of the show's creators who, as I recollect, wrote under the pseudonym of Joseph Polizzi, because he was, at the time, an active LAPD detective. It was that show – and that relationship with Joe Gunn – that inspired my career-long interest in cops and cop shows.

Spring of 1979 was an exciting time. I went to New York in May with all the MTM executives for the annual selling season, called up fronts, where networks present their fall schedules in elaborate stage shows, and advertisers buy ad time for the upcoming season – hence the name up fronts. I had all three pilots in play. When the dust settled, however, only Paris was picked up to series, but I was thrilled nonetheless. I couldn't wait to get back to L.A. and start working.

As previously chronicled, Paris didn't pan out, and was cancelled by CBS after thirteen episodes. Some weeks before we were cancelled, however, I learned a great lesson from Grant.

Life had become miserable for me due to, among other reasons, my ongoing battles with James Earl Jones, so I called for a meeting in Grant's office. Present were James Earl, his agent, Lucy Kroll, Grant, and me. The reason that I knew Jim to begin with was that I had known Lucy Kroll all my life. She was a very close friend of my parents, and was my sister's godmother. When I became successful, she suddenly became my godmother, as well.

Anyway, notwithstanding my personal attachment to Lucy, and Jimmy, too, for that matter, for whom I still hold great affection, I aired out all the laundry, primary of which being Jim's and my conflict, which seemed intractable, and my willingness to leave the show and put it in the hands of someone else who saw things more the way Jimmy did. To my astonishment, Jimmy said, "If you go, I go." I was gob smacked. Actors – go figure.

And then Grant taught me something that has informed my career ever since. Without a hint of rancor, he said, "You know what, guys? If you can't figure this out, I'll pick up the phone right now and call Bob Daley (the head of CBS) and we'll pull the plug. It's just a TV show. It's okay. No one is going to take us out back and shoot us. Life's too short to be miserable. So let's just bag it and go do something else."

I could've kissed him. He had put the entire issue into its proper perspective. It *was* just a TV show. And if we weren't having fun, it wasn't worth doing. Nevertheless, when we were cancelled soon after, I think it was an enormous relief for all of us.

Grant Tinker never, to my knowledge, held the show's failure against me. In fact, he sent me shortly thereafter to meet with Bob Daley, who offered me another pilot script commitment for the upcoming season, which I turned down.

What, you say? You turned down a pilot commitment? Are you crazy?

Well, I might have been, but not for that reason. I knew CBS had given series commitments to other MTM writer/producers: Bruce Paltrow, Michael Gleason, creator and executive producer of Remington Steele; and Hugh Wilson, who'd created and was executive producer of WKRP In Cincinnati. No one could compel a network to program a series it didn't want to. But if you had a series commitment, there was a significant financial penalty for the network if they didn't pick up the series, and so the network was strongly incentivized to program those pilots that had a series commitment attached. My position was that without a series commitment of my own, I wasn't competing on an even playing field. Besides, realistically, who would expect CBS to program *four* series from one small company in the same season. It wasn't going to happen. I knew it, Bob Daley knew it, Grant Tinker knew it. And that's why I turned down Bob's kind offer. If Grant was pissed off at me, he never indicated it.

As the year came to an end, most of the networks had already ordered their pilot scripts for the upcoming season. But in early January, Grant asked me if I'd meet with NBC's head of development, a bright young guy who was Fred Silverman's second-in-command, Brandon Tartikoff, who was even younger than I, though unbeknownst to me at the time, had already battled Hodgkin's disease and won. I had just turned 36, and Brandon was five years younger.

NBC was looking to develop a cop show, and with my background in the genre, they were prepared to offer me a pilot script commitment.

Grant asked me if I'd be willing to work with Mike Kozoll, my collaborator on Vampire, who'd been under contract to MTM for the last year. Of course, I said. Mike and I were good friends, he was a terrific writer, and after my Paris experience, I was more than happy to share the workload with a partner I trusted and whose work I respected.

It was already well into January and pilot season had long since commenced. The three networks between them probably commissioned thirty to forty half-hour and hour pilots during this time, and would choose a handful of them in May that would be ordered to series to become part of the networks' upcoming fall season.

At our hastily convened lunch, Brandon, Stu Erwin, Mike Kozoll and I discussed NBC's pilot needs. Neither Mike nor I were all that keen on doing another cop show. I'd already written and/or produced more than my share, as had Mike, and neither of us felt we particularly had anything fresh to bring to the genre. But Brandon persisted. He said that Fred Silverman had recently seen a movie called Fort Apache, The Bronx, a gritty cop movie starring Paul Newman, and had been taken with the movie's emphasis on its cops' personal lives. Could Mike and I do something along those lines?

I told Brandon that Mike and I would discuss it and that I'd get back to him the next day. Mike was still lukewarm towards the idea of developing another cop show, but I had a thought. I said to Mike that if I could get Brandon to agree to give us total autonomy to do whatever we wanted with Fred's basic idea, would that be more of an incentive? Absolutely, Mike said. And good luck – because in that day and age in television, the expectation of autonomy was absurd. No one ever got that kind of freedom. But I thought NBC might just be desperate enough to give in.

Fred Silverman had been the wunderkind of programming at CBS at a very young age. In 1970, at aged 32, he had risen to the top of the food chain and was responsible for CBS's significant reversal of fortune. In 1975, he moved to ABC as president of entertainment, and pulled off essentially the same kind of programming miracle there.

In 1978, he moved to NBC as president and CEO, but his lucky rabbit didn't follow him there. NBC was in the toilet programming-wise, they were last in the ratings, their shows were a critical laughing stock, and Fred was unable to turn things around. But Fred's – and the network's – misfortune worked to our advantage, the first of many lucky breaks we were to benefit from over the next two years.

The day after our lunch, I called Brandon Tartikoff and told him Mike and I would do a cop show pilot for them, with an emphasis on the cops' personal lives, per Fred's desire, on one condition: that we would have complete creative control over the content of the script. To my utter amazement, Brandon agreed, and before he could think better of it, Mike and I went to work.

Over the years, both of us had collected a million different stories, incidents, and characters that were cop show-centric. And, free of network interference, we dipped into our collective trousseau of tidbits and began to invent a set of characters and stories that very quickly began to take shape.

About three days into it, I got a call from one of Brandon's even younger lieutenants, a kid by the name of Warren Littlefield, who years later would become the president of NBC. "So when are you going to come over and pitch us your story?" he asked. I said we weren't going to. I told him to talk to Brandon, who'd given us carte blanche. And besides, I said, "If you wait one more week, we'll be done with the script."

Ten days after we had begun, we finished the pilot script for Hill Street Blues.

The original title of the pilot was Hill Street Station, an urban precinct in an unnamed city. We purposely left the city unnamed so we didn't have to be vetted by a real police department, like New York's, or Chicago's.

The script generated a great deal of excitement both at MTM and at NBC, but NBC's Broadcast Standards department – the all powerful network censors – hit us with five pages of notes, single--spaced. They didn't like the language. They didn't like the story lines. There were too many African American bad guys, and not enough white bad guys to balance it out. We were not politically correct enough – and on and on and on, for five pages. If Mike and I gave in to all their notes, we wouldn't have much of a script left, so I told them I wouldn't make their changes and, consequently, couldn't make the show. Mike and I left their office. They were stunned. We didn't fight them on anything. We just said no to it all and left. By the time I got back to MTM, Grant was beside himself. I'd never seen him angry, but the calls from NBC had gotten him pretty agitated. What did I mean I wasn't going to make the show? They loved it. They wanted it. They needed it. I told Grant that what they loved, wanted and needed would no longer exist if we executed all their notes, and I felt the script was too good to water down. To his credit, Grant backed me, and once he did, NBC folded. We wound up with ninety-eight percent of everything in the script. Finally, Mike Kozoll and I allowed ourselves to think we might have something special. But for the five years I was the executive producer of Hill Street Blues, I fought with Broadcast Standards weekly. The arguments were stupid, but every script seemed to challenge the limits of their endless restrictions. Once, I think it was during the second season, we titled a script "Moon Over Uranus." It was pretty childish, but so what? Our titles never appeared on screen, so no harm no foul. But Broadcast Standards demanded I change the title. I asked why, as no one would ever see it but us. Broadcast Standards insisted. They said that TV Guide, along with all the newspapers, listed the episode title in their log lines. I refused to budge. This went on for days. Finally, I called Brandon Tartikoff and told him to get these idiots off my back. They were wasting precious time and energy that I should have been devoting to writing and producing. Brandon sighed. This wasn't the first call he'd ever gotten from me about Broadcast Standards. Nevertheless, he promised to talk to them and, sure enough, they finally – grudgingly – allowed us to keep the title. I titled the next script "Moon Over Uranus: The Sequel," and the one after that "Moon Over Uranus: The Final Chapter."

Hey, you gotta have a little fun here and there, right?

Before moving on, a few more thoughts about the whole notion of Broadcast Standards: I think I was always at war with them because I was fundamentally offended by the implicit notion that they had to protect the audience from anything they deemed offensive. I had always felt it was a very condescending approach in that it not only discredited the audience, but it treated us, as writers, as if we were these really talented children who had to be controlled. I wasn't a child. I was an adult, doing adult work in an interesting and complex business that I was trying to make better, and more artistic. From my earliest days as a story editor on Columbo and McMillan And Wife, I would go to war with Broadcast Standards. Their notes were, quite frankly, stupid.

I had almost daily battles with Broadcast Standards over Hill Street Blues. We were not politically correct. We were not racially sensitive. We used unacceptable language. The irony was that most of the words they objected to – "hair bag, dog breath," etc., were of our own invention. Our story ideas were constantly being challenged by them. We once wrote a script about a guy who'd died in a motel room, and when our cops arrived on the scene, they found a sheep in the room with the deceased. It was clear that the guy had been having sexual relations with the animal. Broadcast Standards went nuts. I spent weeks arguing with them, and finally called Brandon Tartikoff. I said, "This is absolute bullshit. (Sheep shit?) This is actually a true story, told to me by a cop I knew. Plus, the sheep is just there in the room, it's not like the guy died with his dick in her."

I promised Brandon I'd make sure that the audience knew the sheep was a female, since gender seemed to be high on Broadcast Standards' list of objections. I promised Brandon this was not a gay sheep.

I guess I finally wore them down, because they relented, and we told the story as written, with a little more emphasis on the poor sheep's gender. The Republic didn't fall.

Over the years, I received countless letters from particular constituencies we'd taken shots at: morticians; accountants; lawyers; Indian food restaurants, etc. I always replied, respectfully, I hope, that our job on Hill Street Blues was to be an equal opportunity offender. I think we succeeded.

9

Now that we'd been greenlit to make our pilot, our first order of business was to hire a director. Grant took the liberty of sending the script to his old friend Jackie Cooper, who'd become a friend of mine, as well since having directed the pilot of Paris. I wasn't sure Jackie was the right director for the material, but Grant felt strongly, and I felt I owed him the courtesy. It was, after all, his company.

Jackie turned it down, thank goodness. He just didn't get the material. I can understand why. Jackie was a very traditional, old school TV director, and the Hill Street script was undoubtedly like nothing he'd ever read before. It was densely written, with dialogue down both sides of the page. We'd written all the background dialogue, as well as the foreground material. There were probably three to four times as many scenes in the script as was considered normal for an hour pilot at the time, and there were something like half a dozen story lines clamoring for attention. It was an intimidating piece of material. I had never felt that Jackie would do the material justice.

After Jackie turned it down, Grant sent the script to another good friend of his, a director named Bob Butler, who I had never met, but whose work I was passing familiar with. Bob loved the material, and when he came in to meet, I fell in love with him. We shared a like point of view about the material, what its themes were, etc. He was a truly unique individual, an old jazz buff and unreconstructed

59

hipster. When he got excited about something, he'd always cry out, "Bigness!" When he ate a meal he liked, he'd bless it with the exclamation, "Good groceries!" And several months later, when we were dubbing the show on the sound stage past midnight, I overheard him whisper to his wife on the phone, "I love you, Mouselet." Come on. How could you not love a guy who calls his wife Mouselet?

Tall, sandy-haired, bespectacled and stoop-shouldered, with half-a-grin always lighting up his face, he was a wonderful spirit, and a great counterweight to the darkness of the material.

With our creative team in place, we started casting the show. The first actor Lori Openden, our casting director, brought in to read for the lead role of Captain Frank Furillo was an actor named Daniel J. Travanti. Mike, Greg Hoblit, our line producer, who'd been my friend for many years, Bob and I all thought he was terrific, and we would measure every candidate for the role from then on against Daniel's audition.

I had a lot of actors I wanted to hire who I'd worked with previously: Kiel Martin, Michael Conrad, Bruce Weitz, Charlie Haid, Michael Warren, and my wife Barbara Bosson. Grant Tinker didn't have a problem with any of them, except Bruce. I had hired Bruce to play a very straight, practically leading-man role in a short NBC pilot presentation called Every Stray Dog and Kid, and Grant just couldn't picture Bruce as the unkempt, barely in control character of Mick Belker.

I told Bruce he was going to have to come in and read for Grant, and I was candid with Bruce about Grant's reservations. On the day of the audition, Bruce burst into the room. He was wearing filthy pants and an old, disgusting vest over an equally unwashed shirt. He hadn't shaved for several days, he had the stub of a cigar sticking out of his mouth, and a grungy old wool cap on his head. He read the scene, then jumped up on the desk, started to growl like a lunatic, and leapt straight for Grant. Bruce picked himself up off the floor and stormed out of the room without saying another word. Silence. Finally, Grant said, "Well, I'm not the one who's going to tell him he can't have the job." And that was that.

The only character we couldn't cast was that of Joyce Davenport. She was supposed to be aristocratic, wealthy, a public defender who swam in the sewers of Hill Street's precinct without mussing her hair, and was a deeply committed and politically liberal representative of the indigent. She also happened to be Captain Furillo's lover.

With only our Joyce Davenport candidate missing, we approached NBC with our casting choices: Daniel J. Travanti, Michael Conrad, Charlie Haid, Michael Warren, Bruce Weitz, Kiel Martin, Taurean Blaque, and Rene Enriquez. NBC's head of casting, Joel Thurm, looked at the pictures of all the actors, and said, "They're all too dark. Where are the blonds? You'll hire this cast over my dead body." As calmly as I could, I told Joel that these were our choices, and if he vetoed any of them, I'd pull the show and we wouldn't make it. Did Joel want to take responsibility for that? He finally backed down, and we had our cast. In addition, we hired Betty Thomas, Joe Spano, and my wife, Barbara Bosson, who played Furillo's ex-wife, to fill out our cast, though Betty, Joe and Barbara were not hired as series regulars. They had originally been hired just for the pilot.

Bob Butler turned out to be an inspired choice to direct the pilot. He'd originally wanted to direct the entire piece in a jittery, hand-held style, a la a PBS documentary called The Police Tapes (1977), in which a documentary crew had filmed a bunch of uniformed cops in the South Bronx, both inside the precinct and outside, rolling on calls with them and recording everything they said. I didn't want the entire pilot episode to be that jarring, so we settled on which scenes would be shot hand-held (including the opening roll call), and which would be shot in the more traditional method.

Our only problem was, we still hadn't cast the part of Joyce Davenport, and we had already started shooting. It was more than a little frustrating, and a bit of a high-wire act. We had one more actress to audition. Kozoll and I were in the narrow hallway of our office building throwing a Nerf football back and forth, when this gorgeous, regal-looking woman showed up and asked where our offices were. Her name was Veronica Hamel, and I thought to myself, "Please God. If this woman can walk and chew gum at the same time, she's the one." Well, she more than walked and chewed gum at the same time. She was terrific. She was The One. Our cast was finally complete.

On stage, the actors loved Bob. He would always generously let them have a take or two that indulged their own impulses, then he'd shoot the scene the way he wanted it. Of course, given the complexity of the material, we were at least a day or two over schedule, and considerably over budget, but the film we were seeing every day was, we thought, brilliant, and the extra time and money was worth the effort.

When we were finally finished with principal photography, we all anxiously awaited Bob's director's cut. It was a chilly, spring evening in May, when a small group of us – me, Kozoll, Greg Hoblit and Bob, trooped over to the CBS Studios administration building, where the main screening room was, to watch the first cut of Hill Street Station. It was a disaster. It was something like sixteen or seventeen minutes too long, there were so many stories we couldn't keep track of the narrative, and when the lights came up after the screening, there was a deathly silence.

I didn't know about anyone else, but I felt like my career was hanging in the balance, and the air was going out of the room like a balloon losing its helium. I knew if I didn't do something quickly, we were all fucked.

I got to my feet and said, into the silence, "This is great. It's too long, it's a little rough in spots, but I know exactly what to do to fix it." Of course, I had no clue. I was trying to buy a little time to think. I said, "Let's go over to my office and I'll run it down for you."

As we left the screening room, I asked the editor to have his assistant jot down one or two lines describing each scene on a 3X5 index card.

In my office, waiting for the editor's assistant, I kept telling everyone how great the pilot was, and repeated my assurances that I knew how to fix it. When the editor's assistant arrived fifteen or twenty minutes later, he handed me a thick stack of 3X5s, and I laid them all out on the floor by acts, the typical one-hour drama being four acts, in those days. Once laid out on the floor like that, I could immediately see what was wrong with the show. The first act was something like sixteen scenes long. The second act was maybe four scenes long. The third act was a dozen scenes long, and the fourth act was maybe five scenes long. The entire structure was out of whack. I certainly didn't realize it at the time, but this is where my old Universal training in deconstruction and reconstruction of stories was of enormous value to me. I started pulling out whole story lines, and then began to move scenes around. Stuff from act one went into two and three. Stuff from three went into act four. Now, everyone else was getting into it. Within half an hour or so, we had a four act structure in which every act was basically the same length. I had pulled at least two whole story lines from the pilot. I said to the editor, "I have a pretty good clock in my head, and I think this revised structure will probably put us within a minute of time."

In 1980 we didn't have the Avid and Apple computer technology that we have today, and editing was a long, laborious process. We weren't going to see the fruits of our labor until about three days later. It was a nervous three days.

When the editor told us he was ready with our new cut, we all trooped over to the screening room again. I was beyond anxious.

The reconstructed pilot was brilliant. It was less than a minute over length, and what we saw that day was the show that was to become Hill Street Blues. Our second editorial pass was much easier, and much quicker, and when we showed it to Grant and the other executives at MTM, they were genuinely moved and excited by the film.

When we showed it to the NBC executives, they were all thrilled. They had no changes to speak of. The next chore on my agenda was to hire a composer. I told everyone I wanted to hire Mike Post as our composer and, with no objection, I called Mike and told him I was going to send him the pilot to look at.

He called me the next day to say it was the best pilot he'd ever seen. What was I thinking of, music-wise? I told him I wanted a main title theme that played against the action: something quiet, simple, melancholy, in a minor key, that would play against the mayhem of the pilot. A day later, Mike called me and asked me to come over to his house after work. "I have something I think you'll like."

After work, I went to his house. He'd converted a small, detached guesthouse into a recording studio, and that's where I heard the theme for Hill Street Blues for the first time. Played on a lone piano with no other instrumental embellishment, it was perfect: simple, poignant, and beautiful. I told him I loved it and didn't want him to change a note of it. I loved its simplicity. Mike said he had to add a couple of instruments, and of course it had to be longer, as main title themes were traditionally sixty seconds in length, but he promised me he would retain the essence of the piece.

That was the beginning of my long and fruitful friendship and collaboration with Mike. I think we did fifteen shows together, including Hill Street. He was, and remains, the best composer I have ever worked with. I did the pilot of Cop Rock with Randy Newman, but when it comes to song writing, Randy is on another planet altogether. There is simply no one like him. However, when it comes to series main title themes and episodic scoring, day in and day out, under the kind of time pressure that's unique to series television, Mike Post is the gold standard.

The finished product caused a sensation at NBC, and word was starting to get around that the pilot was truly special. When Fred picked it up to series, he called me and said, "That actress who plays the wife – you're going to make her a regular, right?" I don't know if Fred knew I was married to her, but I assured him it could probably be arranged. Kozoll and I had also decided that we wanted Joe Spano (Goldbloom), and Betty Thomas (Bates), as series regulars. We suddenly had a cast that was eleven members strong. That wasn't a cast – it was a menagerie!

In truth, the menagerie was only nine strong. In the pilot, we had shot dead two street cops, Hill and Renko, (played by Michael Warren and Charlie Haid), when they inadvertently walked into a drug buy while looking for a phone to report their vehicle had been stolen. We killed them off because Charlie Haid had been hired to do another pilot, and we had taken him in second position, meaning that if his other show were picked up to series, we wouldn't have his services.

In New York for the up fronts, Hill Street Blues was officially picked up, and Charlie's show wasn't. He immediately accosted me in an elevator, begging me to resurrect his and Mike Warren's roles as Hill and Renko. I knew if we did, we were going to have to re-shoot the end of the pilot to allude to the fact that they weren't dead, but in critical condition instead – which is exactly what we did, and it was quite worth it.

In four months, starting from ground zero, we had written, created and produced Hill Street Blues. But there was no time to bask in our achievement. Mike and I had to immediately start writing episodes. Initially, we had no writing staff, and so it was just the two of us. It was only much later in the season that we acquired the services of writers Tony Yerkovitch and Jeffrey Lewis.

10

Right before we started to shoot the first episode of the series, we had a table reading. Daniel J. showed up in skimpy gym shorts and a sleeveless t-shirt, commonly referred to as a wife-beater, or a Guinea-T. Daniel was a gym rat, and it showed. He was ripped. Nevertheless, I thought it was a somewhat inappropriate ensemble to wear to a first table read, and I remember mentioning it to Charlie Haid, who said, "Didn't you know? Daniel is gay."

I didn't know and, personally, I didn't care what his sexual orientation was, but in 1980, that kind of revelation could have sunk Daniel's career, and our show, as well. But with the AIDS crisis just beginning to arise, there would be complications down the road, as when Veronica Hamel came to see me in my office a few seasons later to request that we not write any love scenes for her where she and Daniel had to kiss. In 1983-4, knowledge of AIDS was not only scarce, but generally inaccurate as well. It was a terrifying time, not just for the gay community, but for the straight community, too. No one knew what the virus was, where it came from, or how it was transmitted – or, just as importantly, *not* transmitted. All anybody knew was that there was no treatment for it, and it was inevitably fatal. Fear ruled the day.

Series television has always been a beast. In the seventies and early eighties you shot episodes in seven days, which meant one workweek plus two additional days. In other words, you were shooting an episode (counting weekends) in nine elapsed days, but once the season started, you were on the air every seven days. It was a telescoping schedule, and over the course of a season, you would wind up going from maybe eight weeks to shoot and post produce an episode (editing, sound, color correction, etc.), to three weeks. And by the time you got to the end of the season, you were often performing the impossible: writing an episode in two or three days, shooting it in seven, and post producing it in two or three, just to make your air date. In network TV, you can't call them up and say, "Uh, excuse me, but I don't think we're going to make Thursday night's show. It just isn't finished. Is that okay with you guys?"

Really? I think if I'd ever done that, I would have been selling shoes at Barney's the next day.

I taught myself how to write at night, lying in bed in the dark. I was so immersed in the show, I would wake up at two or three a.m., my mind spinning with stories, ideas, scenes that I had to write. So instead of lying there worrying about falling back to sleep, I would write scenes in my head – literally write them, in script form, in my mind. I'd "write" them over and over until I'd memorized them. Two, sometimes three scenes, over the course of a couple of hours, so that when I woke up the next morning and went into the office, I could simply type up the scenes I had formulated in my mind in the middle of the night. By ten a.m. I had written five to seven pages of material, sometimes more, and I could spend the rest of the day being a producer. Over the next several years I spent a great many sleepless, productive nights in the dark, writing in my head.

By the end of the first season, I was fried. And Hill Street Blues didn't have a normal first season. We were supposed to debut in September of 1980, but an actors' strike that lasted four months really derailed us. It started in July and didn't end until October, and it was every bit as industry-disruptive as the Writers' strike of 1973 had been. When we went back into production in November, we had to start airing in January. We had a thirteen-episode order, and when we went on the air, we landed with a giant thud. No one was watching, so Fred Silverman immediately moved us to another time slot. We did no better. He moved us to a third slot. Still no

one watched. Clearly, the show was alienating its audience. We
were getting letters by the boatload from viewers who complained
we were too visually dizzying; too noisy; there was too much going
on at once; too many characters. The audience didn't know what
the hell was going on. I also got many letters, mostly critical, from
cops. One cop wrote me a two-page, single-spaced letter taking me
to task: "Everything about your show is wrong. The badges are on
the wrong side of the shirt. The name plate doesn't go above the
badge, it goes below," etc., etc. I wrote him back, basically saying
that I was sure we'd made a lot of mistakes, and I appreciated the
input, but that I had the feeling his preoccupation with our visual,
or procedural mistakes was masking a powerful emotional response
to the show. Within days, a letter came back. In the interim this cop
had watched several more episodes and found them deeply moving.
We'd made a new fan.

I also got a letter from a woman who told me that her husband,
a retired cop with a disability – he'd been shot in the line of duty
– was an alcoholic, who had never spoken about the shooting. The
wife made her husband watch the pilot, and when Hill and Renko
were shot, he broke down and cried and, for the first time, told his
wife about what he'd gone through when he was shot. And then he
joined AA. The woman wrote that we had saved their marriage. So,
among the doubters, there were some devoted fans.

There was no question Hill Street Blues was different, by design.
We were putting so much more information on each frame of film
than the TV audience was used to, that it became sensory overload.
In addition, we had serialized our stories. There was no other way
to service the needs of eleven characters in one single hour. Only
by stretching each character's story over multiple episodes and multiple story arcs were we able to satisfy the demands of a show teem-
ing with so much life. Necessity is the mother of invention.

While the audience was ignoring us, and Fred was moving us
around from time slot to time slot so fast our heads were spinning,
the TV critics were raving about us. Ecstatic is not too bombastic a
word to describe what they were writing. In effect, they put Fred in

a position where he couldn't cancel us. We were the only show on NBC's schedule that was generating such an extraordinary reaction. Plus, in all fairness, Fred Silverman genuinely admired the show. He got what we were trying to do. He never asked us to simplify or modify. His position steadfastly was that we were doing nothing wrong; and that it was his job, not ours, to find the right solution to bringing in the audience.

The last time slot Fred tried was Thursday night at ten o'clock. It made no difference. We were practically the lowest rated show in television. I think the test pattern scored higher than we did.

In desperation, Fred ordered five more episodes. Mike and I were exhausted by then, and Mike said he wouldn't do them. We went up to see Grant, and I wasn't going to throw Mike under the bus, so I told him that both of us had decided we couldn't make any more episodes this season. Grant exploded at us. It was only the second time I ever saw him lose his temper. We were hanging on for dear life, we had just gotten an additional five- episode order, and we were saying we were too tired to make them? Were we crazy? He virtually ordered us to make them.

I was angry with Mike, and I told him that if he didn't want to make the five episodes, I'd do them myself. He finally agreed, but he had his agent squeeze more money out of MTM. They weren't happy about it, but they gave in. I didn't ask for anything additional. I was just happy we were still in the game. But it was the first clue that I had that Mike was going to be a problem going forward.

Mike was not a day person. He was a twitchy kind of guy who wrote all night, came into the office in the morning to drop off his pages, and then went home to sleep. Then he would complain to me that in interviews with the press, I was taking all the credit for producing the show. I said, "Mike. Shows get produced during the daytime hours. You're never here. We get interviewed by the press in the daytime, which is when most people work. You're not here. What do you want me to do? I can show you a file cabinet full of articles about us, and you will never once read that I referred to me. It's always *us*."

I chalked it up to exhaustion. I cared about Mike a great deal, and I didn't want to acknowledge that I was watching a degree of destructive behavior that could sink our boat.

Meanwhile, speaking of boats, production down on the set was no day at the beach, either. This was 1981, and cocaine was all the rage. It turned out that a fair number of our cast members were users, and that our Teamster captain was the dealer. I guess the gold Rolex on his wrist should have tipped me off, but I was naïve about that stuff, to say the least.

Charlie Haid and Kiel Martin, in particular, were constantly baiting Michael Conrad during the show's opening roll call, this one written by Jeffrey Lewis:
FADE IN

BLACK

On which: "Roll Call – 7:05 a.m." Under this, the din of –

INT. ROLL CALL – DAY
A Monday morning, as Esterhaus briefs the day shift.

                    ESTERHAUS
          Item ten, as regards canines. The poop scoop
          law goes into effect today.

          Groans, deeply abdominal grunts, and a vol-
          ley of one-liners: "Belker – they passed
           a law for you – ", "Let the mayor scoop it."
          "Please God do save me from foot patrol."
          Over the fusillade –

                    ESTERHAUS
          To wit.
              (louder; quelling the outbreak)
          To wit –

(reading from clipboard)
Any person causing or permitting any domestic
canine to evacuate on a public sidewalk without
promptly and substantially removing said
evacuation
from same shall be guilty of a Class C misdemeanor.

More outbursts: growls, arfs and "What if he removes it, but not
substantially?"

                        ESTERHAUS
Item eleven. Six more complaints yesterday from Dekker Avenue merchants
concerning vending machine coin
box ripoffs. Somebody's doing a lot of
nickel-and-diming out there. Unofficial reward
for the duo who puts the alleged perp out of
business: an evening's free plays of Space
Invader at Dekker Avenue Playland.
Item twelve – A truce has been
reached with the Night
Shift regarding the use, and misuse, of the
Precinct refrigerator. In accordance therewith,
said refrigerator last evening was cleaned out
of all unauthorized foodstuffs alleged to have been
present therein for a length of time longer than
five days.
        (beat; as the assemblage boils)
If I may inject a personal note, guys – we're
all willing to look the other way vis a vis a
little brown-bagging it given the current economic
realities – but to the anonymous owner of the
marinated artichoke and liver pate on whole wheat
in the rear of the third shelf that had taken on
a life of its own . . .

Amid the boil – "A Belker special – " "That was yours, clam breath."

                    ESTERHAUS
        Last item; be cognizant that Monday night
        Football's on tonight, which means we'll be
        Missing fifteen percent of night shift. Be equally
        cognizant that the welfare eagle flies on
        Mondays, which means our local muggers will
        be out in force. Therefore . . . dou-
        ble shift assignments –

A shot of Renko, on the edge of his seat, as –

                    ESTERHAUS
            (reads off clipboard)
        Bates, Coffey, Shamsky, Figliano, Williams,
        and Obradovitch.

Renko breathes a great sigh of relief, under –

                    ESTERHAUS
        All right, that's it. Let's roll. And let's be
        careful out there.

   Michael Conrad, for all his massive size – he was about six-feet five inches tall, and wide as a truck – I had heard, but was never able to verify, that he had once killed a man with his bare hands – was a sensitive, fragile man, and extremely finicky about his work process. Everything had to be just so. He was always incredibly prepared, but had no real capacity for improvisation, and the roll call scenes, in particular, had a kind of improvisatory quality to them. All the guys would cat call at Mike during his carefully prepared speeches, and it drove him crazy. Finally, one day, he snapped, and leapt across a table at Kiel who, along with Charlie, was the primary provoca-teur, and wrapped one giant hand around Kiel's throat. Kiel was no choirboy himself. He was an alcoholic, a drug addict, and a bar brawler. It was a miracle that anybody even bothered to break up the scuffle. Neither Michael nor Kiel was much loved by the rest of the cast.

"Let's be careful out there." Truer words were never spoken.

I was called to the set, and I took Michael outside and walked him around the stage two or three times, calming him down. Then I spoke to Kiel and told him and Charlie both to knock it off and behave. Fat fucking chance. It was oil and water. And by the time I got back to my office, the National Enquirer was calling. Someone had already dropped a dime.

11

After the first season was finally wrapped, the Hill Street cast was invited to Arizona to be the Grand Marshalls at the Fiesta Bowl parade. At the formal dinner the night before the parade, a ten-year old girl approached Kiel Martin with a program and asked for his autograph. Kiel, half in the bag by then, asked her for a pen. She said she didn't have one. Kiel said, "What am I supposed to sign it with? My dick?" The little girl was apparently the daughter of the mayor, and, needless to say, Kiel was absent from the parade the following day.

By the middle of the second season, Kiel was really a mess. His drug and alcohol abuse was completely out of hand. Strangely enough, as an actor, Kiel never flubbed a line. He was always perfect, take after take. Nevertheless, his off set behavior was so bad that I had quietly done some homework about where the best local rehab facility was, which turned out to be at UCLA. My research was precipitated by the fact that Kiel and some drinking buddies had gone down to Mexico for a weekend, gotten totally shit-faced, and hadn't come home. We had to completely re-arrange our shooting schedule to accommodate his absence, and he finally called me late Monday to tell me, drunk as a skunk, that they couldn't make it back because war had broken out in Mexico, and they were trapped. The short of it was, we had to send a plane down to Mexico to pick him up.

The last straw was when he called me one Friday morning at three a.m. to complain about the previous night's episode, from which we'd cut one of his scenes. I said, "Kiel, it's three o'clock in the morning. Call me tomorrow." And I hung up the phone. A minute later he called back and started in again about the edited scene. I'd finally had enough. I told him I was hanging up, and I wanted to see him in my office the next morning at nine o'clock.

When he showed up the next morning he was apologetic. "Not good enough," I said, and threw down an ultimatum. I told him that if he wasn't in rehab at UCLA by end of business that very day, I'd sit his ass down and turn him into the highest paid extra in show business. "Not only that," I said. "I don't think you have the balls to get sober, but I'm willing to give it a try if you are." And I told him if he didn't get his shit together, I'd see to it that he never worked in television again. Kiel whined and complained, but at the end of the day, he checked into UCLA rehab for two weeks. He came out sober, and never took another drink or drug again. I wouldn't have bet you a nickel he could pull it off, but he did. Sadly, he died about ten years later, of lung cancer.

Another one of our actors who shall remain nameless had a bad drinking problem, and one day, he arrived on set after lunch, totally shit-faced. The director called me. "What do I do? He's central to the rest of the day's work." I told him to shoot one master and one close up, and then shut the company down for the day. And I instructed our film editor to slice off those shots and set them up in a screening room the next day. I called the actor and told him to meet me in my office the following day. When he arrived, I took him to the screening room and showed him the film of himself, drunk as a skunk. He was ashamed and embarrassed. I gave him the film, and promised him it would never see the light of day, but that if he ever came to work drunk again, I'd fire him. He never did. However, some years later, he stole some sleeping pills from my medicine chest during several social evenings at my home. He would ask if he could use our upstairs (master) bathroom, and I'd always say of course. So when I discovered the missing drugs, I was pretty sure what had happened. The next time we had a social event to which he was invited, I put a note into the medicine bottle: "I know you're stealing my drugs. You have a problem. Come see me."

The actor came to my office several days later and sheepishly admitted he'd taken the pills from my medicine chest. I urged him to get help, and gave him the name of an excellent shrink. I don't know if he ever called the shrink, but we never had another incident again.

During the writing of the last script of the season, Mike Kozoll came into my office and slammed a bunch of pages down on my desk. It was a section of the script I had written. He told me the pages were shit; that I was a lousy writer; that he was doing all the work and I was getting all the credit, and that he was the only one who knew how to write the show. It was pretty nasty. I told him if he thought he could drive me off, he was mistaken. Hill Street belonged to both of us, but if he wanted to leave, go ahead – I wasn't going anywhere. He left my office in a fury, telling me he'd finish this last episode, but that was it. He wasn't going to return for a second season.

It felt like a hurricane had blown through. The remainder of the season – what was left of it – was extremely uncomfortable. Mike never apologized, he remained sullen and angry, and I was baffled. He had once said to me, apropos of another subject, that he never felt so powerful as when he'd burned a bridge, that is, severed a personal relationship. He'd been talking about a girlfriend he'd dumped, and I was too stupid to realize that in a subtle way, he was giving me fair warning that at some point, it was going to be my turn.

Nevertheless, we made it to the end of the season, and in April – fully a month before the networks were to announce their fall schedules for the following season, Fred sent me a Xerox (remember those?) of an NBC press release, announcing the second-season pick up of Hill Street Blues. Fred had scribbled a note across the page: "Dear Steven, Hill Street Blues is going to sweep the Emmys and go on to become a big hit. Fred." And he drew a little happy face under his name.

Hill Street Blues was the lowest-rated show in the history of television to be renewed for a second season.

Four months later, the night before the Emmy nominations were to be announced, Brandon Tartikoff called me. He said, " I can't tell you how I heard this, but Hill Street Blues has been nominated for a record twenty-one nominations."

I was stunned. I couldn't believe it. First of all, Emmy secrecy was a big deal. No one ever had advance notice of nominations or winners. Secondly, no one had watched us. The only reason that Fred had picked us up, I assumed, was that it was the only show on NBC that was giving them critical credibility. They simply couldn't afford to cancel us – another incredibly lucky break in my career, because if Hill Street had been on any other network, we would have undoubtedly been long gone – as, presumably, would I.

I woke up at 5:30 the next morning to watch the Emmy nominations broadcast live on TV. Sure enough, Brandon had been right. We were nominated for twenty-one Emmys, the most in the history of television.

In September, Fred's note to me seemed prophetic. We won Emmy's in every major category, eight in all. I won two, for writing and for best show. If you've never seen an Emmy, it's gold (plated), and the figure atop the round pedestal has two very pointy wings. When you're ushered off stage after winning, you're escorted to a pressroom where photographers snap away, blinding you with their flashes, and reporters pepper you with questions. It's all very exciting. And then, as soon as the next winner is announced, you're escorted outside of the building, where you walk along a red carpet back to the building's front entrance. Along the way, there are crowds of fans held at bay by police barriers, yelling and screaming congratulations. As I was making my way back to my seat after the first win (for writing), I waved to the crowd, and held up my Emmy for them to see. As I lowered it and kept walking, swinging my arms with the jaunty stride of a winner, I stabbed myself in the thigh with the damn thing, tearing a gash in my pants and drawing blood.

A great start to the next phase of my career.

12

As we began preparations for our second season of Hill Street (this was in June or July of 1981), we were all still feeling the effects of the previous season's work. We were tired, we were grumpy, and no one really wanted to suddenly jump back onto the train we'd so recently jumped off of. Nevertheless, I knew how quickly we'd have to be ready to resume production, and – Mike Kozoll's moodiness notwithstanding – I began to organize writers' meetings. By then we had a legitimate writing staff, consisting of Tony Yerkovitch, a brilliant young writer we'd hired toward the end of the first season, after reading ten pages of a Starsky and Hutch script he'd written – Jeffrey Lewis, and a young, whacky guy named Michael Wagner, to whom we'd always assign our weirdest stories. He had written a film script called Captain Freedom, which was what brought Michael to my attention, and while I wasn't crazy about the script, I was crazy about the character, and I thought we could do a wonderful four-story arc around him.

We hired Michael on staff, and he wrote the story line over the course of four scripts. We cast Dennis Dugan as Captain Freedom, a delusional civilian who'd fashioned a super-hero suit for himself and fancied himself a crime fighter. Dennis had played Richie Brockelman, the teenaged private detective, for me and Steve Cannell four years earlier, and he was inspired in his portrayal of Captain Freedom.

When we'd all sit down in a room together to work on stories (we usually congregated in Kozoll's office), Mike would sit behind his desk, feet up, reading the trade papers. It was rude, distracting, and counter productive. It took about two months of this behavior before I finally confronted him. "Michael, are you in or out? Because if you're out, there's no point in continuing this charade."

We got into it pretty hot and heavy, and Michael finally said to me, "If I leave, the show will fall apart," the clear implication being that I wasn't up to handling the job myself.

This was the first time in my career I'd ever had to handle a situation like this, but my natural inclination was that I wasn't going to be bullied. I told him that if he wanted to leave, be my guest, but I wasn't going to be pushed out.

When Grant heard from Michael's agent that Michael was leaving, he became very concerned. Here we had managed to survive the rockiest of first seasons, we'd just won a boat load of Emmys, there was every reason to believe the future of Hill Street was very bright, and suddenly one of its key creative elements was leaving the show. I assured Grant it would be okay. I *promised* Grant it would be okay.

After I had spoken with Grant, I gathered the writing staff in my office. I said, "Listen. Michael Kozoll is leaving the show. He doesn't think I can write. In fact, he doesn't think that highly of any of us. He believes that in his absence, the show will fall apart. We're losing a big piece of talent, but I believe we can do this by ourselves, and if any of you don't think so, now's the time to go, because this is going to be a shit show for a while."

Everybody said they were in, and we started working. I developed a system whereby we'd all get together every day and work out our multiple story lines per episode, until every one of us knew the story and the characters backwards and forwards. Then I'd assign different pieces of each script to different writers, who'd give me the material when it was finished, and I'd be responsible for stitching everything together (hopefully in a seamless fashion). What this accomplished was our ability to write a full script literally in a matter of days, if necessary. And the most important thing I learned from that time forward was that the key to a happy and productive cast and crew was being able to give them finished material in a timely manner, so everyone had a sufficient amount of prep time.

At the start of every new season of production, particularly if I had a new group of writers, I always began our first writers' meeting with a conversation about how I ran a writers' room and what my expectations were.

Every writers room is different. Some rooms are run by creators who've never run a show before and are terrified of sharing their "baby" with this new group of foster parents.

Other rooms are dysfunctional. The creator or show runner is hostile, or bullying, or dismissive of other's input.

Sometimes the room is populated with abandoned children because the show runner is so frightened of his new responsibilities that he retreats to his own office to write, leaving the writers room rudderless.

There are other, far more productive ways to steer the process. Running a writers room is not unlike how I've always tried to run my company. I work hard to create an environment that makes people feel safe and protected. If you work for me, you know my door is always open. If there are conflicts – and there always are – never let them fester. Resolve them quickly. Always let people know they're appreciated. An attaboy often means as much as a boost in the paycheck. Never hang people out to dry. There's an old saying that failure is an orphan but success has many fathers. In my company, when things went wrong, I took the blame. In success, I always gave others the credit.

A writers room is pretty much the same. On my shows, the writers knew several things explicitly: a) no matter what's said, whatever intimacy is shared in the privacy of the room, it never goes out of the room; b) no idea is too silly or wrong headed to put on the table for consideration; c) egos get checked at the door; d) every story gets fully worked out in the room before anyone goes off to write; and e) no one is assigned a script that they're not one hundred percent enthusiastic about. Nothing guarantees a half-hearted effort more than a fundamental mistrust of the story.

In a room full of writers who trust each other, there are going to be a lot of laughs, a lot of arguments, a lot of shared intimacies and a lot of great stories. I've been a show runner for over forty years, and to this day, nothing is more fun for me than sitting in a room with a bunch of smart writers and breaking stories. And our writers room on Hill Street Blues was as good as it got.

I cannot begin to praise our writers enough. Tony Yerkovich was inspiring. He wrote characters with a flare I couldn't even begin to imagine. He wrote material for the character of Howard Hunter, the lunatic Swat Captain, played brilliantly by James B. Sikking, that was remarkable, and original. He did more to define that character than any of us. The afore-mentioned Michael Wagner was brilliantly screwy. And Jeffrey Lewis was a rock – steady, solid, organized and disciplined – and a fine writer, to boot.

We received something like 18 or 20 Emmy nominations the second season, and – once again – I had been nominated twice, once for Writing and once for Best Show. We cleaned up, and I won both Emmys, which allowed each of my kids to hold one at the after-parties for the second year in a row. Fortunately, no one got stabbed.

All told, Hill Street Blues, over the course of its seven-year run, was nominated for 98 Emmys, won 26 of them, and won Best Show four consecutive years. We won Golden Globes, Peabody awards, People's Choice Awards, Writers' Guild awards, and on and on. By the time we won our fourth Emmy for Best Show, I was genuinely embarrassed. My friend Brucie Paltrow was nominated every year for St. Elsewhere, which came on the air a year after Hill Street, and always lost out to us. He was incredibly gracious every time, but I knew it rankled him, because St. Elsewhere deserved Emmy recognition. Unfortunately, it ran into the Hill Street Blues juggernaut.

Speaking of the Emmy Awards, if I was appointed Emperor of show business tomorrow, I would issue a proclamation that no television show or actor could win the Emmy more than once for the same show. For one thing, it's a bore watching the same people pick up the same statuette year after year. For another, once you've been acknowledged by your peers, it's time to get off the stage and let someone else have a turn. It would make for a much more exciting – and inclusive – Emmy Awards ceremony. That said, I have ten Emmys on my shelf and I'm not going to give any of them back.

A number of years later, after the success of L.A. LAW, Michael Kozoll called me. I hadn't spoken to him since he'd left Hill Street Blues behind. We met for lunch, and he apologized for his behavior, which I thought was enormously generous of him, and acknowledged that the problems we had were pretty much due to his own issues.

We had a pleasant lunch, I wished him well, and I resisted the urge to say, "let's work together again." As talented as Michael was, and as much as I had loved working with him, the price, ultimately, was too high. Plus which, to be perfectly honest, I had learned that I could not only do this job alone, but that in fact I loved being the boss. It's important to create a good environment at work – it frees people up to do their best – but I also realized that television is not a democracy. You can't put every issue to a vote. At the end of the day, you want to have everybody's input, but then you have to make a decision. Ultimately, I think the whole enterprise works best when there's one leader at the top who finally says, "This is how it's going to be." Over the years to come, I was to experience several dysfunctional partners, and it became easier and easier to look them in the eye and say, "Don't threaten to quit unless you mean it. Because I can, and I will, do this job without you."

During our second season of Hill Street Blues, which debuted in September of 1981, Grant Tinker left MTM to become Chairman and CEO of NBC. Fred Silverman, our champion from day one, had been fired. Actually, no one ever gets fired in show business. People resign over creative differences; or a better job offer; or, the ever popular, "I need to spend more time with my family." That said, I owe Fred a debt of gratitude I will never be able to repay him for, for his faith in me and in Hill Street Blues.

I can't over emphasize what a loss Grant's departure was for every writer in the company whose creative freedom had been won by a boss who would put himself between us and the network, so that we always felt free to bend the so-called rules of the medium. It was one among the many lessons I learned from Grant and always tried to emulate: protect your talent. Fight their battles for them. Don't let the "suits" distract them from their artistic endeavors. Because, with Hill Street Blues, television had made a leap in popular culture from being a medium people were embarrassed to admit they watched, to – you should pardon the expression – an art form.

Grant's departure was also a huge loss because it left Arthur and Mel in charge of the company, with none of the mitigating spirit that Grant always brought to every proceeding, whether creative or business. Arthur gave lip service to the MTM credo of creativity first, but the bottom line was, he was all about the money, first and foremost. Suddenly it was no longer so much fun going up to the fifth floor of the executive building. There was no Grant Tinker in the corner office. And, just as soon as he left, suddenly there were electric door closers in all the executive offices, and whenever you'd go up to the fifth floor, all the doors were closed. It was a perfect metaphor for the difference between a Grant Tinker-run company, and an Arthur Price-run company. Door always open, door always closed.

We missed Grant terribly from day one, but the only consolation — and it was a big one – was that he was at NBC, where I did all my shows. At least Grant was still in my immediate universe, and it was of significant comfort to me.

Sometime late during our second season, my original three-year deal expired, and MTM had somehow forgotten to exercise their option on my services for an existing show (Hill Street). Suddenly, purely by virtue of their incompetence, I was a free agent. Of course, as I explained to The Doberman, it was no doubt a simple oversight that MTM would correct as soon as they were made aware of the situation. But Frank saw it as an opportunity to get me a big raise, and he pranced me through a dog and pony show that had me meeting with every studio and independent production company in town.

Arthur Price and Mel Blumenthal were apoplectic, but they had no choice but to negotiate a new deal for me that increased my fees tremendously.

Strike one.

But regardless of Arthur and Mel's anger, for the first time in my life I was making in the neighborhood of a million bucks a year.

I had been, at best, a mediocre student at the High School of Music and Art in New York City, where I grew up. I was a singing major, and I had no performance gene whatsoever. As for academics, that seemed to be a gene gone AWOL as well. My college advisor told me I ought to seriously consider skipping college altogether, as I really wasn't college material. If right after she had said that to me, someone in the next office had said, "Listen, Kid. Forget that old bat. Someday you're going to make a million dollars a year," I'd have hee-hawed all the way to gym class. If I could remember her name, I'd set up a lunch for her with Lee Rich.

With my contractual situation resolved, we finished our second season of Hill Street Blues in late April or early May of 1982. The Emmy sweep of season one had put us on the map, as it were, and we were a hit from then on, and we became the anchor of an astounding Thursday night that evolved under Grant's tenure at NBC. Cosby. Family Ties. Cheers. Night Court. Hill Street Blues. Under Grant's guidance, along with that young and hugely talented head of development, Brandon Tartikoff, who had by now been elevated to President of the network, Thursday night became a juggernaut for NBC. It was arguably the best night of the week for television fans, and each one of those shows was a huge hit. The significance of that Thursday night can't be understated. It was one of the highest advertising nights of the week, because the major studios would buy an enormous amount of ad time to promote their weekend movie openings. And of course, with his typical modesty, Grant never took the credit he should have. He credited Brandon. He credited me. He credited Gary Goldberg. He credited all the writer/producers. The truth is, he was the architect of NBC's turnaround, because he did the same thing there that he did at MTM:

he recognized talent, he empowered talent, and stepped in front of talent when they were being challenged by The Forces Of Evil, Broadcast Standards being one of them.

Brandon Tartikoff was no slouch either, by the way. Young, smart, and very savvy, he was a creature of television. It was his life. And he understood that his talent lay in areas different than, say, mine, or Brucie Paltrow's or Tony Yerkovitch's. He never tried to do our jobs or micro-manage us. But he'd gently steer us, in a big-picture way. It was Brandon who handed Tony a scribbled note on a napkin that read, "MTV Cops. Miami," or words to that effect. And then Tony created the great hit, Miami Vice.

I'll have more to share about Brandon a little later in the narrative, but for now, I want to return to Hill Street Blues, and the arrival (actually, more like an explosion) of David Milch.

13

Here are some adjectives to describe David, which I came to appreciate in fairly short order: genius; sociopath (self-described); crazy; funny – more so than anyone I had ever met.

In the summer of 1982, as we were just beginning to prepare scripts for season three of Hill Street, one of our writers, Jeffrey Lewis, asked me to give a writing assignment to his old college roommate from Yale, David Milch, who was currently teaching English Lit at Yale. I was certainly impressed with the credentials, and I prided myself on finding writers outside the narrow confines of the TV industry. I was always attracted to playwrights, journalists, novelists, lawyers – in short, anyone who'd actually had a life outside the hothouse of our inbred industry. I figured I could always teach them the form of television writing. It wasn't rocket science. But what you couldn't teach, and what I always prized most highly, was a unique voice that had something to say.

I agreed to meet with David, who flew out from New York. My habit, in hiring writers, was to always include in their script contract an option for their exclusive services on the show, in the off chance that they were really special.

Fat Dave, as he referred to himself, presented as a typical college professor: eye glasses, somewhat overweight, tweed jacket, shirt and tie, khakis – almost a cliché of the college professor. David was deferential, but clearly bright, and creatively, we were immediately attracted to one another. Our first meeting was very productive.

David had an idea for a script about a nun who was raped and murdered. It was bold, and dangerous, but I liked it enormously, and within a few days we had worked out that story, and a couple of other minor stories to flesh out the script. David went to work, and two or three weeks later, he came back with a draft. It was okay. It wasn't great. But my feeling was that the problem wasn't so much an issue of writing – David could clearly write – but more an issue of story. To me, story is everything. If the story is right, it's almost impossible to write a bad script. But if there's something wrong with the story, you can't write a good script because the story won't let you, because there's something fundamentally unsound. David's script – really, the story – was missing something, and we spent several hours trying to figure out the problem. Finally, at the end of the day, we agreed to get together the next day and take another whack at figuring it out. But as David left, a light bulb went on over my head, as they say, and I chased after him and found him in the hallway, and brought him back into the office. I had an idea for a small story that I thought would act as a tragic counterpoint to the story about the murdered nun. I think both David and I knew right away that this little story would provide the missing piece to the script.

The main story was about a nun who'd been raped and killed, and the local community was up in arms. They wanted vengeance, and quickly. It was a real lynch mob mentality. So when the cops finally catch the guy and put him in an interrogation room, he clams up and refuses to confess. Davenport is his public defender. Furillo essentially says to the suspect, "There's an angry mob of three hundred people outside this police station, because they know we've made an arrest and they're thirsty for blood. If you walk out of here, that mob will tear you to ribbons. You're safer in here than out there. But I can't keep you in here unless you confess to the crime." Terrified, the guy confesses, and later, in his office, Joyce Davenport, the confessed killer's public defender, confronts Captain Furillo, with a mixture of anger and sadness about how he coerced the confession.

It was a strong story. But what was missing for me was some sense of how life isn't fair – how the sensationalism of one particular case inevitably short-changes the resolution of another, less inflammatory case. So we added a small story about another murder, of a bodega owner named Rodriguez who had been gunned down in a robbery. It happens every day on the Hill, and is far less sensational than the rape-murder of a nun, which is why the bodega murder doesn't get the cops' full attention. What you realize at the end of the day, is that the so-called celebrity event got all the attention at the expense of the second murder, because it just didn't generate the heat the nun's murder did, so it got short-changed. What we come to realize is that the bodega murder will go unsolved: the price of catching the killer of the nun. The kind of systemic cynicism that the two stories, side-by-side, exposed dramatically made the hour terrific, conceptually. It went from being a story that was just about a terrible event to being a story that had an *idea* behind it.

Without going into endless detail, David came back a week later with a second draft that was brilliant. Not only had he incorporated the new story, but he had internalized all the dozens of other notes I'd given him, and the second draft of his script – entitled Trial By Fury – was one of the best scripts I ever read. Here are the final few scenes:

ANGLE - DAVENPORT

Crossing towards Furillo's office.

INT. FURILLO'S OFFICE – FURILLO

Sees her, gets to his feet, continues with the paperwork at his desk - the gesture somehow communicating respect for Davenport's position in the argument both know is to come. Furillo's eyes stay down after both know he's aware of her presence: the opening is to be hers.

DAVENPORT

> I want you to know that what you
> did today frightens me.

                    FURILLO
I understand.

                    DAVENPORT
Do you?

Furillo finally meets her eyes –

                    FURILLO
This is the kind of crime that tears a city
apart, Joyce. It brings out what's
savage in thousands of people. It has
to be dealt with very quickly.

                    DAVENPORT
So the book goes out the window.

                    FURILLO
I went by the book. I pushed a little hard at the bindings.

                    DAVENPORT
That's a crock of the well-known article, Furillo. You bulldozed...

                    FURILLO
I did what I've seen you do for your clients fifty times. I used every resource...

                    DAVENPORT
Furillo! I'm a public defender. I play
a role in a system of checks and
balances, and other people are supposed
to play theirs with the same kind

of energy. You with your jungle justice
threw that all out of whack today.
Gerald Chapman would have confessed
to killing Abraham Lincoln to
avoid that mob tonight.

There's little anger left in Davenport; mostly a mix of weary resigna-
tion and despair. A BEAT.

FURILLO
(quietly)
I can live with what I did, Joyce. I trusted
my instincts and they were right. Under
these circumstances I'd do it again.

DAVENPORT
You can trust your instincts, Frank. Maybe even
I can trust your instincts. But I don't want to
trust everybody's instincts. I want there to be
rules, and I want them obeyed - especially by
people who wear badges and guns You per-
verted the law today. And you're so damn happy
about snagging your confession you don't even
begin to see it yet... Please, Frank... see it.

Furillo's steady gaze effectively hides whether she's struck home
with him or not. A BEAT.

DAVENPORT
Frank, I don't think I can be with you tonight.

FURILLO
I understand.

Their eyes meet – without antagonism or apology, and with mutual regret. Davenport turns to leave. Furillo stops her with –

FURILLO (CONT'D)
You know, Joyce, Gerald not only gave us a confession, he gave us the location of the murder weapon. There's no mistake. These are the killers.

DAVENPORT
(hurt)
Is that where you make your stand finally, Frank – with the oldest excuse in the world? The end justifies the means...?

She leaves; walks slowly through the squad room, leaving Furillo with his chin in his hands. Goldblume pokes his head in.

GOLDBLUME
Frank, on the Rodriguez robbery-homicide, I went over there with Mrs. Rodriguez. No witnesses. And there's no way we're going to get ongoing S.I.D.

FURILLO
Let's at least try, first thing tomorrow.

GOLDBLUME
I'll do my best. But we're really jammed.
(beat)
I don't think we're gonna make this one, Frank.

Wearily, Furillo grabs his coat, departs his office, crossing Calletano in the squad room.

FURILLO
How'd it go with the I.R.S. today, Ray?

CALLETANO
I called the District manager, and explained our
situation. I see them at four thirty tomorrow...
(a beat)
The men are proud of what you did today, Frank.

Off Furillo's half smile of sad acknowledgement –

CUT TO:

EXT. CHURCH – NIGHT

Furillo hurries up the church steps to the door, opens it, as we

CUT TO:

INT. A CONFESSIONAL - CLOSE ON FURILLO

He waits. The sliding door opens. He hears breathing behind the
mesh. Kneeling, he addresses his Confessor:

FURILLO
Bless me Father, for I have sinned...

FADE OUT

I immediately exercised my option on his services for the full
season.

We shot David's script that, in the order of things, was going to
be our fourth episode of the season. But the episode was so good, I
decided to open the third season with it.

When it went on the air in September of '82, Howard Rosenberg,
then the Pulitzer Prize winning TV critic for the L.A. Times, wrote a
very disappointing review. He had been a staunch supporter of Hill
Street early on, and so this sudden reversal surprised me. He said,
among other things, that Hill Street Blues had become a caricature
of itself, that it was no longer the fresh and original show it had

started out to be, etc. It was my policy to never respond to critics. Sometimes you got great reviews, sometimes you got lousy reviews (remember Kevin Thomas – Vampire Movie A Pain In The Neck?), and sometimes you got reviews that praised you for work that was bad, and criticized you for work that was good. But Trial By Fury was a *great* episode; one of the handful of best shows I think I have ever produced. So after I read Howard's shitty review, I wrote him a note: "Dear Howard. I guess the bloom is off the Rosenberg." I never got a reply, but I don't think I endeared myself.

Trial By Fury was the episode we submitted to the TV Academy which won us our third straight Best Show Emmy and which won David his first writing Emmy.

Milch came out to Hollywood and began working on Hill Street. After about two weeks, he came into my office and said that he hadn't gotten his first paycheck from MTM, and could I lend him five thousand dollars, which he promised to pay back in two weeks. I said sure, and wrote him a personal check. Two weeks later, he repaid me in full, in cash. Cash? He explained to me that he hadn't opened a checking account yet.

Two weeks later, David asked me for another five thousand dollars, which he promised to repay in a week's time. This time, he said he had to buy a car, and he was waiting for his next check. So I wrote him another check. Sure enough, one week later, he paid me back, again in cash. I knew something was screwy, and I confronted David. "What's the deal here with the loans and the cash repayments every two weeks? And finally David admitted to me that he was living in a hotel casino in Las Vegas and commuting to work every day. He would take an eight o'clock flight out of Burbank to Vegas every night, and take a six a.m. flight back to Burbank the next morning, and he would basically stay up all night gambling. It was the first time I'd been exposed to the fact that David was (in his own words) a degenerate gambler. The stories that emerged about David over the next months were astounding to me. He had been an alcoholic since childhood, and had become a heroin addict in college. He'd never passed a sober day in his life while in school and graduated first in his class at Yale. He was famous at Yale, not only for his brilliance as a student and then a teacher, but for his drunken escapades, which ranged from exposing himself to the Dean's wife to shooting out the light bar of a police car with a shotgun. Holy shit. What – who – was I dealing with here?

Simply put, I was dealing with a half-deranged genius who quickly became one of our writing stars. Any story meeting with David and the other writers was always a show, with David the star attraction. His mind was always racing. He had great ideas, he had terrible ideas, and they all poured out of his brain with no censor whatsoever. And David never missed an opportunity to drop his pants and expose himself. We were once in a story meeting, David was on his feet expounding about one thing or another, and suddenly he dropped his pants, pulled down his boxer shorts, and slapped his ass against the office window. The window washer was out there on a ladder washing our windows, and David couldn't resist mooning the guy. On more than one occasion I'd be driving David home in my car, and he'd somehow manage to stand up on the passenger seat, drop his pants, and moon the drivers in the next lane. I laughed so hard it's a miracle I didn't wreck the car.

One Saturday, all the writers convened in my office for a story meeting. When David arrived, and before entering my office, he made a slight detour to my assistant's desk, where he grabbed up her pencil cup and urinated in it. Disgusting, but in the sheer audacity of the act, very funny.

The flip side to David's manic brilliance and comic lunacy was the gambling, and the occasional drug and/or alcohol relapse. David, for all his brilliance, for all his pure shining talent, was a deeply flawed man, driven by demons he couldn't control. Some years into NYPD BLUE, which David and I co-created, I was being honored by the Writers Guild of America, West, on a Sunday evening in winter. I think it was either a lifetime achievement award, or the Paddy Chayefsky award. Whichever it was, it was a big deal, and David was going to be a speaker at the event, along with Dayna, who at the time was still married to Marc Flanagan, an Emmy winning comedy writer I'd known for twenty years. Just down the street from the theater where the event was to be held, there was a restaurant the Guild had bought out for the night, where food and drink were served to all the event's attendees. David was particularly manic that night, gave the bartender five hundred bucks, and took over the bar. It was quite a performance.

As we were walking up the street to the theater for the main event, I realized he was holding a tumbler filled to the brim with scotch. "David," I said. "What the fuck?"

And he sheepishly admitted to me that he was a little freaked out. He'd lost a million dollars – *a million dollars* – betting on football games that day.

A few days later, having lost another two hundred thousand dollars on the Monday Night game, he asked me for an advance against his salary of six hundred thousand dollars so he could pay off the bookies. I told him I would loan him the six hundred thousand, but not as an advance. Rather, I was going to make him a personal loan so that he was beholden to me, not the company, or the show, or the studio. And I told him I would lend him the money only if he promised to quit gambling. He swore up and down.

As they say, the check is in the mail, and I won't come in your mouth.

David's demons had him by the throat.

But here's the thing about David. He is somehow irresistible. He's volatile, he's tough on writers, he can be witheringly cruel to people when he feels threatened, but there is something redeeming about David that has always bonded him to me.

One day, he came into my office and demanded a raise. I thought he was being paid extraordinarily well, but I loved David, and I had to acknowledge his importance to NYPD BLUE, so I gave him a raise. A month later, he was back in my office asking for more. Don't ask me why – I don't really know – but I gave it to him. I'd forgotten the old AA quote: "A little is too much, and too much is never enough."

When, several months later, David asked for yet another raise, I blew my stack. David was a volatile man capable of violence. I generally was not, though I did have a temper that I very rarely lost. But I lost it big time, and accused David of trying to extort me. Dayna happened to be in the office, and David and I got so nose-to-nose angry at each other that Dayna fled the scene. I told David enough was enough. He was already the highest paid writer/producer in Hollywood – he was making more per episode than I was, for God's sake – and I wasn't going to give him another nickel. The fight ended with David telling me he was going to quit and storming out of my office.

I couldn't sleep that night. I felt terrible. We had a hit show on our hands, and instead of reveling in the pleasure of our success, we were fighting like cats and dogs over money. At three o'clock in the morning, my trusty light bulb went on over my head, and I knew what I had to do.

The next morning, I called David and asked him to come down to my office. When he got there, dark as an impending hurricane, I said I'd thought about it overnight, and I was prepared to give him anything he wanted. I invited him to go back to his office, call his agent, and come up with a list of demands. I said that whatever they were, I would give them to him. He turned around and left, and shortly thereafter, Dayna came into my office. I told her what I had done, and she looked at me as though I were crazy. Maybe she was right, but I just had a feeling. About an hour later, David came back down to my office, and said he knew what he wanted. I took a pad and pencil and prepared to write down his demands. "Okay," I said. "Fire away."

David said, "Promise me you'll have lunch with me once a week." I said okay, and he left my office. I'd been right. It wasn't money. David was looking for love and approval, and in his whacked-out world, money was the only tangible evidence of it. Somewhere deep inside, he came to understand that our relationship wasn't – and couldn't be – about money. It was about trust, mutual regard, and a creative relationship that was extraordinary. And crazy as he was, he didn't want to jeopardize it.

That was David, in a nutshell.

I can't give you an exact dollar figure, but I signed checks to David in the many millions of dollars. His profit participation in NYPD BLUE was 25% – and it was real, not a studio definition of profits. In addition, David made a phenomenal amount of money from his producing fees, over the years. He also made a ton of dough in a deal with Paramount after he left MTM, and then, At HBO after he left NYPD BLUE. And, so far as I can tell, most of it is gone. David would throw money around like a drunken sailor. He carried thousands of dollars on him at all times, and just tossed money at people. Hundred dollar tips to parking valets and food servers; countless thousands to losers and sycophants he surrounded himself with that he collected from AA or God knows where else. If I told David I needed money to send my kid to college, he would've had his business weasels (and yes, I thought they were weasels) write a check for a hundred thousand dollars. It was easier for David to give you a thousand dollars than sit down and have a meaningful conversation. David would promise jobs to strangers, and then they'd never hear from him again. He was a mass of contradictions. His loyalties were powerful, but even with those he was most loyal to, his promises were confounding, and not always to be trusted.

David perfected what I call the Art Of Performance Writing. He would lie on the floor, surrounded by his adoring followers, and dictate his scripts to a script typist at the computer. A monitor would be in front of David where he lay on the floor, and he would dictate, then re-write, then re-write again and again, all verbally, for the amusement and edification of his adoring audience. Personally, I couldn't watch it. It was a display of narcissism that I found impossible to be witness to. This was his paid audience.

Eventually, David did a show called Luck for HBO. It was a horribly ironic title, given that it was the vehicle by which David's luck essentially ran out. He lost a fortune gambling on horses during that time, and then suddenly HBO canceled the show, using the death of several horses, and the publicity furor that those deaths aroused, as the excuse.

Luck broke David, in more ways than one. I think it broke him financially and, to a certain extent, emotionally as well. And it broke my heart to see this enormously talented man brought low by his demons. But as long as David draws breath, there is always the chance that he'll produce something truly brilliant and memorable.

For all his contradictions, his insecurities, and his foibles, David was – and is – the best writer I've ever known, and I will always love him.

14

With Hill Street Blues well staffed and running more or less efficiently (with thirteen regular cast members it was sometimes like herding cats), I started thinking about other ideas. One Sunday afternoon, I was at a Dodgers game with Jeffrey Lewis, and I suddenly thought to myself: how about a series about a minor league baseball team? I instantly fell in love with the idea, and told it to Jeffrey, who was likewise enthralled. We told the idea to Milch the next day, and he came aboard and we fleshed out enough of the concept that I felt confidant we could go over to NBC and pitch it (no pun intended).

David, Jeffrey and I went to see Grant a few days later, told him our idea, and he bought it, giving us a thirteen-episode on the air commitment. I guess it pays to know the Big Dog.

Anyway, David, Jeffrey and I wrote the script, NBC seemed happy with it, and we folded Greg Hoblit into the mix as the producer and director, with myself as the executive producer and David and Jeffrey as supervising producers.

We began to cast the show, and at the same time we started building the greatest set I've ever seen: a real, minor league baseball stadium. My son Jesse, who was eight or nine at the time, was our Bat Boy. In his Bay City Blues uniform, he was adorable.

We cast Michael Nouri, Kelly Harmon, Sharon Stone (yes, *that* Sharon Stone), Dennis Franz, Bernie Casey, the former great tight end for the San Francisco 49ers and the Los Angeles Rams, Michele

Greene, who would, several years later, become a star on L.A. LAW, Ken Olin, who went on to TV stardom in Thirty Something, and numerous others. It was a huge ensemble. The show was a disaster from day one. Impossibly difficult to produce, we were almost immediately behind schedule and over budget. There was no chemistry between Michael Nouri and Kelly Harmon.

Sharon Stone was, to say the least, difficult. During one early episode, she cut her hair off and got it permed. We were halfway through the episode and she still had a great many scenes to shoot. We had to get her a wig so her scenes would match. Sharon thought she was a star before Bay City Blues ever went on the air, and I guess in her mind, a star wasn't bound by the same rules of professionalism as the rest of us were.

Several years later, when Sharon *was* a star, my wife at the time, Barbara Bosson, was cast opposite her in a Movie Of The Week. Barbara played a married photographer whose husband was having an affair with Sharon Stone, and Sharon and the husband were plotting to kill Barbara by flooding her dark room with kerosene, and lighting it on fire. It was late on a Friday night when they were rehearsing the scene, and everyone was pretty tired. Sharon mimed flooding the floor with the kerosene, and then, with a lit Bic lighter in hand, confronted Barbara with a long speech about how the fire was going to look like an accident, etc. After about thirty seconds of dialogue, Barbara, trying to demonstrate how silly the staging of the scene was, simply leaned over and blew out the flame on the Bic lighter. Sharon was so furious she retreated to her trailer and wouldn't come out.

I thought, notwithstanding our myriad difficulties, that the Bay City Blues pilot was quite good. Dennis Franz, who played the pitching coach, Carbone, in one memorable scene (written by Jeffrey Lewis), explains to a young pitcher how to throw a spitball.

CARBONE
First off, the spitball is not named exactly right
because there's a lotta different substances could

be used. You could use yer spit of course, you could
use yer sweat, you could use yer va-ze-lines and oils,
you could use yer snot, you could use earwax, you
could use toe jam, say fer instance
you got a pebble in
yer shoe. Of yer various spits I pre-
fer the spit you get
after you been drinking a lotta milk, you get a
gooey, slippery, white spit. Though even that
could be inferior to the queen
bee of illegal substances
which would happen to be the
slimy buildup you get
from in back of yer ear back here.
    (indicates back of earlobe)
This stuff don't smell too good, but is primo for
Spitball, provided the ump don't deduce where the
smell come from. Second of all there's the question
of where to hide the illegal substance, which could
be here
    (touching forehead)
or here
    (touching back of cap)
or here
    (touching brim of cap)
or in your glove or right in here
    (indicating belt)
or if you're like some wisenheimers I know,
in the area of your support system, which is
also where you could find a couple other substances
'could be used. Now let's load 'er up and see
how you do.

Dennis was hysterical. But it was all down hill from there. I had
forgotten what later became for me the cardinal rule of writing:

the *easiest* part of writing is . . . writing. The hardest part of writing is . . . *thinking*.

I don't know nearly as much about writing as I'd like to. But I know a few things gleaned from fifty years of writing and producing roughly a thousand hours of television.

I know you have to master form (not so hard). I know you have to master craft (harder). I know you need to find your voice (harder, still). And I know you need to have a passion for writing (passion can't be taught). Thinking (hardest of all) about what you write before you write it – what is my story about? Who are my characters? What is my theme? – will hopefully lead you to the conclusion that good writing is all about understanding the logic of behavior. Lazy writers – who unfortunately abound in Hollywood – start out with a preconceived premise and, maybe, an ending, and then try to arbitrarily craft scenes that get them from A to Z, regardless of the logic of their characters' behavior. Most of the time it's like trying to jam a square peg into a round hole. Without fundamental logic, stories tend to unravel pretty quickly.

Let's say, for instance, you're writing a story about Charlie Manson. He's crazy, right? Wrong. It's wrong because Charlie Manson doesn't think he's crazy. He doesn't wake up in the morning saying to himself, "Boy, I am one crazy motherfucker, and I am going to fuck up somebody's life today." To the contrary, Charlie wakes up every morning thinking *you're* the crazy one, and he's the only sane one on the planet.

There's a great story about Charlie Manson, probably apocryphal, but pretty funny. He was to hold a press conference in jail shortly after his conviction, and about a dozen reporters were crowded into a small room with no air conditioning. Finally, Charlie Manson was brought in and placed in a chair facing the reporters. He stared at them for an uncomfortably long moment, before finally saying, "Is it hot in here, or am I fucking crazy?"

The point is, no one wakes up in the morning thinking, "Oooh, I'm a heartless prick, I'm really going to be *bad* today." On the contrary, most people wake up feeling righteous, convinced that their behavior in life is always just, and justifiable.

So when you think about the logic of behavior, you have to buy into your character's logic, not your own. It's a harder, more complex thinking challenge. But if you can master it, you'll not only be a better writer for it, but you won't be afraid of figuring out your story, because the logic of your characters' behavior will show you the way.

And then there's the passion trap. You need passion in order to write with conviction, but I would suggest it's also a trap because your passion usually suggests a strong point of view. You're against the death penalty, for instance. And so you write a story that proselytizes that point of view. But the job of a fiction writer – at least in my opinion – is not to tell you what to think. It's not to provide answers to questions. The job of a good story is to *ask* the questions in a provocative way so that you'll think about what you've just watched or read, and maybe come up with your own answer.

Thinking. It's the hardest part of the job.

I've been very fortunate in my career to have been given a great many awards and honors for my work in television. I'm proud of all of them. But if you put a gun to my head and demanded that I choose the one award that means the most to me, I think I would have to pick the Writers Guild of America's Paddy Chayefsky Laurel Award for Television Writing Achievement, which I received in 1994. Why that one amongst the dozens of others?

Paddy Chayefsky represented to me the epitome of great television writing. He was emblematic of the generation of writers who literally created the TV drama. He, Reginald Rose, Howard Rodman, Rod Serling and Gene Roddenberry, among others, all came out of theater and film and were the architects of the original Golden Age of television. The anthological dramas of the fifties and sixties, along with the great dramatic series of that era – The Defenders, Naked City, Trials of O'Brien (starring, by the way, a young Peter Falk) – were my earliest influences in terms of shaping my sense of drama, morality, thematics, and the law. And while these great dramatists were taking up residence in my liberal Jewish consciousness, the great TV comics of the era – Berle, Martin and Lewis, Lucille Ball, Jackie Gleason, Red Skelton, Sid Caesar and Imogene Coca, Carl Reiner and Mel Brooks and, somewhat later, Lennie Bruce, Redd Fox and Mort Sahl, excited my clownish sense of humor. I like to think that Hill Street Blues, with its strong drama, cheek to jowl with its often clownish and puerile humor, was the first genuine reflection of all those early voices clattering around in my brain.

I don't mean to imply that Hill Street Blues was mine alone. Hill Street reflected not only my sensibility, but Michael Kozoll's, as well. And regardless of our subsequent estrangement, our collaboration was a great example of the sum being greater than the parts. But Mike left after that first tumultuous season, and the addition of fresh voices – Tony Yerkovitch, Jeffrey Lewis, David Milch, Michael Wagner – in combination with my own, nurtured and crafted a show that redefined the future of television.

I love good writers. I only want to work with writers who are better than me. And I've been very lucky. Rod Serling (ha!). Stephen J. Cannell, Michael Kozoll, David Milch, Tony Yerkovitch, David E. Kelley, Billy Finkelstein, Alison Cross, Jonathan Abrahams, just to name a few. If you put all those writers in the same room, you'd have the best writing staff in the history of television. I'd throw Vince Gilligan (Breaking Bad) in there, but I've never had the pleasure of working with him. I was pretty good myself, but they were – are – better than me.

I think my greatest talent as a writer – aside from my understanding of story and structure – was my ability to guide a group of writers toward the way a story had to unfold, regardless of how *we* wanted it to unfold. A great story has a life of its own, and great writers let that life guide them to a logical conclusion that the reader (or viewer) instinctively understands the truth of.

Here's another fact of life regarding writing, and in particular, television writing. You work incredibly hard figuring out your story, and all most viewers remember are the characters. But if you don't get the story right, all the viewer remembers is that the show stunk up the room.

I used to work my ass off on Columbo, trying to come up with great stories and clues. And all anybody remembered was Columbo turning back toward the villain, cigar in hand, saying, "Oh, by the way . . . " One season, we gave Columbo a dog. I think it was a beagle. Did anyone remember the story? No. But everyone fixated on the dog. But if the stories hadn't made sense – if the plots didn't hinge on the characters' logic of behavior – then the viewer, maybe unconsciously, would've been distracted by the lack of logic and wouldn't have committed to the charm of the character. Or his dog. Am I making any sense to those of you who may have aspirations to write? I hope so.

I'm seventy-two years old, and I'm still learning how to write. And I'm still hoping to work with, and learn from, writers who are better than I am.

Great storytelling, by definition, always involves the exploration of themes. Not to say that all my shows have been great, but the best of them have always explored big themes. One of the reasons I've always been attracted to police and legal dramas is the opportunity to tell stories about how the law defines us as a society. Law, in theory, represents everything that's best about America. But in fact, the law, as a practical matter, is often a blunt instrument that exposes the worst of our societal impulses.

Whether you're a cop on the beat, a homicide detective in New York City, a prosecutor, a judge, a criminal defense attorney or a civil litigator, you're a vital member of a judicial system that is the skeletal foundation of our democracy. And on an almost daily basis you're faced with potentially life altering decisions that test your fundamental values.

When a prosecutor offers a defendant the option of a plea bargain, is that a fair application of the law? From the defendant's point of view, it's a no-win situation. Assuming for the sake of discussion the defendant is not guilty, taking a plea bargain may free him from jail, but it can also saddle him with a felony conviction that will brand him for life. But what if he's not guilty of the crime for which he's accused, and he *refuses* a plea bargain? He may be facing a trial and conviction that will put him behind bars for many years. Is that a fair application of law, or is it the blunt instrument by which the legal system hammers those who run afoul of it?

Few would argue that the legal system favors the wealthy and disadvantages the poor and people of color. It's a fact of life that keeps the wheels of justice turning. If every defendant, guilty or innocent, demanded his or her right to trial, the entire legal system would grind to a halt. But is it fair – is it really justice – to negotiate away one's fundamental rights? Is it morally defensible? I've made my living telling stories that ask those questions and challenge the viewer to answer them.

The best police and legal dramas are a staple of television because every generation's perception of social justice changes. Ten years ago, the concept of gay marriage was unthinkable. Today, largely thanks to television shows that have unraveled the demonization of gays and lesbians, gay marriage is the law of the land.

Hill Street Blues in the eighties was a specific reflection of its time. NYPD Blue, a dozen years later, mirrored a different time and sensibility. Anyone developing a police drama today would be compelled to explore the complex issue of racially tinged police violence. Without taking a definitive stance pro or con (at least from a writer's point of view), Black Lives Matter would be a necessary theme to explore in any 2015 police drama.

I've created and produced legal dramas exploring upscale civil and criminal cases from the lawyers' point of view (L.A. Law, Murder One). I've made legal shows about criminal defense attorneys and public defenders who represent the underprivileged and indigent (Philly, Raising The Bar). I've produced police shows that dealt with the frustrations of cops who have crushing responsibilities and not enough authority (Hill Street Blues), as well as cop shows that emphasized racial tensions and the politics of the work place (NYPD Blue). Every generation seems to spawn a cop show or legal drama that uniquely mirrors the social and legal tensions of the moment. I've been blessed to have a platform from which to explore these themes for the last thirty years.

No matter how our tastes in entertainment change, or how technology alters the way we access content, I hope the awesome power of television never turns its back on its responsibility to inform and enlighten, as well as entertain. In the best of all possible worlds, those responsibilities are not mutually exclusive.

Speaking of writers who are better than I am, I had dinner with David Kelley recently, and it was his suggestion that I spend a few pages talking about the process of writing. So if the last several pages have bored the crap out of you, blame David.

Anyway, the point of this lengthy aside about writing is that I had never thought hard enough about Bay City Blues as a series. Had I not been so impatient, not to mention arrogant – with the success if Hill Street Blues, I wouldn't have fallen into the trap of believing that anything I touched would turn to gold – I would have realized that a show without a strong and reliable franchise, i.e. cops, lawyers, doctors, or gangsters – has to be reinvented every single episode. When you saw the pilot of Hill Street Blues, or L.A. LAW or, years later, NYPD BLUE, you could tell from the pilot what the series was going to be. Off the pilot of Bay City Blues, we didn't have a clue. And neither did the audience.

Here's one last thing I know about writing for television. I can guarantee you that once the flush of initial success has worn off, certain actors are going to look at their material and say, as David Caruso famously did years later, "who wrote this shit?" Or, they'll try to take possession of their character, as if the writer had nothing to do with its creation. Peter Falk would famously re-write all his scenes and bring them into Dick and Bill's office the morning of the day they were to be shot. It made them crazy.

One evening, Daniel J. Travanti (who played Furillo in Hill Street) came up to my office, script in hand. He wasn't happy with a scene he had to shoot in the next hour. "My character wouldn't say this," he said, pointing to the pages in the script. I took the script, looked at the scene, and said, "You're right. Your character *wouldn't* say this. But my character *would* say this, and the guy you're playing is *my* character." I closed the script and handed it back to him.

Meeting over. I suppose I could have been more diplomatic about it, but hey: writers have egos, too.

Bay City Blues was not only enormously expensive, but it performed dismally when it went on the air. After eight episodes, Mel Blumenthal told me that he was going over to NBC to negotiate us out of the deal. NBC didn't want a ratings stinker on its schedule for thirteen weeks, and MTM didn't want to continue absorbing the enormous deficits we were wracking up. All of us agreed it was a right decision.

When we were budgeting the pilot and the series, as hard as we tried, we couldn't get the numbers to work. I volunteered to contribute my executive producer fee (fifty-thousand dollars an episode) toward the production budget. MTM accepted my offer, with the understanding that if we failed, I'd be out the money. But in success, I would be reimbursed for what I'd contributed. I thought it was fair, though essentially I was working for nothing. Given my Hill Street Blues fees, however, no one was organizing a bake sale on my behalf.

All the writers, producers, key crew members and cast had thirteen episode guarantees, meaning they were all going to be paid in full whether we made thirteen episodes or not.

We suspended production, and Mel Blumenthal negotiated an agreement with NBC whereby all the contracts were honored. And, as a kicker, NBC gave MTM another series commitment.

When Mel told me the deal was closed, I asked him, "What about me?"

He said, "What do you mean?"

I said I realized I had contributed my episodic fees toward the production budget, and having made eight episodes, I understood that was lost money. I had, essentially, made a bad investment and was willing to pay the price (four hundred thousand dollars – not exactly chump change). However, I said, what about the remaining five episodes that we weren't going produce? Since everyone else was being paid for thirteen episodes, shouldn't I be compensated for the remaining five, as well?

Mel saw the logic of my argument, but insisted the deal was already closed. He wasn't going to go back to NBC and try to get another 250,000 dollars on my behalf. I asked Mel if he minded if I sent The Doberman over to NBC to plead my case. "No," he said. "Be my guest." Those were his exact words.

So Frank went over to NBC and met with John Agoglia, NBC's head of Business Affairs. Frank reported back to me that Agoglia had agreed to pay me fifty cents on the dollar. I proposed an alternative to Frank: tell Agoglia to forget the money, but instead give me, personally, a series commitment that would be valid for one year beyond my contractual commitment to MTM.

Frank said he seriously doubted that NBC would go for it, but I said, "What the hell? Give it a try."

Not only did The Doberman get the series commitment, but he also got the fifty cents on the dollar for the last five episodes of Bay City Blues.

Three days later, Frank called me to say that NBC had reneged on the deal. I knew exactly what had happened. When Arthur Price found out about the series commitment to me, he must have gone berserk, called Grant, and gotten NBC to pull out of the agreement. Frank was dead-ended.

I told him not to worry, that I'd take care of it. I called John Agoglia first. I told him if I didn't have my series commitment back by the end of business that day, I was going to walk away from Hill Street Blues. They could sue me, I'd sue them back – I'm no lawyer, but I know what restraint of trade is – and in the meantime, while we buried each other in legal paperwork, Hill Street Blues would fly off the rails.

I then tracked down Brandon Tartikoff, who was in New York, and told him the same thing: that I knew what had happened, and if they didn't make it right by the end of business that day, I was going home with the worst sore throat in the history of show business. I had never made a threat like that before, and I've never made one like it since, but I meant every word of it. By end of business that day, I hadn't heard a word, and when I left work that night, I told my assistant I'd be at home indefinitely and would only take calls from Frank Rohner.

I stayed home for four days. I spoke to no one. I wouldn't take calls from anyone on staff at Hill Street Blues. The only person I spoke to was The Doberman. Within days, Hill Street Blues was in chaos. There was no one there who could – or would – make key decisions.

Finally, late Friday afternoon, Frank called me. NBC had caved. They'd given me back my series commitment, and Frank said I could go back to work on Monday. I said no, I wanted something in writing, since NBC already had reneged on our verbal agreement once.

Frank said he wouldn't be able to get a written agreement that quickly, but he promised me the battle had been won. I relented to this extent: if John Agoglia would call me personally and apologize, and give me his word that our deal had been reinstated, I'd return to work Monday morning.

Agoglia called me twenty minutes later. "Steven, so sorry. It was all a misunderstanding. Of course you have your series commitment."

A misunderstanding. Right.

I went back to work on Monday, but I knew that Arthur and Mel had to be seething that I'd challenged them and won.

Strike two.

Strike three came soon after. Particularly now that Grant Tinker was gone, Hill Street's budget became a chronic sore point with Arthur. We were an expensive show, no doubt about it. With thirteen regular characters that needed to be serviced in multiple story lines over the course of twenty-two episodes, the production costs exceeded our license fee (the amount of money MTM would get from NBC per episode) by a considerable amount. I believed that, long-term, MTM would make a fortune on our show in syndication. But in the short term, on a per episode basis, Hill Street Blues was losing money.

At the beginning of the fourth season, Arthur called me up to his office to lecture me about costs, and he asked me what I was prepared to do to decrease our budget. "Look, Arthur," I said. "I know we're an expensive show. But we're responsible producers. Every dollar is up on the screen. We're not wasting a dime."

Arthur suggested that if I reduced the number of story lines per episode, I would also reduce costs. I pointed out that if I reduced story lines, I wouldn't be able to service all of our characters. Arthur further suggested (with true, bean-counter logic) that if I reduced the number of characters (i.e., fired some of our regulars), I'd save even more money. I countered with the argument that we were the most honored show in the history of television. We'd won the Best Show Emmy three years in a row. Why on earth would I want to preside over the dismantling of what was, arguably, the best one-hour drama in the history of television? I finished with this: "Arthur, I'm an employee. I work for you. If you're really unhappy with me, you can fire me. But I'm not going to gut the show just to reduce its costs."

The next morning, Arthur called and asked me to come up to his office. When I got there, he said I'd cost him a night's sleep (boo hoo), but that he'd decided he was going to let me go. I was a little shocked, but I said okay, that was his right and he should call Frank Rohner to negotiate my release.

As I was leaving his office, I said, "Arthur. I just want to caution you about what's going to happen now. The press is going to get wind of this very quickly, and my phone is going to ring off the hook, and I'm going to tell them exactly what happened. And I'm going to tell them the reason I've been fired is that I refused to knuckle under to the demand that I reduce the density and complexity of the show. What's going to happen then is you're going to get pilloried in the press. And with Grant gone, the inevitable ripple effect is really going to be detrimental to MTM's reputation. You're going to be accused of dismantling the best show on TV." I left his office, and by the time I'd gotten to the elevator, I was called back to his office. He folded like a guy holding a pair of deuces. "Just do the best you can." I assured him I always had, and would continue to do so.

Strike three.

From that day forward, I knew my days were numbered.

In November of 1983, Michael Conrad finally succumbed to cancer. He'd been diagnosed mid-season three, had responded to chemotherapy at first, but then it was discovered the cancer had spread, and Michael began to descend the slippery slope. By the beginning of season four, he was painfully thin, he'd lost his hair from the treatments, and he was physically very ill, both from the cancer and from its treatment. Nevertheless, he insisted on coming to work every day. We made every accommodation for Michael that we could, reducing his workload to just roll calls. It was heartbreaking to watch, but also moving in its display of raw courage in the face of death.

When Michael finally died, we wrote him out of the series by having him die while making love to his paramour, Grace Gardner, played by the lovely and talented Barbara Babcock.

And at the end of the episode, all the Hill Street cops gathered late at night to say goodbye:

EXT. CITY STREET – NIGHT

A desolate patch of the Hill, boarded-up or burnt out, a junkie hangout but at the moment empty of junkies. The street shines blue-wet under the streetlights. Hill, Renko, Belker, Bates, Hunter, Calletano and Furillo all in civilian clothes, no rank apparent among them, are congregated on the sidewalk. Hunter is holding the container of Esterhaus' remains. No one is very talkative. Furillo surveys the faces. Goldblume arrives hurriedly, having parked a few feet away.

GOLDBLUME

Sorry.

FURILLO

(nods; half a beat)

This everyone?

Silence. Furillo takes it as an affirmative.

FURILLO (CONT'D)

Howard.

Hunter pops the lid on the tin. Happens to look inside . . . Frowns.
Shakes it.

HUNTER

Large aggregate particles here, Frank.
High adhesion factor.
(hands container to Furillo)
We may have a problem getting a uniform distribution.

RENKO

(grouchy from his muscle pull)
What'd he say?

HILL

The Sarge is a little gritty.

RENKO

Oh.

BELKER

(thinking about the plan)
Putting him in the street. I dunno.

BATES

A cop in this town lives on the street. It's home . . .

ON FURILLO

Over this, Furillo has stepped off the curb into the street. He pours
himself a handful of ashes from the container. Tosses the handful
into the street, out beyond the parked cars. Those on the sidewalk
hush up, wise to what he's doing.

FURILLO

Ray.

Calletano steps out beside Furillo. Furillo pours him a handful of ashes. Calletano tosses it into the street.

CALLETANO

Goodbye, good friend.

Calletano returns to the sidewalk. Goldblume comes next.

GOLDBLUME

Goodbye, Phil.

Hunter comes next.

HUNTER

Home is the sailor home from the seas,
Phil . . . and the
hunter home from the hill.

Then it's Bates. She says nothing as she tosses the ashes. She's followed by Hill and then Renko.

RENKO

So long, Sarge.

Belker gets the last handful. He holds it for a beat. Then tosses it. Furillo upends the container and taps the bottom to get out the last of it.

THE SIDEWALK

As Furillo rejoins the silent crowd waiting there. A long, meditative beat follows. All eyes are on the street, their thoughts with the soul they've just laid to rest. And then, without a word, Hill breaks away and moves slowly to his car down the street. Renko follows. Bates moves away in the opposite direction toward her car. Then Hunter, Goldblume, then Calletano. Belker is fixated on the street, frozen in time . . . And then he's gone, vanished into the night. Furillo and Esterhaus are alone. Furillo gives the street one last look. A simple, whispered –

FURILLO

Phil.

CAMERA PULLS BACK

Giving us a full view of the street and the block as Furillo walks to his sedan. He gets in, starts it up, pulls away from the curb. As he turns the corner, a street sweeper appears from the opposite direction and pivots onto the street. It moves toward us – lights flashing, brushes turning, its sprinkler shooting out a gentle spray of water – and passes innocently over the remains of Sgt. Esterhaus.

FADE OUT

It was an emotionally wrenching scene.

In all honesty, I have to admit that Hill Street Blues was never quite the same once Michael was gone. He was the true zany spirit of the show, and a great, great character. None of us could imagine anyone else having played the part. We tried Joe Spano (Goldbloom) behind the podium. We tried Betty Thomas (Bates) as well. No one could really pull it off. Michael Conrad's shoes were too big to fill. We finally cast the great actor, Robert Prosky, as the new roll call Sergeant. Bob was excellent, but it just wasn't the same. Larger-than-life Michael, with that weird wandering eye of his (we'll add him to the lunch with Peter Falk and David Victor), was irreplaceable.

With Michael's death, some part of the show's brilliance died with him.

15

When I refused to cut the budget of Hill Street, I knew when I left Arthur Price's office that it was just a matter of time until he got rid of me.

That time came about a month before the end of the fifth season. We had just passed the one-hundred-episode mark, the traditional point at which a television series becomes a true syndication asset, and syndication is where the real money is in television. We were shooting our next to last episode of the season and in the midst of prepping our last one.

Arthur called me up to his office and fired me. He said the show was too expensive, I was profligate, I had refused to listen to his pleas for more austerity, and it was time for us to part ways, and that David Milch and Jeffrey Lewis would take over as executive producers for the sixth season and beyond. I can't say I was surprised by the firing. I pretty much knew it was coming, it was just a matter of when. But I was surprised – and angry – that, obviously, Arthur had spoken to David and Jeffrey, and neither one of them had let me know what was going on. Given our friendship and our close working ties, I felt betrayed by both of them. I knew I could forgive David. He's a self-described sociopath. He actually said that to me, once. And he's just not capable of the kind of integrity that I think most of us would feel compelled to act upon. It would be like being angry with someone for not having blue eyes. It's not their fault. There's nothing they can do about it. But Jeffrey was another story.

He *was* an adult, and he should have been a more stand up friend. But life is short, and grudges are toxic. I'm too old to hold onto them. Jeffrey and I remain friends today.

I told Arthur to talk to Frank Rohner about settling out the deal, because technically, they couldn't fire me, as I was contractually tied to the show. But we all knew it was time for me to go, and I certainly didn't want to stay where I wasn't welcome. Besides, I had my NBC series commitment in hand, so it wasn't exactly like I was going to be out on the street. In fact, Grant Tinker had recently called me and suggested I might want to give some thought to the possibility of some kind of law show.

In terms of the cast and crew, my firing was a wrenching experience. We had all taken this extraordinary ride together, and now the engineer was being kicked off the train. Our wrap party at the end of the season was particularly emotional.

I was more than a little concerned for my wife, as neither Jeffrey nor David particularly liked her character. But I urged her to stay, and not let whatever my issues were with MTM distract her from her work.

But that was wishful thinking. As the company commenced production on its sixth season, it was clear that Barbara was essentially being written out of the show. She finally quit. And then Greg Hoblit, who had always been the steady production and directing hand, quit as well. Production costs soared by something around twenty-five to thirty percent, and without Greg's and my presence, the overall quality of the show dropped precipitously. At least that's what I was told by others. I never watched another episode of Hill Street Blues for the last two years of its existence.

The Doberman did what Dobermans do. Financially, he tore MTM to ribbons, exacting from them a payment of seventy-five thousand dollars for every episode of Hill Street produced going forward. The show lasted two more seasons (forty-four episodes), and I was paid seventy-five grand times forty-four for *not* coming to work.

America. What a country.

16

When I was a kid, I was a terrible student. I was also shy. The only time I felt comfortable was when I was playing sports. I was a good athlete. Not great – but pretty good. And while I was small for my age (I didn't have a real growth spurt until my senior year in high school), I was fiercely competitive. I hated losing. But all in all, I wasn't very noticeable – or notable – through my childhood and adolescence, and even into my young adulthood, though fortunate nonetheless to have a job in television that I loved. That said, I didn't really find my voice as a TV writer and creator until Hill Street Blues came along in 1980-81.

I provide this autobiographical observation because it seems to me that my personal evolution was roughly parallel to that of TV's.

When TV was "born" in the middle to late 1920's, it was an oddity, its childhood barely marked. By the late 1940's, however, after WWII, television had become available to the public, or at least those lucky enough to afford a TV set.

The first TV I ever saw belonged to Jewel Kaufman, a woman who lived in our apartment building at 46 W. 83rd Street in New York City. My life-long friend, Peter Hyams (who grew up to attain success as a film writer and director) and I would go down to her apartment to watch Howdy Doody and Kookla, Fran and Ollie. I was thrilled. The TV shows of the late 40's and 50's were enormously influential in the development of my sense of humor. I loved them all: Milton Berle, Red Buttons, Red Skelton, Sid Caesar and Imogene Coca, Lucille Ball, Dean Martin and Jerry Lewis, Jack Benny, Jackie Gleason and Art Carney in The Honeymooners. These artists (and many more) fueled the popularity of the barely adolescent medium, and by the mid-fifties there were something like seven million television sets in America. (Today, sixty years later, 98% of all homes have TV.)

My parents couldn't afford a set, but a group of their friends chipped in and gave us a TV for Christmas in the early fifties, when I was nine or ten. I couldn't get enough of it. I remember my early interest in politics (not to mention ethics and morality) was ignited by watching the McCarthy hearings in 1954.

When Joseph N. Welch said to McCarthy, "Have you no sense of decency, Sir? At long last, have you left no sense of decency?" I was electrified. I think that might have been the first time I became conscious of the power and eloquence of the spoken word, and it cemented the foundation of my future career as a writer.

Television in the 50's and 60's evolved into a mass soporific. There were some fine dramatic shows, but it was the comics who defined the era. It was also during that era that the so-called intellectual elite came to define TV as a lowbrow entertainment; something only the great unwashed indulged in. It was a medium that drew their contempt.

In the 70's, television visionaries such as Norman Lear began to shift the public perception of the medium. All In The Family not only raised the bar for writers and producers, but it began the inexorable shift in the audience's perception of what TV was capable of contributing to the public discourse. Through his comedies, Norman raised the public's consciousness about racism, class warfare, abortion, etc.

The comedies coming out of Grant Tinker's MTM were also altering the public's perception of the medium. Shows like The Mary Tyler Moore show (a divorced, single, working woman – shocking!), The Bob Newhart show and Rhoda, to name just a few, were not only funny, they were smart. And then there was Maude, and MASH, and Taxi.

It would be unfair not to mention that the most popular series of the 70's was the admittedly low brow Happy Days. Henry Winkler as The Fonz mesmerized a generation of kids, including my own daughter, who was about nine. (As an aside, Henry and I became friends at the height of his Happy Days fame. He was, and is, a wonderful man. When I first met him at a family party, with kids running all over the place, I told Henry I had a nine year old daughter floating around somewhere. Henry went and found her, and in full Fonz persona, took her aside for a ten-minute chat. After they chatted, he swore her to secrecy. She's forty-five and to this day won't tell me what they talked about.

Anyway, I used to have a recurring dream that for some reason was logical only in dream reality. In it, I had to leave my family and career behind and return to college to complete a class in order to graduate. In the dream, which I'd been having for years, I'd have to return to Pittsburgh, rent a small apartment, and complete the class I had missed. The dream would always end with me sitting in the classroom not understanding a word the professor was saying. I would bolt awake in a panic. One night, after Henry and I had become friends, I had the same dream, except that this time, I didn't awaken. The dream went on. I was sitting in the classroom and I thought to myself, "This is bullshit." I got up from the desk and left the room, walked through the lobby of the Fine Arts Building at Carnegie Tech, and as I was exiting the building, Henry was entering. "Henry," I said. "What are you doing here? It's so great to see you!" And I embraced him. That's when I woke up, and I instantly knew I'd never have the dream again. To me, in life as in my dream, Henry was the very symbol of great success. And when I embraced him in my dream, I was finally embracing my own success.)

The point I'm getting at, dream analysis aside, is that television was in an interesting time of discovery in the 70's, both within the medium and without. TV had always been viewed as an escape from the realities of life – kick back, have a beer, and watch Uncle Miltie or Bonanza. Now, suddenly, television was becoming a driver of culture, asking a mass audience to do something it had never expected TV to demand of them: *Think.*

And then, in January of 1981, the Hill Street Blues bomb exploded. Or, more accurately, fizzled. Critics loved it. The public hated it. As Yogi Berra said, if they don't want to come, you can't stop 'em. But then we won eight Emmys, sweeping virtually every creative category, and became a hit – not just in terms of ratings, but in terms of the culture, as well. Television was no longer a kid. It had quietly (and then suddenly, loudly) morphed into a mature art form. Those of us who wrote and produced series television for a living no longer had to admit to our profession sheepishly. We could say, with pride, "I'm a television writer."

Television had finally evolved into an art form that, at least for adults, was beginning to eclipse the motion picture as a topic of water cooler conversation.

I'm not big on tooting my own horn. There are no one-man bands in our business. There's an army of gifted men and women behind every great show. But through the eighties and nineties, I had four big hits, each one created with a different collaborator: Michael Kozoll on Hill Street Blues, Terry Louise Fisher on L.A. Law, David Kelley on Doogie Howser, M.D., and David Milch on NYPD Blue. And notwithstanding the great talent I was surrounded with, there was only one common denominator on all those shows: me.

Hill Street ran on NBC for seven years. L.A. Law ran on NBC for eight years. Doogie Howser ran on ABC for four years, and NYPD Blue, also on ABC, ran for twelve years. In all, from January of 1981, continuously through May of 2005, I never had less than one show, and sometimes two or three, on the air at any given time. And during that span of almost twenty-five years, television became *the* place for quality story telling. If the live dramas produced between 1948 (The Actors Studio) and 1963 (Chrysler Theater), including NBC Television Playhouse, Kraft Television Theater, Studio One, Playhouse 90 and The Twilight Zone were considered the first Golden Age of television, then I would argue that shows like

Hill Street Blues, L.A. Law, ER, NYPD Blue, The West Wing, The Sopranos, Breaking Bad, and Mad Men defined a Platinum Age of television.

Hindsight is 20-20. At the time Mike Kozoll and I created Hill Street Blues (1980), we had no real overview of what we were doing, and we certainly had no idea of the impact the show would have on American, and ultimately international, culture. In 1980, society was still very much in its post-Vietnam era. The political turmoil of the civil rights movement, the urban riots of the 60's and the war-protest movement of the 70's (Kent State particularly comes to mind) were still recent memories. Cops weren't people. They were Pigs. In particular, the Chicago riot at the Democratic National Convention in 1968 put an indelible crease in young people's brains about police brutality, a subject still being vividly revisited today.

But in the years I'd been working on and creating cop shows, I had come to know a good many cops personally. And I became familiar with a psychology that's common to most police departments: Us versus Them. Cops have always felt, to some degree, beleaguered and misunderstood. Certainly not all, but most cops I've met, came from lower class, blue-collar backgrounds where some form of racial and gender based bias was common. And for most cops who deal day-to-day with crime, particularly in urban environments, it's all too easy for those biases to be reinforced. This is not to apologize for what is often outrageous or egregious behavior. But certainly as a writer, you want to look at things in their proper context. And in the 60's and 70's there were ample reasons for African Americans to fear and distrust the police, as in fact there are today. I guarantee you that the overwhelming majority of cops start their careers with genuine, altruistic intent. But cops are human. They're under tremendous stress. They have very high divorce rates. Alcohol and substance abuse is significant. Corruption – morally, ethically, or financially – is often a corrosive by-product of a cop's day-to-day interaction with the public. We have an unrealistic social compact with the police: you keep us safe, and we won't really look too closely at how you do it. We'll eat the sausage, but we just don't want to see how it's made.

In this age of cell phones, videos, and ubiquitous surveillance cameras, that's changing. And while there's debate about police reluctance to act forcefully under such scrutiny, it is, in the long run, in all our best interests.

But in 1980, none of that existed and, as I mentioned, cops were routinely referred to as Pigs.

The vast majority of us never run afoul of the law. An occasional traffic violation is about it. But cops deal with serious lawbreakers every day. They have a lot more reason than most of us to fear for their physical safety. They work in a highly politicized, paramilitary environment. They have high stress levels, often without sufficient background or training to deal with it. It was widely perceived, certainly in the eighties and earlier, that if a cop went to his department for psychological counseling, he was "branded." And so cops kept their fears and stresses to themselves, often medicating their anxieties with drugs and alcohol. (I used to meet a cop friend for lunch frequently, and he would always want to meet at eleven-thirty in the morning so he could have a couple of martinis.) Cops, like the rest of us, had wives and kids and parents to support and bills they couldn't pay. Often they moonlighted as bodyguards or bouncers or small business owners. Being a cop was no picnic. Their rate of suicide was higher than that of the general population. And, in general, the population didn't much care for them. If that's a misstatement of fact in the 60's, 70's, and 80's, don't tell that to the cops themselves. They felt that they were living a different reality than the rest of us.

When Kozoll and I created Hill Street Blues, I think both of us wanted to pierce the veil of common perception and portray cops – good and bad – as real people with real problems who were burdened with fulfilling a social contract that they often weren't prepared for.

Most cops I know hate cop shows. They're filled with unrealistic procedures, and their cops are one-dimensional characters who never suffer the personal consequences of their actions. Do cops have prejudices? Yes. But unlike many of us who, when confronted, can't really explicate them, cops can. For instance, many male cops don't want to partner with females. Misogynistic? Maybe. But it's a bias that, in their minds, has a legitimate rationale. More than one cop has told me that a female partner usually isn't big enough to physically intimidate a belligerent suspect and will therefore be too quick to go for her weapon, unnecessarily escalating the risks to both suspect and cops. Is that true? I don't know. I've never been there. But I can understand how a cop who's been in that situation might extrapolate the experience into a general mistrust of female partners.

There's always more than meets the eye when trying to understand the psychology of cops and how it effects their behavior. In Hill St. Blues, we were trying to humanize "Pigs." And judging by the response we got from hundreds of cops in the U.S. and abroad, I think we did a pretty good job of it.

In London, if a bobby loses his helmet, he has to replace it at his own considerable expense, in addition to whatever other disciplinary action he might face. In 1984 or thereabouts, my then wife (who played Furillo's ex-wife on Hill Street Blues) was in London promoting a film she was in. A bobby came up to her in the street, took off his helmet, and handed it to her. "Please give this to your husband with my thanks," he said. I was deeply touched by the gesture, and it – as well as many like it over the years – convinced me that in some small way, Hill Street Blues went a ways toward humanizing cops. I like to think that ten years later, in a different time and to a different generation, we did the same thing with NYPD Blue. If for no other reason, I'll always be proud of both those shows.

17

With the extraordinary success of Hill Street Blues behind me, and a thirteen episode on the air commitment from NBC in my pocket, I was in demand all over town. I met with Paramount. I met with Universal. I met with Disney. I met with Twentieth Century Fox. The Doberman was demanding a three-year, five million dollar contract. No one had ever made that kind of demand before, but Frank was undaunted, and I never wavered in my support of his tactics. He had made me wealthy. I had no idea he was to make me rich over the next several years.

I narrowed my choice to either Disney or Fox. I'd had a great meeting with Jeffrey Katzenburg and Michael Eisner, and their enthusiasm was infectious. I'd also had a good meeting at Fox, and though I didn't know Barry Diller very well, I thought very highly of him. I learned, some years later, that before I was to meet with them, Arthur Price called Barry Diller to warn him off, saying I was difficult, and profligate. In my meeting with Barry, when the subject of money came up, I was frank with him. I said that I believed I was a good and responsible producer. If you asked me to produce a Chevy, I would make it for what a Chevy appropriately cost. But if you asked me to produce a Rolls Royce for Chevy prices, I couldn't – and wouldn't – do that.

When I went back for a second meeting at Disney, Michael Eisner, who I really liked, told me that he thought a three-year, five million dollar deal was exorbitant, and that he didn't think anyone in town would pay that kind of money. He said to me, "But if you find someone who will, grab it, because that's a home run." Two days later, The Doberman closed the deal with Fox for three years, at five million dollars. I sent Michael a note: "Dear Michael, I hit a home run. Best, Steven."

With the Fox deal closed, I had lunch with Brandon Tartikoff to discuss what kind of show he might have a preference for me to develop. Brandon channeled Grant Tinker. He said it was up to me. Whatever I wanted to do was what he wanted to do. I couldn't have been happier at being given that kind of freedom. At the same lunch, Brandon told me that Arthur Price had said that I had come to him, saying that I was burned out, and asking to be released from any further obligation to Hill Street. When Brandon expressed concern for the show's ongoing welfare, Arthur assured him that the show would be in great hands with Milch and Lewis. And only then, after he had received Brandon's blessing, did he fire me. Brandon asked me not to repeat what he'd said to me, and I promised him I wouldn't. Thirty years later, I'm breaking my promise. If Brandon were alive, I don't think he'd mind.

I had several series ideas in mind, but I had learned my lesson from the fiasco of Bay City Blues. I was going to take my time. But among the various ideas that were floating around in my head, the notion of a law show kept coming back to me. It wasn't just that I liked the idea of doing something I knew Grant Tinker would like. I also liked the idea of doing a show that had a franchise, so that an audience would know what it was going to get every week. And, stealing more than a page from my experience with Hill Street Blues, I wanted to do a show with a large ensemble cast. With an ensemble, one rotten apple isn't going to spoil the barrel. The more I thought about it, the more intrigued I became, and I began to think about creating a show around a boutique law firm that was a full service firm: criminal law, civil law, and domestic law. I'd never seen a show like that on TV, and I thought that if I made it a glossy, Los Angeles-based show with a cast of beautiful, bright, sexy, and successful lawyers, I'd in effect be making a show that was the polar opposite of Hill Street Blues, in the sense that I was still exploring the justice system, but through the opposite end of the telescope, as it were. Where Hill Street was about a group of men and women fighting a losing battle in the war against crime (or at best, a holding action: trying to keep the lid on the garbage can, as it were), this show would be about winners: lawyers who charged into battle armed with education, experience, money, and intelligence. The more I thought about it, the more I liked it.

I began to see the characters: the avuncular head of the firm; the younger administrative boss – Mel Blumenthal came to mind; a young, handsome divorce attorney who never thought twice about bedding down an unhappy female client in the midst of a bruising divorce; and a handsome, committed young partner, a criminal attorney who would fall in love with his female counterpart in the firm.

I had always wanted to work with Michael Tucker and his wife Jill Eikenberry. They had done an episode of Hill Street called The Out Of Towners, about a couple of tourists who get mugged, lose all their money and identification, and wind up in the Hill District, their troubles escalating from there. They'd been terrific, and now I saw a chance to create two roles for them as a married couple in the firm; he, a financial whiz who specialized in wills, estates, etc., and she a high-powered civil attorney with a high-end corporate clientele.

I also imagined a Hispanic attorney who'd come from a poor background and had fought his way through law school to become an attorney deeply committed to the notion of defending the less fortunate among us who, under normal circumstances, would never be able to afford the services of a top tier attorney. Throw in a couple of young associates, and there's your law firm: McKenzie, Brackman, Chaney and Kuzak.

I checked onto the lot at 20th Century Fox to begin this new phase of my career. It was June of 1985. I was greeted by the President of 20th TV, Harris Katleman, and his team, consisting of Peter Grad, Michael Klein, and Dayna Kalins (her maiden name, before she married Marc Flanagan).

Dayna was a tall, very attractive blond and, in those days, women wore skirts that stopped inches above their knees. Dayna had legs that had eyeball magnets in them. It was hard not to look. If this was a fairy tale, or a bodice buster, or a rom-com, I'd have said to myself, "I'm going to marry that woman some day." The truth is, I didn't say that to myself. I was a married man with two kids who didn't fool around. That said, fifteen years later, I did marry her. But that's another story I'll get to later.

Harris had told his team, and I guess Barry Diller had told Harris, that I had a reputation for not wanting to talk to executives, that I just wanted to do my thing, and after saying hello, I was to be left alone. So everyone was very nice, they showed me to my new office, and left. I thought to myself, "Now what do I do?" I didn't even have an assistant yet, so when the phone rang a few minutes later, I picked it up myself. It was Dayna Kalins. "They told us to leave you alone," she said, "but I just want you to know, if there's anything you need, please don't hesitate to call."

I told her how pleased I was that she'd called, and that I didn't *want* to be left alone. In fact, if she had the time, there *was* something I needed. I told her about the series commitment, which of course she knew about, and I told her I had a very specific idea for a law show I wanted to develop, and I'd love to find a writer to work with who had a law background, and could she help me with that? She said she'd get right on it, and the next day there was a stack of scripts on my desk, every one of which had been written by a lawyer. As soon as she'd hung up the phone with me, Dayna had called every agent in town, looking for writers with a background in law.

Now I had something to do, and I started plowing my way through the stack of scripts that, for one reason or another, didn't appeal to me. I felt like Justice Potter Stewart, who famously said, "Pornography is hard to define, but I know it when I see it." I didn't like any of the scripts, but I figured that eventually, I'd know the right one when I saw it.

In the meantime, I went over to NBC to pitch my law show concept. We got together in Brandon's office, along with Warren

Littlefield, a woman named Michele Brustin, and one other NBC executive whose name I don't recall. The three of them started peppering me with questions: "What's the show? Why do you need all those characters? Is that really a legitimate law firm? Why do you think this show will work when there's never really been a successful law series?" I felt like I was fighting off three muggers in an alley, and Brandon was just sitting there, silently taking it all in.

This back-and-forth went on for about thirty minutes until Warren, as I recall, said to Brandon, "What do you think?" It was obvious to me that they were skeptical of the idea, to say the least.

But Brandon just smiled, and said, "I like it. Let's do it."

And that was that.

The next time I talked to Dayna, I had refined my thinking somewhat. I felt that because we had so many good female characters, it would be a good idea to concentrate on finding a female writer with a law background, which considerably narrowed the field.

Within days, Dayna sent me a Cagney and Lacey script (Barney Rosenzweig's terrific cop show with Sharon Gless and Tyne Daley), written by Terry Louise Fisher. Bingo! She was the one.

Brandon wanted a two-hour pilot that could air in his Sunday Night Movie slot, so once I filled Terry's head with everything I had come up with to that point, we went to work on the stories, and within a couple of weeks we started writing the script. We divvied up the writing chores the way I had with Kozoll, the idea being that once we had each written our half, we'd swap them and polish each other's work.

When we'd finished writing the first hour of the script, I took Dayna to lunch and gave it to her to read. She read it that afternoon, and called to tell me she loved it. That gave us a real boost into the second hour.

Everyone loved the finished script, and I hired my friend Greg Hoblit to direct the pilot. Greg had produced and directed on Hill Street Blues for five years, and I thought we were in very capable hands.

Casting went pretty well. We knew we wanted Jill Eikenberry and Michael Tucker – the Tuckerberrys. We went to New York and met Corbin Bernsen. Young and handsome and quintessentially Californian, he was the perfect Arnie Becker. We hired my brother--in-law, Alan Rachins, to play Douglas Brackman, the stuffy firm administrator. Alan was perfect for the role, and eventually, we hired my sister to play his wife, Sheila Brackman, in nineteen episodes. It was a family affair. We cast Richard Dysart in the role of Leland McKenzie, the patriarch of the firm. Dick was perfect – powerful yet avuncular; we cast Susan Dey (grown from her days on The Partridge Family into a beautiful woman and a terrific actress) as Grace Van Owen; Michele Greene (who'd earlier worked for me in Bay City Blues) as young Abby Perkins, an associate in the firm; Jimmy Smits as Victor Sifuentes, a tall, handsome Hispanic lawyer; Susan Ruttan, as Roxanne Melman, Arnie Becker's secretary; and, lastly, Harry Hamlin as the young, named partner in the firm whose specialty was criminal law. It was a wonderful cast, and they were all wonderful people. After the emotional chaos of Hill Street Blues, this cast of adult actors, not a crazy in the bunch, was a pure delight. Were some of them a little more needy than others? Sure. A little more neurotic? A little more insecure? Of course. Show me a team of ten people in any endeavor, and I'll show you those characteristics in varying measure. But they were all grown-ups, they were a pleasure to work with, and every single one of them developed a strong chemistry to the ensemble. It was truly a case of the sum being greater than the parts, and the parts were pretty damn good to begin with.

We started production with high hopes, but within four or five days I was very nervous. My great friend Mr. Hoblit was scaring the crap out of me. His dailies were disturbing. Everything was in short pieces, as if he were making a patchwork quilt. There were no sustained scenes, or master shots, in the traditional sense. I finally took him aside and expressed my concerns. I probably wasn't too diplomatic. I'd known Greg too long and we'd been through too much together for me to be politic with him. We got into it pretty intensely, and finally he said to me, "You hired me to direct this pilot. I know exactly what I'm doing. Every piece of this puzzle will fit together. Now leave me alone. I have to go back to work." O-kaaay.

I suppose if it had been someone I didn't know, or hadn't worked so closely with in the past, I might have fired him. But I made a decision right then and there to trust him. Television is a collaborative medium. You either embrace that reality, or you're going to have a miserable (and short) time of it. You have to delegate. You have to trust. You have to empower. I had learned those lessons, partly from others (Grant Tinker, anyone?), and partly through painful, personal experience. And I knew Greg to be a great talent with a personal vision that, though not always in sync with my own, always had a well-thought out rationale. So I crossed my fingers, and held my breath, and – lo and behold – Greg was right. Every piece of the puzzle fit perfectly. It was a wonderful two-hour film. He had brought our stories to life.

Our guest star in the two-hour pilot was Alfrie Woodard, and she won an Emmy for her portrayal of a poor African American woman who was dying of leukemia. She had also won the Emmy years earlier for a role on Hill Street Blues. She was then – and remains today – one of the finest actresses in America.

I was as lucky with pulling together my writing staff as I had been with the way our cast came together. Having had such great success with Terry Louise Fisher, we set about trying to find other writers with a law background, and Dayna put out the word to agents around town. We were inundated with scripts. One of them was a play by a lawyer in New York named William Finkelstein. It was a very interesting and different piece of work, and I reached out to him with an assignment. Billy came to L.A., and we spent a couple of weeks working up several stories for his script, and then he returned to New York. Before he left, he asked if we had a fax machine. A fax machine? What's that, I asked. (This was 1986. Thirty years ago. And look at our technology today.) Apparently, there was *one* fax machine on the entire Fox lot, somewhere in the Administration Building. We found out the number, and gave it to Billy, who said he'd fax us pages as he wrote them.

And then I read the first ten pages of a screenplay called From The Hip, written by a young trial lawyer in Boston named David E.

Kelley. I immediately reached out to him as well, and David came to Los Angeles to meet with me and Terry Louise. We gave him an assignment also, and off he went back to Boston, to write. In the meantime, locally, we had hired a bright young writer named Jacob Ebstein, and Terry and I figured that if either Finkelstein or Kelley panned out, we'd have a small but decent writing group. I would say Finkelstein and Kelley more than panned out. Both of their scripts were brilliant, we exercised both their options, and within weeks, Billy and his wife Barbara were relocating to Los Angeles, as was David and his partner, Hogan. David wasn't gay, and Hogan wasn't his partner in that sense. Hogan was David's inseparable companion, a standard poodle that I guess David had had since the pooch was a pup. Hogan went everywhere with David. At work every day, he'd follow David around wherever he went, except in the morning, when he'd make the rounds of all the offices, scrounging for donuts and bagels. If you had nothing for him, he turned up his nose and left. He was as much of a New Englander as David was. You had to really work hard to earn his trust and affection. But when you did – if you did – it was more than worth the effort.

Between me, Terry Louise, David, Billy and Jacob, we had a pretty damn good writing staff, and the scripts we were churning out were terrific. They were smart, complex, and funny. There was a real buzz and excitement in those early days of L.A. LAW, kind of like we were all inhaling the pheromones that get pumped out in a new romance.

We debuted with our two-hour pilot on Sunday night, September 15th, 1986, and we were number two in the Neilson ratings for the week. Over thirty million people had watched the premiere. In today's world, good luck getting thirty million people to watch a hanging.

Brandon put us in the Friday night at ten p.m. time slot, against the CBS hit show, Falcon Crest. We got our brains beat out that first week. We got our ribs broken the second week. They should have called it The Friday Night Mugging. It was a rapid descent, to say the least, and a deflating one, to boot. On the Monday morning after our second Friday airing, Brandon called me. "I have some good news and some bad news," he said.

"What's the good news?" I asked.

"I'm moving L.A. LAW to a better time slot," he said.

"That's fantastic news," I said. "What's the bad news?"

"It's Thursday night at ten. You're replacing Hill Street."

Don't ask me why Brandon thought that was bad news. Maybe he felt he was shortening Hill Street's lifespan. But the truth is, since I had left, the show had rapidly gone down hill, and so had its ratings. In its seventh season, it looked like it was headed for the bone yard, anyway. Brandon was actually hoping to resurrect two important assets: the Thursday ten p.m. time slot, as well as L.A. LAW.

And it worked. Boy, did it work. We killed the competition on Thursday night, and for that week's ratings, we ended up in the top ten. We were an instant hit.

On the other hand, Hill Street Blues, now on Wednesday night, continued its accelerated descent in the ratings and in its quality, and was canceled at the end of the season. It had run for seven years and had changed the course of my life forever.

Having a hit series is a miracle; like catching lightning in a bottle – and it was no less thrilling for me the second time than the first, not the least of reasons being that I felt I had vindicated myself against Arthur Price's bullshit accusations of profligacy, and had validated Barry Diller's and Fox's belief in me.

But life always throws you the Clown Ball. Right before we were supposed to start series production, Jill Eikenberry and Michael Tucker called me to tell me that Jill had breast cancer. They were afraid that if Jill needed chemotherapy, she wouldn't be able to do the show. But when she found out that her therapy regimen would involve radiation instead, I said come do the show – we'd work her schedule around her radiation treatments. Jill's cancer had been caught early, and her treatment put her into total remission. As I recall, she didn't miss a day's work. But it was, however briefly, a nasty intrusion of reality, a reminder to all of us not to get too cocky. I tried to heed the lesson. Well, sort of.

By the late winter of 1986, I was on a career roll. LA LAW had become a huge hit. Law school applications had increased exponentially. Hill Street Blues was limping toward the finish line after seven years, but was still deeply embedded in the cultural zeitgeist. Best of all, I could pretty much get into any restaurant in L.A. on short notice.

One day, I was having lunch with 20th Century Fox's head of TV development, Peter Grad. He mentioned that 20th had a deal with John Ritter, of THREE'S COMPANY fame, to develop a half-hour comedy series starring John, for ABC. Off the top of my head, I said why not make John a cop? By the end of lunch I'd fleshed out the concept, and Peter was sold on the idea. By the end of the day, Peter had spoken to Ritter and sold him on the idea. I went over to ABC with Peter a few days later, and sold them on the idea of a half-hour comedy/drama with John playing a cop named Hoooperman. I then approached my co-creator of LA LAW, Terry Louise Fisher, and asked her if she'd like to write the pilot with me, and she readily agreed. Everyone loved the script, and we commenced filming later that Spring, with my friend and co-producer, Gregory Hoblit, directing. ABC was so pleased with the finished product that they approached Frank Rohner, the aforementioned Doberman, about entering into an exclusive arrangement to create shows for ABC. I was in the second year of my three-year contract with Fox, and so I told Frank to explore the possibilities with ABC. Frank was looking for some guidelines and asked me what kind of deal I'd be interested in. For some time I'd been thinking about starting my own company, and I told Frank that were I to do so, I'd want a guarantee of enough shows to make financing my own company feasible. Grant Tinker had recently left his position as Chairman of NBC, and he'd made a deal with CBS to produce ten series, an unheard of commitment. So I told Frank I wanted the same deal with ABC. Frank cautioned me that Grant's deal wasn't all it seemed. There were all kinds of conditions attached to the deal, and among other caveats, the ten series weren't guaranteed on-the-air commitments. I told Frank to see what he could do, and in relatively short order he'd entered into negotiations with ABC, and fashioned an extraordinary deal that ABC seemed amenable to. In simple terms, the deal was as follows: 1) I was to create and produce ten 13-episode series, guaranteed on the air, over the span of seven years. 2) Every series' production overages (deficits) were to be borne by ABC, up to 65 episodes. (Since virtually all one-hour dramas were produced at substantial deficits, having a network agree to cover those deficits was an incredible element of the agreement.) 3) The newly formed Steven Bochco Productions would only be on the hook for deficits after any given show had reached 66 episodes, which was the generally accepted number of shows that qualified a series for syndication, where the real profits were. In other words, this deal was, from a financial point of view, virtually no risk to me in failure, and in success, the profits from syndication would more than accommodate the accumulated deficits. 4) Frank demanded, and got, the unprecedented agreement that I would essentially have complete creative control of my shows. And finally, 5) ABC would throw in 5 million dollars for the privilege of owning exclusive rights to my services. There had never been a deal like this one in the history of television, and to my knowledge there's never been one like it since. It came to be known not as the Bochco Deal, but the Rohner Deal. Not for nothing had I dubbed him The Doberman.

Before the deal was sealed, however, life threw me an unforeseen curve ball (not to be confused with The Clown Ball, always a harbinger of bad news). I received a phone call one day from Bob Batscha, who was at that time Director of the Museum of Television and Radio, an institution founded and initially funded by William Paley, one of the true godfathers of the broadcast industry. With branches in New York and Beverly Hills, the Museum was a highly regarded organization devoted to the celebration and aggrandizement of our business.

I had known Bob for a number of years, and had contributed to the Museum what was, for me, at the time, a pretty good chunk of change. In fact, I had been invited to join its board of directors, which I'd accepted. On the phone that day, Bob asked me if I'd meant it when I'd casually said to him, on more than one occasion, that I'd like to run a network. I had felt for sometime that I'd be able to do a better job of it than most network executives, by virtue of the fact that I'd created and produced so many shows over the course of my twenty years in the business. Anyway, not knowing exactly where this was going, I said yes – I did mean it. Bob then asked me, confidentially, if I'd come to New York to meet with William Paley. I inferred from the conversation, however opaque it was, that CBS was looking to replace its current network president with fresh blood.

I hung up the phone, my head spinning. This was the last thing I'd ever expected to come up – and right in the middle of negotiating the most extensive and potentially lucrative deal in the history of television! I immediately called The Doberman and asked what I should do. Frank, in his early days in the business, had been head of CBS Business Affairs under Frank Stanton, who ran CBS for Mr. Paley. He said to me, "Are you kidding? Get on an airplane, go to New York, and meet the man who is the founder of your industry."

And so I went.

William Paley lived in a grand apartment on 5th Avenue, opposite the Central Park Zoo. The elevator opened directly onto his apartment foyer, and the first sight that greeted me as I stepped off the elevator was a famous Picasso I'd only seen pictures of, Boy Leading A Horse, painted in 1906. It was breathtakingly beautiful.

I was ushered into the apartment by Mr. Paley's uniformed maid, and there stood the man himself: tall, patrician, formal in a dark suit, white shirt and red tie. He apologized for having our meeting in his home, but, as he explained, he'd had some recent health issues and was still recovering. He ushered me over to a small table by a window overlooking the park, and said, "That law show of yours. It's a great show. That's the kind of show I'd like to have on my network." I thanked him, and then he said, "Tell me about yourself." And this is what I told him, virtually word for word. (Just for fun, check your watch and see how long it takes you to read the next few lines.) "I was born on the other side of Central Park,

I went to the High School of Music and Art, college at Carnegie Tech in Pittsburgh, then I spent twelve years at Universal Studios, seven years at MTM, and I've been at 20th Century Fox for the last two and a half years." (I clocked that statement at around eleven seconds.)

Mr. Paley leaned across the table at me. "That law show of yours," he said again. "It's a great show. That's the kind of show I'd like on my network." I thanked him again. "Tell me about yourself," he said. Uh oh.

For the next two-and-a-half hours, I steered William Paley like a bus with a flat tire. He was all over the road, lucid one moment, heading for a ditch the next. Finally, he asked me, in one of his more coherent moments, if I'd come back after lunch to meet with Mr. Tisch. (Larry Tisch was the owner of CBS.) I said of course I would, and when I returned after lunch, the three of us – William Paley, Larry Tisch, and me, little Stevie Bochco – sat down at the same small table. Larry Tisch kept looking at his watch, and when he talked to Mr. Paley, he'd shout: "BILL, DID YOU SPEAK TO SO AND SO?" I thought to myself, Bill Paley may be a little dotty, but he's not deaf. Why is Larry Tisch screaming at him? In any event, within minutes, Larry leaned over to me and whispered, "Can you have dinner with me tonight?"

"Of course," I said. "That's why I'm here." And with that, Larry Tisch left, leaving me to steer the bus for another hour.

At dinner that night with Larry, his wife Billie, and one of their sons, Tisch picked my brain at length about CBS. What did I think about their shows? How did I feel about the network and the way it was run? What would I do if I were in charge? With nothing to lose, I was completely candid. Among other things, I told him that while it wasn't the only solution, it would take a lot of money to turn the network's fortunes around, and it was generally perceived by the industry that Mr. Tisch was, to put it bluntly, cheap. Unfazed, he told me that when it came to CBS, money was no object. The crown jewel in the Tisch empire, he was prepared to spend whatever it took. In my mind's eye, I was beginning to see the ABC deal sprouting wings and flying off into oblivion.

When the dinner check came – we were dining at a neighborhood Italian restaurant often frequented by the Tisch family – Larry took a pen from his breast pocket, put on his reading glasses, and checked every single item on the bill before signing off. In poker, that's what they call a "tell," and I knew right then and there that the man would never change, regardless of his protestations to the contrary.

As we were leaving the restaurant, Larry's wife, Billie – a bright and charming woman – said to me, quietly, "We would love for you to run our network." Wow. There it was for the taking: an oft-expressed dream come true. I told Billie that I'd take forty-eight hours to ponder their offer and then let them know.

By the time I returned to L.A., I'd made up my mind. I told The Doberman to close the ABC deal, and I called Larry Tisch to tell him the timing wasn't right for me, and I was reluctantly turning down his offer. Within hours, William Paley was on the phone, screaming at me that I'd screwed them; that I'd taken advantage of their offer to get myself a better deal at ABC. I literally banged the phone receiver on my desk half a dozen times – try it, it'll get your listener's attention, big time – and then I calmly told Mr. Paley not to shout at me. I'd done nothing wrong or unethical. To the contrary, I'd suspended a negotiation in progress in order to consider the CBS offer. Mr. Paley instantly backed off, telling me he'd be happy to match the ABC deal. I thanked him and hung up. I never heard from him or CBS again.

Several months later, I went to New York for a Museum of Television and Radio board meeting. Mr. Paley by then was wheel chair bound. I went over to him, shook his hand, and greeted him. He stared at me, blank-eyed. He had no idea who I was. A few months later, he died.

By now it was summer of 1988. The ABC deal was completed, and The Doberman was "shopping" it, by which I mean he was seeking a studio partner for us. The idea was that we would bring our company, the newly formed Steven Bochco Productions, along with our ten series commitments, to whichever studio would pay us the most. It was an extremely attractive deal for a studio, for the usual risks associated with series television production were all being borne by ABC. Essentially, there was no downside to the deal for a studio. They shared in any profits. Frank was looking for a sixty/forty percent profit split in our favor. They would control distribution of our product, they'd have an exclusive partnership with me for seven years, and they'd make additional money from us by virtue of our exclusive use of their equipment and facilities. Multiple studios were interested, including Fox, which rightly thought that by virtue of our ongoing relationship, they had the inside track.

While all this was going on, I took my family for a vacation to Hawaii. After all the excitement of the preceding six months, plus the normal rigors of production, ten days in Hawaii was just what the doctor ordered – except for the fact that, in my absence, Terry Louise Fisher, along with her leather-coated boyfriend and her agent, announced to Fox that when I left LA LAW for ABC, she and her non-industry boyfriend would be taking over the show. All of us had already signed off on Terry taking over the show. As co-creator, we all felt the show would be in capable hands. What nobody was on board for, however, least of all me, were the conditions that Terry and her boyfriend, Chuck, who now was insisting on being addressed as Charles, were demanding, including but not limited to, their insistence that I be banished from any further involvement with LA LAW. No advising, no consulting, no authority whatsoever as to hiring of new writers, etc. Terry was to be the ultimate boss, with her boyfriend, Chuck-call-me-Charles, as second in command – a fellow who knew as much about writing and producing television as I knew about brain surgery. Maybe less.

Dayna called me in Hawaii to alert me as to what was going on. I was coming home that weekend anyway, and told Dayna I'd deal with it on my return. The next Monday morning, I had a ten a.m. story meeting scheduled with our writing staff, consisting of David

E. Kelley, Bill Finkelstein, and Jacob Epstein, when Terry waltzed in as if nothing had happened in my absence. I told her I knew what she'd done, and that I was herewith firing her. When she refused to leave my office, I gathered David, Bill and Jacob, and *we* left.

I told Fox what I had done and, anticipating their anxiety about what would happen to LA LAW if both of us were gone, I promised them that I would postpone commencement of my ABC deal for a year and continue to run LA LAW. Within 24 hours, Terry sued me, Fox, Dayna and, for all I knew, the guy who trimmed the trees outside my office. The suit accused us of collusion, conspiracy, restraint of trade, and God knows what. All I remember is that Fox's first response was to try and settle the suit out of court. There was no impulse to defend my position, nor was there a single expression of gratitude for my willingness to postpone the ABC deal for a year in order to assure LA LAW's continued success. So, in a fit of what I felt was justifiable pique, I instructed my lawyer to strike Fox from my list of potential suitors.

Enter Barry Diller, the head of 20th Century Fox. Though in 1988 20th Century Fox was owned by Rupert Murdoch, for all intents and purposes Barry ran the joint. I'd always liked Barry, dating back to when he had made my original Fox deal in spite of efforts by MTM's head honcho Arthur Price (who had fired me in 1985) to convince him that I was an undependable and profligate producer. So when Barry invited me to lunch to discuss our situation, I readily agreed.

Barry, as always, was direct and to the point. He said Fox had mishandled the Terry Louise Fisher situation, and he apologized. He went on to list the reasons why I should bring my ABC deal to Fox, not least of which was that we already had a strong working relationship, the Terry Louise Fisher kerfuffle notwithstanding. Like the line from the movie Jerry Maguire, Barry had me at hello. I told my attorney to re-engage with Fox, and within weeks it was clear that they were our most ardent suitor.

One evening, after a marathon negotiating session, The Doberman came into my office looking like he'd been in an alley brawl. It was late June of 1988. His hair was mussed, his tie was askew, his white shirt was wrinkled and half pulled out of his pants. "I think we have a deal," he announced.

I won't bore you with all the fine points of the deal, of which there were many, most of which I didn't understand myself. What I did understand was when Frank said, "They're going to give you fifty million dollars, thirty of it upfront." I started to laugh. Fifty million dollars was outrageous. Where did Frank ever get the balls to demand such a sum? I realize that nowadays, with professional athletes signing contracts for as much as 200 million dollars, fifty million doesn't seem laughable. But in 1988? In television? It was unheard of.

I never missed a meal as a kid, and I never went without shoes, so I can't say my family was dirt poor. But there were times when my Dad had to borrow money for the rent, and I remember a period early in my childhood when he had to declare bankruptcy. And in his best years, he never made more than ten thousand dollars annually. And now, here I was, someone was going to pay me fifty million dollars for doing what I would've done for rent money, and I couldn't stop laughing at the absurdity of it.

On July 2, 1988 – it was a Thursday, and the studio had mostly emptied out already for the long July 4th weekend – Jon Dolgen, a Fox executive who became a good friend of mine over the years, came to my office. He handed me a check for thirty million dollars – the down payment on our newly minted deal. My wife had taken our children to Hawaii, so I called Dayna, who'd become my close friend and who'd already agreed to leave her position at Fox to run our fledgling company, and told her she had to come over to my office and take a ride with me to Beverly Hills. There was a watch at Cartier's that I'd had my eye on for several years, and with thirty million bucks in my pocket, I was going to treat myself to a present.

At Cartier's, I asked the sales lady how much the watch was. She said it was twelve thousand, five hundred dollars. Smart mouth that I was, I said, "How much for Jews?" She looked at me frostily and said, "Twelve thousand, five hundred dollars." I explained to her that there wasn't a high-end jewelry store on Rodeo Drive that wouldn't give me a fifteen or twenty percent discount on such a high-priced purchase. She wouldn't budge. "Look," I said. "I'm going to buy this watch today, either here or someplace else, but I want a discount." She still wouldn't budge, so with a thirty million dollar check in my pocket, Dayna and I walked out of Cartier's, drove over to Norman's Jewelers in Brentwood, and I bought the watch for ten thousand dollars. I'd gotten my twenty percent discount.

Who said Larry Tisch was cheap?

For its second season efforts, L.A. Law was rewarded with nineteen Emmy nominations. The awards ceremony, as usual, was held at the Pasadena Civic Auditorium. It was September of 1988. Sitting in our seats, we watched, with rising dismay, as we lost award after award to other shows. We had only won two Emmys out of all those nominations when, at the end of the evening, Thirty Something won the Emmy for Best Dramatic Series. I leaned forward and whispered into the ear of our co-executive producer, Rick Wallace, sitting in the seat directly in front me, "Work harder."

Shades of Bill Sackheim.

The following year we again won the Emmy for Best Dramatic Series.

18

One morning in late 1988, I was sitting on the throne reading an article in New York Magazine written by a pal of mine, Tony Schwartz, about child prodigies. My father had been a child prodigy. His parents had stuck a violin in his hands when he was six years old, and within three or four years he was concertizing. No such prodigious talent had been inherited by either my sister or me, but I was always fascinated by the phenomenon. And so, sitting there on the can, an idea came to mind for a television series, about a child prodigy who becomes a doctor by the age of sixteen.

By the time I'd showered and dressed and gotten to work, I'd pretty much figured out the whole story. The boy, who I named Doogie Howser, had been stricken with life-threatening childhood leukemia, and during the several years he spent in and out of hospitals fighting for his life, his prodigious intellect was, of necessity, channeled toward medicine, to the point that by the time he was cured of the disease, he had developed an obsession with medicine, and was as knowledgeable about his disease as his doctors were.

I called my friends the Woottons, both doctors. I asked Barbara Wootton (she was a UCLA radiologist of some renown under her maiden name, Kadell) if the notion of a sixteen-year old doctor had any credibility. She said absolutely. She was on the Board of Admissions of UCLA Medical School, and while their policy was not to accept kids, she'd had applicants as young as twelve. She also told me that other universities, such as USC, didn't share their policy, and would accept the occasional young applicant.

I said, "You mean it's realistic that a sixteen-year old doctor could write a prescription for morphine, but couldn't buy a six-pack of beer at the grocery store?"

"That's right," Barbara said.

And with that, I knew that Doogie Howser, M.D. would be my first show for ABC under our new deal.

I'm sure ABC wasn't expecting my first effort with them to be a half-hour comedy about a sixteen-year old doctor, but knowing what I'd done with Hooperman, they certainly weren't afraid that I couldn't execute it. In fact, they rather liked the idea, although I think they had a somewhat different show in mind than I did. They were expecting a broad, three-camera type comedy with lots of jokes. They weren't expecting a story about a sixteen-year old kid who winds up having to give his girlfriend a pelvic exam when she has symptoms of appendicitis.

After ABC approved the general idea, I approached David Kelley and asked him if he'd like to write the pilot with me. David had a wonderful sense of humor, and I thought between the two of us, we could produce a delightful script. I wasn't wrong.

David Kelly was, and is, a star. I think a talent such as his comes along once in a generation. I could see his growth almost daily, and he was one of the few writers I've ever known who could go into a room and come out two days later with a shootable script. David was a New Englander. He was quiet, almost unflappable. He'd been a professional hockey player in Europe, and he had an easy self--confidence along with a dry sense of humor that was totally winning. After the Terry Louise Fisher fiasco, I knew that when I left L.A. Law, David would be the most qualified to run the show.

There are, essentially, two components to writing a television script: story, and teleplay. There's a reason why the Writer's Guild of America makes that distinction by allocating separate payments for each segment. Over the years, I had become very good at story construction. It wasn't a natural talent, but I had great teachers, and gifted contemporaries whose work I admired and tried to emulate, and by the time I did L.A. LAW, I'd been at my craft for twenty years. David E. Kelley seemed to have a natural gift for story. He was a lawyer. He loved a good argument. He knew how to frame both sides of a position, and he never let personal politics or opinion get in the way of a credible representation of any given issue. Plus, David had a wonderful sense of humor that came across on the page, and it made his scripts an absolute delight to read.

Anyone in my position as a show runner will tell you that when a new script drops onto your desk, you approach it with a confusion of hope and dread; hope that it'll be good, because that means less work for you; and dread because you know that, far more often than not, the script you read is going to require an enormous amount of re-writing. David was one of those writers whose scripts were always good, and always fun to read, first shot out of the box. In the short time he was with me at L.A. LAW, I had come to rely on him heavily.

If David had one weakness as a show runner, it was that he wasn't very good at running the writers' room. At least that's what he told me. Maybe it's because of that New England upbringing. Or maybe it's because he had such a strong internal sense of what every show should be that he didn't know how to communicate it with his writers. If you were a writer on staff at a David E. Kelley show, this is what would happen (or so I've been told by writers who worked for him): Everyone would sit in the room and throw ideas around. David would say, "Okay, I like that one. Go do it," and the writer would go off and write a script. When he or she handed it in to David, he would disappear into his office – or at home, if it was a weekend – and completely re-write it. Monday morning, there was this brand new script, with the writer's name on it, and inevitably better than the one the writer had written.

David was always a little sheepishly apologetic about his way of working, but unlike some other show runners who shall remain nameless because of their terrible reputations for mistreating writers, everyone loved David. How could you not? He made you look better, and you probably became better, because every David E. Kelley script was a lesson in how to write a proper television script.

Billy Finkelstein was also a wonderfully gifted writer, but I felt at that time that David was the more disciplined of the two, and I knew that I would be leaving L.A. LAW in great hands when I left.

During that unexpected third year of L.A. LAW – unexpected in the sense that I thought I would already have embarked on my ABC deal – Twentieth Century Fox was constructing a building on the lot for our company. We gutted an old, existing building, and Fox retrofitted it to our specifications. If I was going to spend the next seven years of my life cranking out series television, I wanted to come to work every day in a physically welcoming environment. Jeff Goldstein, our art director on L.A. Law, designed the interior. It turned out beautifully, with a ground floor atrium that soared several stories high. On the ground floor, off the atrium level, were offices that housed me, Dayna, our Head of Production, Publicity, and Milch. Upstairs, the offices (which by and large were occupied by writers) overlooked the atrium, and the overall effect was light and airy. (Ted Mann, one of our writers and a uniquely whacky fellow, once chucked a typewriter over the railing that ringed the second floor of the building, and smashed it to smithereens on the atrium floor.) I'd spent too many years in too many old studio buildings with dark, narrow corridors, working in small offices with small windows. I wanted the people I worked with to look forward to coming to work every day as much as I did.

ABC wasn't happy with David's and my pilot script for Doogie Howser, M.D. It was neither as broad nor as funny as they'd hoped, and so on my very first show for them, we were already in conflict. But the nature of the deal that The Doberman had negotiated was such that, creatively, there wasn't much they could do.

The conflict was exacerbated when I told them I wanted to cast Neil Patrick Harris as Doogie. I had seen Neil in a movie he'd made a couple of years earlier (Clara's Heart, with Whoopi Goldberg), and he was already an accomplished actor. He brought the perfect blend of youth, innocence, and intelligence to the role of Doogie.

I could believe that he was a prodigy. In 1988, Neil was a terrific, fifteen-year old young man from a lovely family in Alberquerque, New Mexico. And, he was a young fifteen. His voice hadn't really changed yet, and he didn't have a hair on his face. Physically, he resembled a twelve or thirteen-year old boy, which was perfect.

ABC strongly resisted casting Neil, and I just as strongly insisted on him. They finally relented, but from day one they were reluctant about this show. They didn't know what to do with it, and they didn't know what to do with me. I think they might have been feeling a bit of buyer's remorse.

I surrounded Neil with a strong supporting cast. As his best friend and neighbor, we cast Max Casella, who was thirty but looked sixteen. It was always jarring when Max would go outside the stage for a smoke. Jim Sikking, who'd played Howard Hunter in Hill Street Blues and was one of my closest friends, played Doogie's dad, David, also a doctor. Belinda Montgomery played Doogie's mom, Larry Pressman (also a close friend) played his boss at the hospital, and Katherine Lang played Nurse Spaulding. It was a great and caring group, and I felt we had surrounded Neil with a surrogate family.

ABC didn't like the pilot episode at all, but it tested well – far better than they had expected – and so they programmed it on Wednesday night at 9pm. We premiered on September 19, 1989, and became virtually an instant hit, despite a general critical drubbing, although Howard Rosenberg, surprisingly, gave it a strong review. I always knew Howard was a smart guy! I think critics just didn't expect a comedy about a sixteen-year old doctor from the same guy that had brought Hill Street Blues and L.A. LAW to television. My own sense of it was that Doogie was an underrated show. I loved it, and most of the audience did, too. My instincts had been vindicated, and Doogie's success went a long way toward assuaging ABC's fears about my "unconventional" ideas.

I can't argue that Doogie Howser, M.D., had the cultural heft of either Hill Street Blues or L.A. Law, but the name Doogie Howser became part of the vernacular and, to this day, it is synonymous with any particularly youthful professional. The show was unique, in the sense that there'd never been anything quite like it on TV before, and there hasn't been since. It exists – at least so far – in a category of one.

Candidly, my feeling was that if I was lucky enough to have the unprecedented opportunity to create ten series that were guaranteed on-the-air commitments, I'd be crazy not to try and stretch the limits of my imagination and make at least some shows that were outside the box of conventional TV programming.

But then I proposed a musical cop show, Cop Rock. ABC thought I was off my rocker. And so did everyone else. But I was fixated on the concept. Some years earlier, a woman who was a Broadway producer had approached me with the idea of bringing Hill Street Blues to Broadway as a musical. I loved the idea, but for numerous reasons it was impractical. But the notion of a musical cop show stuck with me, and I figured if I couldn't take the cop show to Broadway, maybe I could bring Broadway to the cop show.

Bob Iger, then head of ABC Entertainment and now the CEO of Disney, thought I was nuts. Yes, he wanted a cop show from Steven Bochco. Nothing would have made him happier. But a *musical* cop show? Really? I had spoken to Mike Post, who also thought I was nuts, though I didn't share that nugget with Bob, but he thought that logistically it could be done on a series schedule.

I had never met Randy Newman before, but I tracked him down and we made an appointment to meet at my office. I was in awe of Randy, and I felt then as I do now, that he is an American treasure, one of the finest songwriter/performers of our generation.

Randy listened to my pitch for Cop Rock, and told me bluntly that he thought it was a terrible idea. Undaunted, I continued to pitch him, and eventually brought him around to the point where he agreed to write five songs for the pilot. Now it was really getting exciting. I brought in Greg Hoblit to direct. Greg thought I was crazy, but what the hell? I had three hit shows under my belt, maybe we could pull off a fourth.

So the four most important people I had spoken to thought Cop Rock was a crazy notion: Bog Iger, Mike Post, Randy Newman, and Greg Hoblit. I should have listened to them, I suppose, but I was besotted with the idea and couldn't stop thinking that if we got it right, people would flock to their TV sets. Ha!

Undeterred, I plowed on. God bless Bog Iger. He gave us the go ahead, and we commenced writing the script. By we, I mean myself, and Billy Finkelstein, who had become a very close personal friend ever since our LA LAW days.

The pilot was one of the most difficult we'd ever attempted. We had a sound truck outside the stage, and all the songs were performed live without reliance on lip-syncing. It was a high-wire act, culminating in a production number staged in a courtroom where the jury morphs into a gospel choir for a song Randy wrote called He's Guilty. As far as I was concerned, it was worth the price of admission, right there. It took almost all night to shoot, but the results were spectacular. Randy won a well-deserved Emmy for that song the following year, the only award the show ever received.

When we premiered in September of 1990, it was instantaneously clear that Cop Rock was circling the drain from day one. Bob Iger at one point said to me that Cop Rock was a good show, and that if I removed the music, it would probably be a viable show. I resisted. For one thing, we had, of necessity, hired singers who could act, versus actors who could sing. I was fearful that without the songs, the ensemble cast wouldn't be that strong. The ratings plummeted every single week, and by episode eight, ABC threw in the towel. We were gone. They played off the remainder of the episodes during the summer, when no one was watching TV anyway.

I have been asked a thousand times why I thought Cop Rock failed, and I quickly came to the painful conclusion that singing cops, at least on TV, just embarrassed the hell out of the viewer. Unlike a show such as Glee, whose music was built into the very concept of the show, Cop Rock imposed music on what was otherwise a fairly straightforward police procedural. It was like having your drunken uncle Bernie bellowing Fly Me To The Moon at your

Thanksgiving table. That said, I will never regret making Cop Rock, and to the same degree I will always be grateful to Bob Iger for letting me do it when all his instincts, and for that matter, everyone else's, told him it would fail. Cop Rock wasn't the cop show he wanted from me. He got it a couple of years later when David Milch and I created NYPD BLUE, but getting that show on the air was no walk in the park, either.

When Cop Rock skidded to a thudding halt, I decided to do something more accessible to the general viewing office. (Hell, a series about weekly executions would probably have been more accessible.) I had an idea for a law show called Civil Wars. It was about two lawyers who run a small domestic law firm specializing in divorce, child custody suits, etc. I figured it couldn't miss. After all, everybody's either been through a divorce, or knows someone who's been through a divorce. Six degrees of separation. Divorce is a legal proceeding rife with drama, black comedy, and built-in conflict.

I wanted Billy Finkelstein to write it with me, and Greg Hoblit to direct and produce it, but both men wanted to move on. Basically, they no longer wanted to work under me, as both felt they were ready to strike out on their own. I offered them a deal: if they stayed and wrote and directed Civil Wars, I'd completely stay out of their hair. It would be their show, win lose or draw. It would not be a Steven Bochco show.

I remained true to my word, but during the casting process, a fairly well-known actress said she wouldn't come in to read for the lead role unless I was there, so Billy and Greg invited me upstairs to Billy's office, where they were casting. Billy, Greg, and I were sitting on the couch, and our casting director, Junie Lowry-Johnson, was in a chair nearby, so she could read with the auditioning actress. I had never met her before and, as I do with every actor that comes into the casting room, I stood up to greet her. She pulled me into a tight embrace and whispered into my ear, "You're the handsomest man I've ever met." Uh oh. I thanked her, more than a little embarrassed, and sat back down on the couch. The actress sat in a chair directly opposite the couch, with a coffee table separating us. After a moment or two of chit chat, we got down to the audition, and while the actress was reading, I could clearly see that she wasn't wearing underpants. I snuck a look over at Billy and Greg, and it was clear that they were also aware of the visible breezeway. In all my years in Hollywood, which by then numbered almost twenty-five, I had never been exposed, you should pardon the expression, to anything like this. Clearly, this was an intentional act and, needless to say, it was completely distracting and totally un-sexy. When she left, we all agreed that she wasn't right for this particular role.

The actress, whose name I won't disclose because I wouldn't want to embarrass her, went on to become a star some years later in a successful series that ran for years. I hope they paid her enough so she could afford some underpants.

Civil Wars turned out to be an excellent show with a fatal flaw. There was absolutely no chemistry between our two leads, Mariel Hemingway and Peter Onorati. Peter is a good friend of mine, and we've worked together many times over the years. He'd also been a principal player in Cop Rock. But Peter isn't a romantic lead. He's more of an Italian street guy; blue collar, working class. And Mariel was this gorgeous, natural American beauty, not particularly urban and never totally comfortable with the legalese of the show. In short, it was a fatal mismatch. I tried to talk Greg and Billy out of casting them opposite one another, but they insisted, and so I honored my commitment to them. Alan Rosenberg and Debi Mazar rounded out the cast, but the show, at its center, didn't gel.

It lasted parts of two seasons, debuting in November of '91 and finishing its run in the winter of '93.

19

In the summer of 1993, NYPD BLUE – before a single episode had ever been aired – created a furor, fueled by three sources: advertisers, ABC's (mostly) southern affiliates, and Reverend Donald Wildmon, leader of the American Family Association, a self- -appointed watchdog of American television's contribution to the nation's precipitous slide down the greased pole to hell. Advertisers objected to the show because of its sexual content as well as its rela- tively R rated language. ABC's affiliates, mostly in the south, objected on the same grounds. TV 101: neither advertisers nor affiliates are in the controversy business. Generally speaking, they're frightened of boycotts, negative publicity, and loss of revenue, certainly an under- standable concern. Wildmon, on the other hand, through his AFA, had taken upon himself the role of America's moral watchdog, and commenced a countrywide newspaper ad campaign condemning the show's content and urging a viewer boycott. It was apparently of no concern that he'd never even seen the show. He was also using his ads, taken out in virtually every major newspaper in America, to solicit money for his association. He'd included a coupon in sup- port of the boycott that could be clipped and mailed, and over the course of the summer, I received thousands of them, delivered in mail sacks that cluttered every spare inch of our offices. In 2015 it seems quaint, but in 1993 it was a very big deal. No one had ever programmed anything like NYPD BLUE in prime time, and ABC, understandably, was in something of a panic.

In 1991, Dan Burke was the head of Cap Cities, which owned ABC. (Dan's son, Steve, is now CEO of Universal-Comcast.) Bob Iger and I had lunch with Dan at the now defunct Maple Drive restaurant in Beverly Hills, to pitch him my concept for NYPD BLUE. I liked Dan enormously. He was bright, direct, and no nonsense. You always knew where you stood with him. He was also a devout Catholic, and I had serious doubts whether he'd be willing to go out on a limb in support of our show.

In 1991, the bottom had pretty much dropped out of the one--hour drama business, replaced by much cheaper to produce news magazine hours. The last bona fide network hit had been my own LA LAW, in 1986. The lack of subsequent one-hour hits had two very immediate consequences: new one-hours were floundering in the ratings, and syndication revenues for one-hour series had become anemic, at best. Plus, cable programming, with its lax to non-existent censorship, was eating broadcast TV's dramas for lunch.

In May of 1991, in New York for up fronts, Dayna and I were strolling up Park Avenue, and I was bemoaning the situation. One-hour television drama was the backbone of our company and, notwithstanding Doogie Howser, it was what I did best. We had a serious problem on our hands.

NYPD BLUE was my proposed solution. I felt that an adult themed one-hour drama with adult sexuality (nudity, in other words) and a far more liberal use of the kind of "street" language we were all familiar with in our normal lives would bring viewers back to so-called free TV and rejuvenate the medium.

In Bob Iger's presence, and with his blessing, I made my pitch to Dan Burke, who listened carefully and didn't interrupt me once. When I was done, he paused for fully thirty seconds before turning to Bob. "Do you really want to develop this show?" Without hesitation, Bob said yes, and that he believed it could be a great hit for ABC. Dan said, "You better be right. Because if you're wrong, my skirts won't be big enough for you to hide behind." And with that, NYPD BLUE was born.

David Milch, who I had worked with on Hill Street Blues, had left MTM after Hill Street was cancelled, and had spent a couple of years at Paramount Television. When his deal expired, I asked him if he wanted to do a cop show with me, and I explained to him what I thought it should be. It was essentially the same pitch I'd made to Dan Burke, and David loved the idea and agreed to co-create the show with me.

David had an idea about an undercover cop who'd infiltrated one of the Mafia families in New York, and he wanted to do a show about wiretapping, mobsters, etc. It was exactly the show I didn't want to make, but David was so committed to the notion that I suggested he go off and write it. If it was great, we'd do it.

A month or so later, David's script landed on my desk. It started with a close-up of a reel-to-reel tape recorder, and a Voice Over conversation, heard but not seen, between a couple of mobsters. This scene went on for pages and pages. It was awful, as was the rest of the script. I told David I didn't like it, and that I thought we should start from scratch. Having gotten the undercover cop story out of his system, we commenced working on the story that became NYPD BLUE.

At some point during the writing of the script, David flew to New York and, through a friend of his, the journalist Michael Daley – currently with The Daily Beast, and in those days The Daily News as well as New York Magazine, and a really terrific guy – met a New York City homicide detective named Bill Clark. David and Bill instantly bonded. David found Bill irresistible and invaluable, and – with my permission – promised Bill a position as our technical consultant should the show get picked up to series.

Bill Clark, or Walter, if you wanted to give him some shit, had been a cop for almost twenty-five years. I met him for the first time in New York, where we'd gone to do some casting for the pilot of NYPD Blue. We were supposed to meet him outside ABC's casting offices on West 67th Street, and I was going to give him a lift back to Los Angeles on my plane. It was a Hawker, the former 20th Century Fox jet that Barry Diller had acquired as part of his exit deal from the studio. He was trading up to a Gulfstream and had sold the Hawker just days before I called him to inquire about it. Barry gave me the name of the buyer and told me he thought the guy would sell it to me for a hundred thousand dollars more than he'd paid for it.

After I'd been fired by MTM, The Doberman, to add insult to injury, sued them for Hill Street Blues profits we maintained they had withheld from us. We settled the case out of court, finally, in 1988, for two million dollars, and I used that money to buy the plane.

Meow.

I remember that day particularly well because Bill arrived a little late, and harried, without luggage. His department issued sedan had been broken into, right in front of the station house no less, and the thief had stolen his suitcase.

On the flight back to Los Angeles, Bill and Dayna got into an argument over why Bill didn't like female police officers: they couldn't physically intimidate a male suspect, etc. It got pretty hot. Dayna backs down to no one. I was pretty sure this guy and I weren't going to get along. I didn't like his politics, and I didn't much care for his attitude about women, and his in-your-face style was off-putting to me.

What can I say? Over the course of the next twelve years, Bill became one of my closest friends, and remains so to this day, even though he's a self-described "broken down flatfoot."

Bill loved animals, birds in particular. He literally had hundreds of them in cages, along with a couple of talking parrots we taught to say a few terrible things. He also had a particular love of dogs. When he'd served in Viet Nam, he had walked patrol in the pitch-blackness of night with his dog as his only companion. He still puddles up when he talks about that dog.

Bill would cry at weddings. He lost his brother to drugs as a young man, and whenever he talks about it, he starts to cry. He was (and is) the most sentimental man I've ever known. He was also the toughest. In his twenty-five years as a cop (during which he also moonlighted as a bouncer in a gay bar, as well as a body guard), he'd been in dozens of brawls and never lost a fight. He was absolutely fearless. I could (and still can) listen to Bill's stories endlessly. He never bragged. It was always just matter of fact. Bill was a true warrior.

If you earned Bill's friendship and loyalty, you knew he would without hesitation put his life in front of yours to protect you. When we would go to New York, he'd always hector me about not hiring a bodyguard. I told him that just wasn't me. I'd grown up in the city, in a pretty tough neighborhood, and I always felt safe walking the city's streets.

"You don't understand," Bill would say. "There are shit birds out there who'd kill you for a hundred bucks and not give it a second thought."

It was always amazing to me to walk around New York with Bill. He owned the street. Always. He'd point out person after person. "That guy's a scum bag. That guy's a dealer," Etc., etc. I, of course, saw nothing.

During our first year of production, Bill commuted back and forth. I was always clear about Bill's role: he was *our* cop. He kept us honest. If Bill said we were doing something wrong, we'd change it without argument. I was always proud of how realistic NYPD Blue was, and so was Bill. I like to think, in spite of our many flawed characters, that we never dishonored the badge.

In December of 1994, Bill took his twenty-five year retirement and moved to Los Angeles to become a producer on the show. Over the twelve-year life of the series, he rose to the rank of executive producer.

In late December of 1996, I gave Bill a Christmas card and told him not to lose it. In the card, handwritten and signed by me, I'd assigned him a one percent profit participation in NYPD Blue. Now, one percent may not sound like much, but over the long syndication life of the show, it amounted to several million dollars. And Bill earned every cent of it.

The pilot script of NYPD Blue was spectacular. I loved it, 20th Century Fox loved it, and the programmers at ABC loved it. But when the script went to ABC's Broadcast Standards department, the shit hit the fan. We got back pages and pages of notes regarding language and nudity. Had we agreed to them, they would have gutted the script of its uniqueness and realistic grittiness.

And thus commenced my war with Broadcast Standards which, finally, caused me to yank the script. I told Bob Iger I wasn't going to make their watered down version of the show we had all agreed upon. Bob was desperate to have a great cop show on ABC, but I was adamant. Essentially, it was going to be my way or the highway, my reasoning being that I'd already made what was generally considered to be the best cop show ever (Hill Street), and I had no motivation to do another one that, in its own way, wasn't every bit as distinctive. To make a long story short, I stuck to my guns, and the pilot script went back on the shelf.

Six months later, Bob invited me over to his office to have another conversation about NYPD Blue.

During the interim, however, in 1992, we were producing an animated half-hour series called Capitol Critters. It was a cute idea about insects, rats and mice, living behind the walls and under the floor of the White House. Animated shows were becoming all the rage. The Simpsons was a huge hit for Fox. We all thought maybe we could catch some of that lightning in a bottle. Fat chance. I had no way to know how complex and difficult animation was. You'd send a script to Taiwan, or someplace like that, where their animators would bring the script to life. Then they'd send it back for notes. Then they'd take another whack at it. It was incredibly time consuming, not to mention expensive, between writing and animating, re-writing and re-animating. Our head writer, Nat Maulden, and I, clashed often about scripts. He was headstrong in his vision of the stories and characters, as was I. But our conflicts were overwhelmed by the sheer difficulty of making the show on a series schedule. I don't know how The Simpsons did it then, and I don't know how they do it now, but I learned one important lesson: animated comedy was not my strong suit, even less so than musical drama.

Capitol Critters aired a total of seven of its thirteen episodes between January 31, 1992, and March 14th of that same year. Between Bay City Blues, Cop Rock, and Capitol Critters, I was becoming the king of the seven-episode flop. Not exactly what ABC had been hoping for when they coughed up all those commitments to me in 1988.

NYPD Blue had already missed the 1992 season, and development was well under way for the new shows of 1993. I told Bob I hadn't changed my mind about watering down the content, and he invited me, Dayna, and Frank Rohner to meet with ABC's top executives in Dallas, in hopes that we might change their minds. What they were doing in Dallas, I don't know. I didn't have much faith that I'd change anyone's mind, but we flew there in any event, and spent two hours arguing the issue with ABC/Cap Cities' highest-ranking lawyers, who had ultimate authority over the Broadcast Standards department. At the end of the meeting, we'd gotten nowhere, and Dayna, Frank, and I left Dallas. I, for one, was sure the show was deader than Kelsey's balls.

Another two or three weeks went by, and I was actively thinking of other concepts to pitch to ABC when Bob Iger called me and asked me to come over to his office. I went, and he once again asked me to reconsider making the pilot. And, knowing how adamant I was about content, the two of us sat in his office for over an hour, with scratch pads and pencils, drawing "dirty" pictures like two nine year old schoolboys – breasts, buttocks, and torsos. Neither of us could draw worth a shit, but we finally agreed on how much nudity ABC would be willing to tolerate, and it pretty much conformed to my own thinking. As I'd said all along, I wasn't trying to make porno films. I just wanted to depict adult sexual relationships more realistically than anyone else on broadcast TV ever had.

Once Bob and I signed off on the nudity issue, we turned our attention to the language issue. Obviously, we couldn't say "fuck" or "shit" or several other words that your mother would smack you for using. But everything else was on the table. Bob and I finally agreed to a glossary of "acceptable" words, and for reasons I simply cannot recall, we agreed to a cap of thirty-seven uses of those words per episode.

I was quietly ecstatic. After a year and a half of stubbornly holding out, I had gotten about ninety-five percent of everything I wanted. And I probably wasn't appreciative enough of how hard Bob Iger had fought for us with his own bosses.

The pilot for NYPD was a go. We commenced casting right away. We had Dennis Franz's commitment from day one, but we couldn't find the right actor to play his partner, John Kelly. Finally, our casting director Junie Lowry-Johnson, brought up David Caruso's name. I had worked with David on Hill Street Blues, and thought he was a very interesting (and different) sort of leading man: red-haired, a classic Irish mug, and a wonderful voice. Twenty years earlier, you would only have cast him as a heavy.

Caruso read for the role and was terrific. I was ready to hire him, but David Milch begged me not to. Caruso's reputation as a malcontent (to say the least) had preceded him, and Milch was convinced that Caruso would be nothing but trouble. I told David, "You may be right, but he's a wonderful actor. I'm going to hire him anyway." The fact of the matter is, we were both right. Caruso was a big time malcontent, but he was also terrific in the role.

Greg Hoblit produced and directed the pilot for us, and was very committed to a visual style of constant, jittery camera movement that I found very disturbing. Nevertheless, it also added to the uniqueness of the show, so I let Greg have his way. Mike Post wrote a spectacular main title theme, and when the pilot was finished, we knew we had something really special. I'd never seen anything like it on network TV, and I was as proud of NYPD BLUE as I had been of HILL STREET BLUES.

Every May, the networks announce their fall schedules to the affiliates, press, and advertisers in New York to great fanfare. NYPD BLUE caused a sensation among the affiliates – a negative sensation. It's not that they hated it. But it scared them to death. They were convinced the show would tank, and that they'd lose advertisers, audience, and revenue, all due to the language and the nudity.

Back in Los Angeles, the networks would hold their annual affiliates conventions in late May or early June. All the owners, station managers, advertisers, and cast members of the networks' shows, would participate. These were lavish spreads that everyone enjoyed immensely.

An hour before I was leaving for ABC's big bash at The Century Plaza Hotel, I got a phone call from Dan Burke. He was suddenly getting a little wobbly. The affiliate reaction to the show had been so negative, particularly the one big sex scene between Caruso and Amy Brenneman, that he had told them the pilot was still a work in progress and that the show was still to be extensively edited.

I went nuts. I told Dan that I wasn't coming to the event, and that I would go to the press and tell them that ABC had reneged on its promises. Poor Dan was caught between a rock and a hard place. He begged me to agree to tone down the sex and language. I refused. We argued for twenty minutes. He finally asked me if I would at least agree to trim the main sex scene by about ten to fifteen seconds. The scene itself was almost three minutes long, and I felt I could accommodate a fifteen second edit without diluting the scene, so I agreed to that one change, and Dan backed off the rest of his demands.

The moment I arrived at the event, I was mobbed by members of the press. My wife had to bring me a glass of wine because I couldn't escape the crush for over two hours. Clearly, NYPD Blue was the most controversial show on the coming fall schedule, and it was all the press wanted to talk about.

When the show premiered on September 21, 1993, we held our collective breath. It was obvious to me, given the pressure we were under from advertisers and affiliates that ABC wasn't going to give us a lot of rope. Thankfully, we were an instant hit, despite the fact that seventeen percent of ABC's affiliates refused to air us. In addition, we had precious few of what could be considered top tier advertisers. My own sense of it was that the controversy provided us with a degree of notoriety and publicity that we never could have generated on our own, and I was tempted to send Donald Wildmon a bottle of champagne by way of thanks.

At some point during the first season, we were shooting parts of four or five episodes in New York City. One of the scenes we were supposed to shoot involved setting up a roadblock at an entry ramp to the West Side Highway. Sipowicz and Kelly were trying to apprehend as escaped felon. The scene called for traffic to back up, antagonizing the drivers, who were yelling at the cops and honking their horns. At one point, Sipowicz was supposed to yell at one of the drivers, "Hey, asshole!" and the driver, as it was written, was supposed to flip Sipowicz the finger. Broadcast Standards said we couldn't do that. Somehow, with our obsession over tits and ass and language, Bob Iger and I had never bothered to negotiate the flipping of the bird.

I responded to Broadcast Standards with the observation that if they didn't let me have the guy flip Sipowicz the bird, I would have Sipowicz call this guy an asshole thirty-seven times that, per our agreement, I could do. They folded, and the guy flipped Sipowicz the bird.

By the end of season one, I was dealing with two opposing realities. The first was, thankfully, that NYPD BLUE was a hit. The second was that David Caruso had become impossible. His clashes with David Milch were occurring on an almost daily basis, Milch was having serious heart issues, and every time I'd call Caruso into my office for a conversation about his problems, he'd shut down like a sullen teenager.

Caruso's behavior was, simply put, cancerous. He was emotionally unavailable to everyone, and he was volatile, moody, or sullen, depending on the day. You never knew who was going to show up on the set from day to day in terms of mood, or attitude towards the material. It was destabilizing, but that's how Caruso defined his power. Most people don't function well in a dysfunctional environment, but Caruso loved it because he was the source of all the discontent, and it empowered him.

He never said it to me directly, but the simple truth was, Caruso felt he was too good for television. He wanted to be a movie star. And his plan was to alienate the writers, producers, and his fellow cast mates, in hopes that we would dump him from the show. Fat chance. He may have accomplished the former, but not the latter. Against all odds, we had turned NYPD BLUE into a hit, and I wasn't about to unravel that sweater just because of an actor who thought he was too good for the room.

About a month into the summer hiatus, David Milch and I were already working on second season scripts when Caruso's agent called. Caruso wanted to be let out of his contract. Of course, I said no, and that if he decided not to show up for work, we would sue his ass. In that case, said the agent, could we all sit down and talk about re-structuring his deal? I agreed to that, of course, since it was common practice to renegotiate an actor's deal in success.

Several days later, we met in Dayna's office. In attendance were Caruso's lawyer, his agent, his manager, me, and, of course, Dayna. The meeting started with Caruso's agent saying that Caruso had felt persecuted all year, and that he felt Milch had reduced the size of his role out of personal animus. He again asked that we let Caruso out of his contract. Dayna, in no uncertain terms, said that wasn't going to happen, and she suggested they cut to the chase. What were they looking for on Caruso's behalf?

Caruso's lawyer, with a straight face, said that their demands were based on the theory of diminished opportunity. Huh? Diminished opportunity, explained the lawyer, rested on the fact that Caruso was currently in New York working on a movie, making seventy-five thousand dollars a week. Returning to NYPD BLUE for a second season at his contractual rate of forty thousand or so represented a big pay cut – hence the concept of diminished opportunity.

I pointed out that if it weren't for NYPD BLUE, Caruso would be in New York for the summer working in a car wash.

Dayna saw the red creeping up my neck, and this was no heart attack. I didn't often lose it, but I did have a temper, and Dayna saw that I was quickly getting to that point. She tried to steer the meeting back on course. "What exactly are you looking for," she persisted. Caruso's lawyer ticked off the following: one, a hundred thousand dollars per episode. Two, Fridays off. Three, a thirty-eight foot trailer. Four, an office suite on the lot, replete with his own development executive, for whom we had to foot the bill, to the tune of a thousand dollars a week. Five, two hotel suites in New York when the company went there on location, plus a dozen first class plane tickets. And lastly, Caruso had to have additional security to shield him from his adoring public.

I said, "You've got to be kidding me," or words to that effect.

Now the lawyer said, "Well, if you're not willing to meet those demands, here's a second set of demands Caruso could live with." And he went on to ask for sixty-five thousand dollars an episode, Fridays off, the office suite, the development executive, the hotel suites, the plane tickets, and lastly – and here's the kicker – Caruso wanted the last seven weeks of the season off, so that his window for doing feature films would be larger.

I'd had it. I said, "Your client is under contract, we've exercised his option for a second year at forty-two-five an episode, and if he doesn't show up for work on the first day of shooting, we will sue his ass for everything he has." And I walked out of Dayna's office.

As declarations of war went, that had gone well.

The short of it is that the lawyer, the agent, and the manager, kept up a daily barrage. Caruso didn't want to return to the show and was threatening to walk. Ted Harbert, then an executive under Bob Iger, tried to meet with Caruso to talk him into returning. It was getting ugly. Milch was getting sicker. By now we had four scripts written that, without Caruso, would have to be thrown in the trash. I finally decided to let Caruso go, but first I tracked down Jimmy Smits, who had been my first choice for the role when we were originally casting the show, but who turned us down in favor of pursuing a film career. Jimmy was currently somewhere in Morocco, shooting one of those sword and sandal epics.

When I finally tracked him down – I think the nearest phone was ten miles away, and he probably had to hitch a ride on a camel to get to it – I offered him the role again. Actually, I begged him. Then I asked him this question: "Do you want to come home and be a huge TV star in a show that's already a hit, or do you want to be making movies in Morocco in hundred degree weather wearing a leather skirt?" Jimmy's no fool. He came home and took over Caruso's role in NYPD BLUE, and made the series even greater.

We then negotiated a deal with Caruso that, in exchange for his release, required him to do the first four episodes so that we could properly write his character out of the show, and further stipulated that he couldn't work in another television series for five years. His agent and lawyer agreed to the terms, and Caruso was officially gone.

When he had shot his last scene of the fourth episode, he turned without a word and left the set, the stage, and the lot. He didn't say a single word of thanks, or a goodbye to his cast mates – nothing.

In the meantime, Milch and I had to invent a whole new character for Jimmy Smits, which we did on the fly. It was a bit of a fire drill, but Jimmy – a consummate pro and a truly fine person – jumped into a fast moving river and hung on for the remainder of that second season. The audience loved him, and by the end of the second season, we were an even bigger hit, ABC was thrilled, and no one missed David Caruso, whose so-called movie career was already circling the drain. Boo hoo.

One last note about Caruso: About two years later, his film career having totally flamed out, his agent called and asked me if I might consider releasing David from the clause in his exit deal that prevented him from working in television for five years. Apparently, he'd been offered a CBS pilot. I've never been much for holding a grudge, and I certainly wouldn't have wanted to ever prevent someone from making a living, so I acquiesced. The CBS pilot was a bust, but the next show Caruso did was CSI: Miami.

He was right back where he'd started, except that instead of being the star of NYPD BLUE – one of the most acclaimed and honored shows on television – he was the star of a standard spin-off of the CSI franchise. But the worst part for David Caruso was that he was . . . David Caruso: a malcontented, self-destructive, emotionally unstable actor who made life miserable for everyone around him, and who was constitutionally incapable of happiness.

I'm not a psychologist. I don't even play one on TV. But I've run into my share of talented, but highly neurotic or dysfunctional types throughout my career. Mike Kozoll; Terry Louise Fisher; David Caruso; Sharon Stone; Daniel Benzali, to name just a few who in my estimation shot themselves in the foot, career-wise. The film and television industry is loaded with men and women blessed with talent and on the cusp of great success who go off the rails. Why?

I can only assume that, short of the true narcissists and sociopaths among us, or those afflicted with crippling addictions, the majority of these self-inflicted wounds are the result of a deeply ingrained sense of unworthiness that success threatens to upend. It's ultimately easier for these people to blow up their own sand box than to live into the responsibilities – and compromises – that sustained success requires.

I think all of us can blame our shortcomings on inherited traits and/or neglectful or abusive upbringing, to a point. But most of us, at some point in life, have the opportunity to reinvent ourselves – to allow our better, or stronger, natures to prevail. It takes courage and hard work, but it's possible. Pissing and moaning about your shitty childhood when you're twenty-five? Okay. At forty? You're a loser. Get over yourself.

There's a certain personality type (David Caruso, unfortunately, comes to mind) that, unlike the majority of us, flourishes in a dysfunctional environment and is therefore masterful at creating it. But like cancer, one of two results is inevitable: the cancer gets cut out in order to save the organism, or the organism is destroyed by the cancer. But in destroying the organism, the cancer dies with it – at best, a Pyrrhic victory.

Becoming successful in the film and television business is tough. It takes talent, opportunism, and hard work. Staying successful is even harder because it requires a couple of additional traits: patience and maturity. In a world that encourages narcissism, generosity of spirit is counter-intuitive, yet the most truly success-ful people I've known in my fifty years in television are thoughtful, kind to everyone, and almost always prepared to assume responsi-bility for failure. Thank goodness, in my experience, those folks far outnumber the jerks among us.

20

In 1994, we produced a show called Byrd Of Paradise. I'd always loved Hawaii, ever since I started vacationing there in 1978. I thought a family drama set in Hawaii would be a great excuse to spend more time there. I'd also never made a true family show, and so, with the help of the writing team of Charles "Chick" Eglee and Channing Gibson – we invented the Byrd family, who relocate to Oahu after Sam Byrd's wife dies. The show starred Timothy Busfield, Seth Green, Jennifer Love Hewitt, Arlo Guthrie, and Bruce Weitz, among others. It was a lovely show, and Chick and Chan wrote a terrific pilot.

As a family drama on ABC, the show had a difficult time. The reviews were, by and large, excellent. But it was a soft show, by design, and on Thursdays at 8pm, it was burdened with having to start off the night. The folks at ABC genuinely liked the show, but reluctantly canceled it after thirteen episodes, victim to marginal ratings. I think they came to regret that decision subsequently, but you know the old saying: you can't get the toothpaste back in the tube.

Byrds Of Paradise was a good example of the distinction I've always made between failing and not succeeding. A good show, which Byrds Of Paradise was, in my opinion, may not succeed. There's nothing you can do about it. That's the gamble of series television: you never know what's going to catch an audience's fancy. There are bad shows that have become big hits, and wonderful shows that have fallen by the wayside, all because the audience either responds or doesn't. Maybe they fall in love with an actor or actress. Maybe they love a particular show's "gimmick." Or maybe it's what they call a time-slot hit: there's nothing better on, and you're looking forward to the show that follows. By the same token, maybe an audience doesn't respond well to an actor, or doesn't much care for the genre, or simply prefers what the competition's offering. If I could figure out what makes an audience tick, I'd never have a flop.

But then there are the flat out failures. Bay City Blues was a flat out failure, not because the audience simply didn't respond, but because I did a lousy job. It was ill conceived and badly executed. That's failure. If people for some reason had loved it, I would still have considered it a failure.

Not succeeding is the luck of the draw. Failing is on me. I care greatly for all my shows, but Byrds Of Paradise was a particularly disappointing cancellation.

When we went to New York for the up fronts, right after the cancellation, Barbara and I were supposed to have dinner with Ted Harbert, who was then co-head of programming at ABC with Stu Bloomberg. I had a car and driver for the evening, so I swung by the Regency Hotel, where Ted was staying, to pick him up. He walked out of the hotel with a bag over his head. However disappointed I was, that made me laugh. Ted was, and still is, an old school executive who loved TV and agonized over programming decisions. He was genuinely invested in and respectful of our efforts, for which I will always be grateful.

Nevertheless, NYPD Blue was firing on all cylinders. By our third season, virtually all of the ABC affiliates who'd initially refused to air the show had come back on board. Money talks and bullshit walks, as they say. We were attracting top tier advertisers, and our transition from David Caruso to Jimmy Smits had, if anything, made us an even bigger hit. It was at this point that 20th Century Fox began to talk to us about selling the show into syndication. 20th claimed there was scant market interest, but they were willing to buy it themselves as a launch pad for their new cable network, FX. After several rounds of negotiations, we agreed to sell NYPD BLUE to FX for four hundred thousand dollars an episode; not a huge amount of money, given the production costs of the show, but enough to insure that our deficits would be covered and that there'd be a decent profit left over to split amongst the participants (me, Greg Hoblit, who'd directed the pilot, our president, Dayna Flanagan, and David Milch, my co-creator). At this point, I was anticipating the show would run at least seven years, and that those of us who shared in Steven Bochco Productions' sixty percent of profits would all make a tidy sum.

About six months after our sale to FX, my attorney, Frank Rohner, came to me, telling me that over the preceding several months, he'd had numerous conversations with the presidents of other cable networks, and they'd all said the same thing: 20th Century Fox had told them they were not accepting bids on the show. At least one of these cable heads told Frank that they'd been prepared to offer as much as seven hundred thousand dollars per episode.

Frank urged me to sue Fox for self-dealing, among other things, but my feeling was that we'd entered into the deal with our eyes open and should live with its results.

Over the course of the next 18 months, however, Frank kept banging on me to sue. His position was that we hadn't gone into the deal with our eyes open, but that, rather, we'd been lied to, and that Fox had taken advantage of us in order to use NYPD BLUE to build up the fledgling FX network. In other words, it wasn't an arm's length transaction.

Finally, with the statute of limitations staring us in the face, I agreed to let Frank file suit. If I'd had any idea what the next two years of my life was going to be like, in all probability I never would've done it.

The suit was filed and, predictably, Fox didn't budge. They simply dug in for a long war, under the assumption that I, like a thousand litigants before me, would fold under the reality of the time and cost of pursuing a lawsuit.

The paper started to fly. Subpoenas were issued back and forth. When it started to come clear to Fox that I wasn't going to fold – that in fact, I was prepared to spend whatever it took to get our day in court – things started to get nasty. Normally, as a courtesy, attorneys will accept subpoenas on behalf of their clients. But when we tried to subpoena Rupert Murdoch, who owned Fox, his attorneys repeatedly refused service. Finally, one day, when Rupert approached the commissary for lunch with Peter Chernin, then COO of Fox and Rupert's right hand, a pleasant little lady saw Rupert and approached. "Oh my goodness," she said with obvious delight. "Are you Mr. Murdoch?" Rupert smiled and responded in the affirmative. The woman slapped a subpoena in his hand and said, "You've been served." Rupert was stunned, Peter Chernin was furious, and from that day forward and for the next two years, I was banned from dining in the commissary.

Recently, I was recounting this episode to an old friend, the renowned attorney, Howard Weitzman, who shrewdly pointed out something I'd never thought of. He said that the likely reason Chernin was so pissed off was that Rupert probably didn't even know he was being sued by us; that that was, among other reasons, what the Peter Chernins of the world existed for – to make sure stuff like our lawsuit never even came to Rupert's attention.

Weeks and months dragged by. Depositions were taken by testy lawyers on both sides. Nerves became frayed. The lawsuit, like most lawsuits, took on a life of its own. Finally, about two weeks before trial was to begin, I said to Frank that I felt we needed to hire a big-time litigator. It wasn't that Richard Ross wasn't a fine lawyer. He was, and is. But courtroom presence – the ability to command and hold center stage – is a talent, and in much the same way that I could never act or direct, I felt strongly that Richard was not the lawyer to litigate this case. Reluctantly, Frank agreed to hire an outside litigator named Brian Lysaght. Brian was a confidant, good-looking attorney with real presence, and I immediately felt comfortable with him. When we met in my office for the first time, he told me that if I was willing to permit him, he felt he could settle the case within forty-eight hours. I asked him why he thought so, when Fox had been so aggressively intransigent for over two years. Brian said, "That was then, this is now. They know that if they walk into that courtroom, they're going to lose." I was stunned by his confidence, wondering how he could be so sure. He explained that, in his experience, juries made up their minds very quickly, based on who had the better story. And as far as Brian was concerned, we did, and he was convinced that Fox knew it.

I had already spent close to three million dollars in pursuit of this case, and we hadn't even gone to trial yet, so I told Brian to give it a shot. At that point, we were about four days from the start of trial. The next morning, Brian called me to tell me he thought he had a reasonable settlement in hand. He walked me through the terms of it, and it sounded pretty good to me. Per the agreement, Fox would pick up all our legal costs, plus an additional sum of money that by no means compensated us for what we believed our lost syndication revenue was, but what made the deal attractive was that Fox was to immediately release their exclusive syndication rights to NYPD BLUE, and was willing to let us take the show back out to the market place and re-sell it. What we didn't know at the time was that Fox's syndication group had indicated to Fox that they believed our future syndication potential was exhausted, and we would find that the show was worth less on the open market than we were already getting from the FX deal.

I told Brian I thought the settlement was a fair one. I only had one remaining issue I needed resolved in my favor. "What?" he asked, a note of caution creeping into his voice.

"They banned me from the commissary," I said. "I want my table back, guaranteed in writing, as part of the settlement."

Pause. Then, "Please don't make me do that. It could blow up the entire agreement."

I didn't care, I told him. "Tell them your client is crazy, and that if they don't give him back his customary table, he'll see them in court on Monday."

Ten minutes later, Brian called me back, instructing me to go over to the commissary and find out what my old table number is and call him back.

I went over to the commissary. I hadn't been inside the place for two years. I was greeted by the wait staff as if I were a long lost relative, which touched me enormously. In the intervening two years, the place had been completely remodeled. I asked one of the waitresses which one was Rupert's table, and then I asked her the number of the table next to his. Thus informed, I went back to my office, called Brian, and gave him the table number so it could be written into the settlement agreement. Petty? Yes. But I enjoyed that single moment more than all the subsequent money that accrued from the settlement.

Speaking of said settlement, the following week Frank, Dayna and I sat down with Fox's syndication team to strategize our approach to re-selling the show. In spite of getting the show back, we were still partners with Fox, and they owned a forty percent stake in any future profits. Once again, the syndication team expressed their belief that we'd be lucky if we could sell the show for a sum even close to the 400 thousand per episode that Fox had paid us in the FX deal.

Seventy-two hours later, under the Turner Network banner, Time-Warner paid us one million dollars per episode for as long as the show was on the air. We ran for twelve years and produced 263 episodes. You do the math.

NYPD Blue was something of a game changer for the nineties. I remember attending a dinner one night in New York at the home of Bob Bascha, the director of the Museum of Television and Radio. At the time, I was on their board of directors. One of the guests was a fellow board member named Frank Bennack who, at the time, was the Executive Vice Chairman of The Hearst Corporation. Frank asked me what shows I was developing, and I told him I was cooking up a cop show for ABC which was going to be as close to a real R-rated television series as you could get. Frank listened closely as

I described the parameters of the show and then said to me with absolute certainty: "Not a chance. That show will never make it onto the air."

Twenty some-odd years later, it seems tame, particularly compared to most cable dramas. But in the early nineteen nineties, the series caused a shit storm with advertisers and broadcast affiliates, and it took a few seasons for them to realize that the sight of a bare ass and the sound of a few common school yard curse words hadn't brought down the republic.

NYPD Blue ran for twelve seasons, the longest run of any show I ever produced. It had a significant impact on television, if not the culture at large, in the sense that it cracked open the door for more adult television drama, if primarily on the cable networks.

For twenty five years, those four shows – Hill Street Blues, L.A. Law, Doogie Howser, M.D., and NYPD Blue were broadcast network mainstays, and I like to think that not only the shows, but the dozens of gifted actors, writers, producers and directors who got their start on them, irrevocably changed the landscape of television.

21

After the fourth season of NYPD BLUE, which by now had settled into a reliable Tuesday night hit for ABC, David Milch's work habits became more and more erratic. Scripts weren't being delivered on time, directors were getting less and less time to prepare their work, and actors were increasingly bothered by their inability to get material in a timely fashion with which to do their jobs. It got to the point where, after several more seasons of this, the quality of the show was suffering. By now, David was literally writing whatever pages were needed for the day, and then he'd hand deliver them to the stage and act out for all the actors how they should portray their roles. It was frustrating for them, and demeaning for directors.

In 1997 I'd been in the throws of separation and divorce and, to be honest, I hadn't been paying as much attention to the deteriorating situation as I should have been, given my own emotional deterioration. I determined to speak to David and, at the beginning of the seventh season, with the show's performance in the ratings beginning to reflect the chaotic environment in the work place, David and I amicably agreed that this season would be his last.

Enter Nick Wootton and Matt Olmstead, our two best staff writers.

My friends the Woottons – Dr. Barbara Kadell and Dr. Gareth Wootton (the wittiest man I've ever known) – who had been my technical advisers on Doogie Howser, had two sons, the older being Tony and the younger being Nick. I had known both of them since they were children. The Woottons and Bochcos had been been friends for forty years, having found each other when our children attended the Crossroads school in Santa Monica. Tony, the older of the two boys, grew up to be a successful tech entrepreneur. The Woottons' youngest, Nick, wanted to be a writer since he was knee high to Thomas Wolfe. He was always walking around with a book sticking out of his back pocket. When he was in high school, I hired him as a summer intern. In those days, having so many friends with kids who wanted to be in the business, my policy was to hire them for one summer only, so as to give all the other kids a chance. I hired Nick for three summers in a row, and then practically every summer he was in college at NYU Film School. I used to half-joke that Nick was my second son. When he went off to college, I told him to send me everything he wrote, and I would give him notes. Even as a kid in college, his writing was special. When he was a sophomore, I told him that when he graduated, if he still wanted to write for film and/or TV, he could come work for me. And when he graduated, he came to work for me on NYPD BLUE. He quickly went from being a general assistant to being a "junior" writer under the dubious mentorship of David Milch. I say dubious because, on the one hand, David was a brilliant teacher. On the other hand, he could be genuinely abusive to the writers under his command. I often found myself doing double duty as these writers' shrink. Somehow, Nick survived this trial by fire. Under David's tutelage, Nick won an Emmy for writing what was arguably the best NYPD BLUE episode we ever made: the episode in which Jimmy Smits' character died of a heart infection. To this day, I can't watch that episode without puddling up.

I've only had two genuine protégés in my career: Nick Wootton and Jesse Bochco (more about Jessse later), and both of them earned every bit of their individual successes.

Today, Nick is a successful show runner on the CBS hit The Scorpion. And of course, Jesse Bochco has become a successful director and producer, and when I'm lucky enough to get a series on the air, I've been able to pry him away from his successful freelance career to come run my show for me. If Nick Wootton and Jesse Bochco were publicly traded stocks, I'd buy them both with every buck I had. (I suppose in Jesse's case, heir-wise, you could say that I did.)

And then there was Matt Olmstead. I hired Matt in season six, as I recall, and over the next six years, along with Nick, he became one of our two primary writers on the show after David left. These were two young writers who absolutely rose to the challenge, and almost single-handedly raised the bar back up for NYPD BLUE, resuscitating the better part of its lost quality. The show ran successfully for five more years.

Today, Matt runs two shows for Dick Wolf, on NBC: Chicago Fire and Chicago PD. I'm enormously proud of both him and Nick. They're consummate pros who have learned their lessons well, and I hope someday one of them will give me a job.

22

Like millions of other Americans, I was riveted to my TV set on January 24, 1995, the first day of the O.J. Simpson trial. I had known O.J. casually, and we both belonged to The Riviera Country Club, where O.J. was and avid golfer. O.J. was a star: Heisman Trophy winner at USC; star running back in the N.F.L.; hugely successful commercial pitchman; and well-known film actor. O.J. had it all: wealth, fame, a spectacularly beautiful wife and a high-end, gated home in Brentwood, California. And yet, here he was, in January of 1995, on trial for the brutal murders of his now estranged wife, Nicole, and a young waiter named Ron Goldman, who'd had the misfortune to be delivering a pair of sunglasses to Nicole that she'd left at the restaurant in Brentwood that Goldman worked at. It was a blood-bath – a shocking celebrity double murder that captured the morbid attention of the American public. It certainly captured my morbid attention. In addition to my passing acquaintance with O.J., I was also a good friend of his first attorney, prominent criminal defense lawyer Howard Weitzman, who resigned from the case shortly after O.J. was brought in for questioning by LAPD detectives. Howard strongly advised O.J. to clam up. O.J. disregarded Howard's advice and yapped at length to the police. They let him go after about an hour. I think Howard saw the shit storm ahead and didn't want to represent a client who a) disregarded his instructions, and b) felt that his fame shielded him from the consequences of his actions. Howard is too ethical of a lawyer to ever voice his opinion, but I suspect he may have strongly felt O.J. was guilty. (I remember Bill Clark saying to me, matter-of-factly, that if he'd had O.J. in that room, he – O.J. – never would have left that room until he'd confessed.)

Personally, I had no doubt that O.J. committed those two murders. Violence was his business, and he was brilliant at it. Additionally, though I had no first-hand knowledge of it, it was widely rumored that O.J. had a significant cocaine habit, which could easily have fueled the explosive rage that resulted in the brutal murders he was accused of.

But I was also fascinated by the trial for its own sake. As the creator of L.A. Law, I had more than a layman's interest in the judicial system. Audiences, over generations of TV watching, had been conditioned to accept the conventions of television legal drama: present the case, quickly bring it to trial, get a verdict, and dispose of the matter, all within the one-hour constraints of series television.

But this trial – O.J.'s trial – was reinventing the audience's perception of how the criminal justice system worked. It was slow. It was methodical. It was procedural. There were long stretches of testimony, sometimes covering days. The lawyers meandered. The judge called for frequent recesses. Progress was glacial. Time wasn't measured in hours, or even days. This trial was taking months. And yet, the public was obsessed with the case. The judge, prosecutors and defense attorneys all became stars. They were household names. Lance Ito, Marcia Clark, Chris Darden, Johnny Cochran, Robert Shapiro, F. Lee Bailey, Alan Dershowitz, and . . . Robert Kardashian (ha!). I was mesmerized along with everyone else. But I was also becoming obsessed with another thought: that no one would ever watch a law show on TV in the same way again.

Inspired by the O.J. trial, I began to think about creating a TV series that would follow one case for an entire season. The seeds of Murder One had been planted in my mind.

I pitched my idea to ABC in late February or early March of 1995. O.J.'s trial was already over a month old, and just getting started. ABC was genuinely enthused by the idea, and gave me a quick thumbs-up.

I asked Howard Weitzman to be our technical consultant, and I recruited a talented writing team who had worked with me on the previous year's Byrds Of Paradise, Charles "Chick" Eglee, and Channing Gibson. What I didn't know at the time was that they were going through the elongated throes of a divorce. The analogy to marriage is not far-fetched. A writing team is often closer than a married couple and, sex aside, prone to all the conflicts and turmoil that any "normal" marriage is heir to.

In any event, between me, Chick and Channing – with a notable assist from David Milch, who wrote one of the pilot's most memorable scenes, we got the script written.

It was good stuff, and better, in retrospect, than I thought at the time. I'd been infected by Chick and Channing's conflict, which they were trying to hide from me but was clear in the work, which was late, and wanting – and by my own anxiety over trying to pull off something that no one had ever done before: tell a single story over an entire twenty-two episode season.

I hired my old college friend and Hill Street Blues cast member, Charlie Haid, to direct. I had started Charlie as a director on Doogie Howser, M.D., and he had blossomed, his difficult personality notwithstanding, into a first-rate director.

In a bold – some might say idiotic – move, I cast Daniel Benzali in the lead role. Daniel was a totally bald-headed, not particularly attractive character actor who I'd known since we made the pilot of NYPD Blue. He played a hard-charging criminal defense attorney modeled after a well-known New York criminal defense lawyer named Bruce Cutler, whose specialty was representing wise guys. In the opening scene of the NYPD Blue pilot, Benzali's character eviscerates Andy Sipowicz on the witness stand.

FADE IN:

INT. COURTROOM – 100 CENTER STREET – LATE MORNING

Detective John Kelly, mid-thirties, fifteen years on the force, is seated in the back of the courtroom, watching uncomfortably as his florid-featured, booze-bellied partner, ANDY SIPOWICZ, is taken through his paces as sole prosecution witness by an identifiably unenthusiastic A.D.A., Sylvia Costas, thirty-eight –

COSTAS
Detective Sipowicz, please tell the court how
you came to arrest Mr. Giardella.

At about which point the camera picks up in the defendant's chair Marino crime-family lieutenant ALFONSE GIARDELLA, late forties, overweight, wearing a hairpiece –

SIPOWICZ
This past August twenty-seventh I was routinely
surveilling the defendant because
he's a known felon.
During the course of the surveillance I observed the
defendant's automobile get a
flat tire, and he got out
of the Cadillace and opened his
trunk. At that time I
approached the vehicle, identi-
fied myself as a police officer
and in the course of a casual observation of the open trunk
I saw twenty-seven cartons of fil-
ter cigarettes which did
not have tax stamps. I ascertained that the vehicle
was owned by the defendant, gave him his rights,
and took him into custody.

COSTAS
Nothing further, Your Honor.

The judge in turn looks at JAMES SINCLAIR, mid-fifties, lawyer for
the Marino crime family –

ANGLE – SINCLAIR AND SIPOWICZ

                    SINCLAIR
          Detective Sipowicz, you've testified you were
          conducting a routine surveil-
          lance of Mr. Giardella at the
          time his vehicle became disabled.

                    SIPOWICZ
          That's correct.

                    SINCLAIR
          You've testified that the car-
          tons of untaxed cigarettes
          for possession of which you
          arrested Mr. Giardella were
          in plain sight in Mr. Giardella's
          trunk when he opened
          it to get a jack out to fix the flat.

                    SIPOWICZ
          Right.

                    SINCLAIR
          Now, there were seven nails in Mr. Giardella's
          right rear radial, Detective. That wouldn't exactly
          produce a slow leak. Yet you say that during several
          hours of antecedent surveillance
          you saw no one damage
          Mr. Giardella's tire.

                    SIPOWICZ

I was surveilling Mr. Giardella,
Counselor, not his car. He'd
stopped at Niglio's Coffee House,
maybe some urban youths
did mischief to his vehicle during that time frame.

SINCLAIR
Your Honor, justified or not, the reputation of the neighborhood
in which Niglio's Coffee House
is located is such that
urban youths do not tend to congregate and do mischief
in its environs –

SIPOWICZ
Maybe he drove past a construction site after he left –

SINCLAIR
(over Sipowcz' interjection)
On the other hand, Detective
Sipowicz here is known
to have a personal vendetta against Mr. Giardella.
I submit the true scenario is that
while my client stopped
in Niglio's, Detective Sipowicz hammered nails into
Mr. Giardella's tire and caused a flat, so when Mr.
Giardella stopped to get out his
spare the Detective could
circumvent probable cause statutes and go
fishing inside Mr. Giardella's trunk. Move to
suppress the evidence as tainted and dismiss the
complaint –

                          JUDGE
          (has been visibly skeptical
          of Sipowicz' testimony)
        Granted.

                         SINCLAIR
          – although if the day were lon-
          ger I'd cross file charges
          of vandalism against this Detective.

                         SIPOWICZ
          (to the Judge)
        What about the construction-site theory?

                          JUDGE
        Pathetic. Adjourned.

Off Sipowicz, angrily red-pussed as the Judge gavels –

INTERCUT – KELLY

rising, reacting with a mix of affection, amusement, and wincing
embarrassment, as we –

                                             CUT TO:

INT. COURTHOUSE CORRIDOR – DAY

As Alfonse Giardella exits from court with his lawyer, who, about to
part company with his client, waves a good-naturedly admonishing
finger in his puss –

                         SINCLAIR
          Pay for your cigarettes Alfonse.

ANOTHER ANGLE

Giardella's seen Sipowicz, hails him –

GIARDELLA
Know what I love about you, Sipowicz? Slow
days, there's always a fifty-percent
chance you're gonna
give me a big laugh.

SIPOWICZ
You want a laugh? – Just check yourself in the
mirror, Giardella.

GIARDELLA
Yeah, now make some bad wig jokes. Meanwhile,
I'm walking out the door, you nickel stiff.

SIPOWICZ
(red-faced)
What is that, a dead rat you got on your head?

Kelly's got a hand on Sipowicz' arm –

KELLY
Take it easy, Andy.

GIARDELLA
Hey, what's your take-home Sipowicz, about
Eighty-eight bucks a day?
(holds a bill out between his fingers)
Buy yourself some clean socks.

SIPOWICZ
I'm going to burn you down! Count on it!

The veins on Sipowicz' neck are bulging. As Kelly steers him to the exit stairs –

> KELLY
> Will you lay off him now, Andy?

To Giardella's receding back, as Kelly pushes him into the stairwell –

> SIPOWICZ
> No shot. That wig-wearing hump rubs me the
> wrong way, and I'm gonna make his life miserable!

EXT. COURTHOUSE – 100 CENTER STREET – FRONT STEPS
– DAY

As the two partners move down the stairs –

> KELLY
> And what happens if you bury your career?

> SIPOWICZ
> Who are you kidding? They already held that
> service.

Sipowicz turns and walks away as under –

A.D.A. COSTAS

passes by, on the way down the steps –

> SIPOWICZ
> Boy, you prosecuted the crap out of that one, lady –

> COSTAS
> I went with the crap I had, Detective.

SIPOWICZ
You calling that a hummer bust? You
saying I queered that guy's tire?

COSTAS
I'd say res ipsa locuitor if I thought you
knew what it meant.

SIPOWICZ
(grabs his joint)
Ipsa this, you pissy little bitch.

And he moves down the steps. Off Kelly –

SMASH CUT TO:
MAIN TITLES

It was the first scene of the pilot, and I thought Daniel was riveting, as was Dennis Franz. I'd never forgotten Benzali's portrayal,
and in fact we hired him a number of times over the course of
the first few seasons, to play the same character. As physically
unattractive as he may have been, he was a powerful actor, and I
needed someone for Murder One who could seize the stage and
hold it for an entire season. Acknowledging that Daniel was an
acquired taste, it was a gamble I nevertheless was willing to take.
Daniel didn't disappoint, either. He was powerful in the role, and
more than held his own against the likes of Stanley Tucci. In one
of the final scenes of the pilot of Murder One, the lead attorney,
Ted Hoffman, played by Benzali, is in a bar having a drink with
one of his young associates. As they're leaving, he's accosted by a
half-drunk patron at the bar:

PATRON
(mock-respectful)

Excuse me, Mr. Hoffman? Could I have a word
with you?

                    HOFFMAN
          Call my office.

Above the bar, the television shows a TV reporter speaking about
the arraignment of Hoffman's client on a murder charge.

                    PATRON
          Hey, Mr. Lawyer, here's fifty bucks – get
          up on the bar and dance.

The drunken patron waves a wad of bills at Hoffman –

                    HOFFMAN
          (low-voiced, to the associate)
          A local wit.

The waiter returns with Hoffman's credit card, receipt, etc. As
Hoffman adds a tip and signs –

                    PATRON
          C'mon, Hoffman, you know this guy is guilty.

                    HOFFMAN
          I'm not interested in talking to you.

                    PATRON
          (waving money)
          Y'know what I think? I think hookers on Sunset
          got more scruples than you guys, is what I think.

Hoffman finally turns to the drunk –

HOFFMAN
My friend, do you think anyone in this bar
believes you've got a head of hair?

PATRON
What did you say?

HOFFMAN
We all know that's a comb-over, but 'til you get
so obnoxious you forfeit your right to civil
treatment, no one in here points
it out. Think of the
trial system like that. We know
accused people aren't
always innocent, maybe not even usually innocent –

PATRON
Yeah, now start to twist things around.

HOFFMAN
(moving closer to him)
– and even though we know that, we treat people
like they're innocent 'til they've had their shot in
court because it makes us better people. It civilizes
us to treat them that way. Civility's important. That's
why no one in here called you a self-deceiving fool
'til you opened your drunken mouth.
(gets his wallet)
Now I'm not gonna dance for
you, but I'll put up fifty
bucks of my own, you put up yours –
(indicates bartender)
and Felix'll hold the stakes.

PATRON

You betting your guy didn't do
it, or you're gonna get
him off?

HOFFMAN
Never bet against me on that.

I filled out the cast with a fine group of supporting players: Stanley Tucci, Barbara Bosson (Mrs. Bochco, at the time), Michael Haydn, Mary McCormack, J.C. MacKenzie, Jason Gedrick, and Patricia Clarkson.

Charlie Haid chose as his director of photography a brilliant and talented young man named Aaron Schneider. And except for the fact that he used so many lights that he actually lit one of our sets on fire, the shoot went surprisingly well and, in all honesty, I have to say that the finished product resulted in one of the best pilots I'd ever produced.

The hardest part of finishing the pilot was the music. I wasn't happy with Mike Post's first try. Or his second. Or his third. Mike, who by this time was one of the most successful television composers in the business – he had done the main title themes for every one of my shows since Hill Street Blues – was getting pretty exasperated with me. (It reminded me of the old joke: a woman goes into a kosher butcher shop and asks for a fresh chicken. The butcher brings one out. She spreads its legs, sticks her nose right up there, and takes a deep sniff before declaring: "It's not fresh enough. Bring me another one." The butcher brings her another one. Same deal. She spreads the chicken's legs, takes a sniff, and says, "This one's not fresh enough, either. Bring me another one."

Exasperated, the butcher says, "Lady, could you pass a test like that?" I based a whole story line in Hill Street Blues on that joke. I put Mick Belker (Bruce Weitz) undercover in a kosher butcher shop, just so I could dramatize the joke. As Mel Brooks said, "It's good to be the king.")

189

So Mike said to me, "I don't know what you want. Come over to the studio and let's find it together." I went over to Mike's studio in Burbank, and we spent an entire Saturday working on the music for Murder One. I'm not a trained musician, but my dad was a professional violinist, and I grew up with music all around me. My father used to have some of his great musician friends over to our apartment in New York on Sundays, and they'd play quartets: Schubert, Hayden, Mozart, Beethoven, Mendelssohn. In fact, Albert Einstein, who fancied himself somewhat of a fiddle player, once wangled an invitation to my dad's Sunday musical soiree. The general consensus was that he wasn't very good. But holy shit – Albert Einstein!

Anyway, by the end of the day, Mike and I had agreed to a main title that informed the score for the entire hour. It was very Baroque in style, and the main instrument was a harpsichord. It sounded unique, the melody was haunting, and I felt that Mike had created one of his best main title themes ever.

Murder One premiered on September 19, 1995, to uniformly excellent reviews. The O.J. trial was *still* going on.

Our ratings sucked. Maybe it was because of the single storyline that asked its audience to delay gratification for an entire season. Or maybe it was because the audience didn't much cotton to Benzali. When you gamble, you often lose.

Our episodic scripts were something of a high-wire act, since I had no idea how the story was going to resolve itself. I'd never done anything remotely as complicated. When I finally figured out the ending – we were about fifteen episodes in at the time – it was like a thousand-pound weight had been lifted off my shoulders.

At about that time – episode sixteen or seventeen – one of our producers came to me, asking for help with a problem. Apparently, Daniel Benzali was an hour late to work every morning. On an eight day shooting schedule, a lost hour a day cost us several hundred thousand dollars an episode. I have always prided myself on being a responsible producer, and so I called Benzali and asked him to come see me when the company broke for lunch. When he arrived,

I said, "Daniel, you're an hour late for work every day and it's hurting us. What can I do to help you with this problem?"

Daniel said to me, "I don't know what to tell you. I live in Malibu. I get up, I have my coffee, and then I have to wait until I have my morning dump."

Unbelievable. I suggested the following: "Get up, have your coffee, and come to work, *then* have your morning dump."

Daniel said he couldn't; that once he'd had his coffee, the drive was too long for him to hold his dump in.

"How about this?" I suggested. "Get up an hour earlier, have your coffee an hour earlier, then have your dump an hour earlier. That way, you'll get to work on time."

Daniel shook his head, no. "I can't get up an hour earlier. I have to learn my lines the night before, and I need to get eight hours sleep."

"Okay," I said. "How about this? Get up at your regular time, but skip the coffee entirely, ergo no urge to dump. Have your coffee at work, and take your morning dump in your trailer. Then you'll be able to start work on time."

"I can't do that. I can only go to the bathroom in my own toilet at home."

Now I was getting mad. Here I was, a fifty-four year old adult male, highly successful, with a shelf full of Emmys at home, negotiating the terms of an actor's morning bowel movement.

So then I said, "How about this? Let us rent you an apartment across the street in Century City. Stay there Sunday night through Thursday night. You can sleep in even later, have your coffee, take your dump, and then *walk* across the street to work."

"I can't," he said. "Malibu is my sanctuary. I have to know it's there for me at the end of the day."

I was flabbergasted. This unattractive, bald-headed dope, in a starring role that was the biggest break of his entire life, was telling me there was no way to solve a problem costing us hundreds of thousands of dollars?

"I don't know what to tell you," Daniel said.

"Well, I'll figure something out," I told him, and sent him on his way.

What I figured out was that at the end of the season, I'd fire him. Who wants to work with an actor who can't figure out how to get to work on time because he can only take a shit in his own bathroom in Malibu?

Welcome to my world.

When we had completed our first season of Murder One not long after, I told Bob Iger that I wasn't going to bring Daniel Benzali back if there was a second season. Our first season's ratings were marginal, though we had become a huge hit in England, I assumed because they were more used to single-story series. Bob renewed us for a second season anyway, and I revamped our concept considerably in hopes of making the show more user friendly for the American TV audience. We replaced Benzali with the fine Australian actor, Anthony LaPaglia, and instead of one story line for an entire season, we told three stories, each running about seven episodes each. We didn't help ourselves. It was sort of like being slightly pregnant. You either is or you ain't. And we weren't. Over the course of the season, Anthony's weight ballooned by about twenty pounds, it seemed.

Benzali couldn't take a crap anywhere but in his own bathroom, and Anthony never met a pizza he didn't like.

ABC cancelled our grand experiment after its second season.

Parallel to the end of Murder One, I was about to leave my marriage of twenty-seven years to my wife, Barbara. Our marriage had never been easy, but over the course of twenty-seven years, we'd raised our kids and had a good life. But with both of them gone from the nest, I could no longer distract myself from how unhappy I was.

More often than not, men experience a mid-life crisis around forty years of age, usually as a function of unmet expectations. They wake up one morning and realize they're nowhere near the goals they set for themselves when they were twenty. Affairs, divorces, Porsches, bimbos ensue. I had never hit that wall. At forty, I had exceeded every conceivable expectation I'd ever had.

Some years later, however, I awoke in the middle of the night, having to pee. Standing at the toilet, relieving myself in the dark, I was suddenly overwhelmed with despair: Jesus, I'm forty-seven, I thought to myself. My life is more than half over, and I'm miserable. I staggered back to bed and fell asleep, but I woke up with a pall hanging over me that didn't lift for days. I figured I ought to seek professional help. It had been a long time since I'd been in therapy. A friend of mine recommended a shrink he'd been seeing, and his best credential, as far as I was concerned, was that his office was two blocks from the 20th Century Fox lot.

I called and made an appointment for the following week, and on the appointed day, I showed up at his office. There was another woman sitting in the waiting room. About five minutes later, the therapist came out of his office. I was a little taken aback at the sight of him. He looked to be at least eighty-five, but I figured he might have some well-earned wisdom about getting older. He looked at me, and then at the woman, and barked at her: "This isn't your appointment time! Leave! Get out! Call me to reschedule our appointment!" The woman slunk out of his office, and he waved me in, apologizing for the mix up. It was an uncomfortable start to our relationship.

I spent the next forty-five minutes or so running down my issues: I was in my late forties, hugely successful, but terribly unhappy. Married twenty some-odd years, burned out, blah blah blah. Familiar, middle-aged complaints, I was sure. The shrink said virtually nothing. It was like talking to a wall. At the end of the session, he suggested we get together again the following week, and though I hadn't felt much of a connection, I agreed to come back.

The following week, I arrived at his office at the appointed time. The same woman was sitting in the waiting room. I took my seat, feeling awkward. Moments later, the shrink came out of his office, looked at the woman, and barked at her again: "This isn't your appointment time! Leave!"

The woman slunk out again. What the fuck? This was getting very weird. I followed him into his office, and he apologized again for the confusion. We started to talk – or, more accurately, I started to talk. As in the previous meeting, he seemed to have nothing to say.

About fifteen minutes into the session, the phone by his chair started to ring. He wouldn't pick it up. It rang and rang and rang. I finally said to him, "Are you going to answer that?" He grabbed up the phone and shouted into the receiver: "I told you never to call me at work! What do you want?"

The phone continued to ring. The cord that connects the receiver to the handset was dangling from the handset, disconnected. He was screaming into a dead handset. Finally, I got up from my chair and reached for the dangling cord. The doctor flinched as I plugged the handset back into the receiver.

Jesus Christ, I thought to myself. I'm spilling my guts to a lunatic. He hung up the phone and said, "Sorry. Where were we?"

I said, "I don't think this is going to work."

He said, "Let's talk about it."

I said no, I was going to leave. I got up from my chair and left. So much for mental health.

Shrinks are like writers. A few of them are great, another few are incompetent, and the vast majority of them are low to high mediocre. I would have to classify this poor old schmuck as being in the incompetent category. Suffice it to say, aside from the bizarre nature of our brief relationship, my emotional welfare remained unchanged.

I muddled through the next several years until Dayna sent me to see her shrink, Phil Stutz and – under his guidance – screwed up enough courage to tell Barbara I wanted to leave the marriage. Over the course of twenty-seven years, we'd been to numerous shrinks, individually and together, but the ship had run aground. In my mid-fifties, I wanted to start a new life for myself.

I rented a house in Mandeville Canyon, and made a pact with myself that I wouldn't date for a year. I'd never lived alone in my entire life, and I thought I ought to figure out how to do that. I also didn't want Barbara seeing or hearing about me having dates with a succession of women.

In fact, I had no interest in "getting out there." After almost three decades, I owed it to myself to make the transition to single life by myself.

For eleven months, my only dates were my mother and my beautiful daughter, Melissa. My mother loved it. We'd never been so close. She and Barbara had always had an edgy relationship and, under the best of circumstances, my mom – though capable of enormous charm and genuine charisma – also had a very dark side. She was no day at the beach, to put it mildly. In fact, speaking of no day at the beach, I literally threatened to put her on a plane back to Los Angeles from a vacation in Hawaii, because she'd had a temper tantrum at Melissa when she was ten years old.

Nevertheless, as emotionally chaotic as that year was, my mother and I enjoyed the best relationship we ever had.

Hollywood is no different than the rest of the world. It thrives on gossip. And let's face it: what's the best gossip du jour? Who's fucking whom, and does the poor, clueless spouse know about it? And in that category, there had been rumors about Dayna and me for years. Forget about the fact that she was married and had an eight-year old son, and that I was the father of two, married for twenty-seven years. That only made it juicier: a successful uber producer, as they used to call me in Variety, and his beautiful, blonde corporate president? They had to be having an affair. No question. Except we weren't. We were both married, we were both raising families, and neither of us was interested in the kind of personal melodrama that rumor had us engaged in. The best solution was to simply dismiss the rumors and not respond. But after Barbara and I separated, the rumors started anew.

It was a rocky time. In addition to the swirl of gossip and innuendo, when my long-term marriage to Barbara went belly up, it was enormously disruptive to the tight social circle we had been part of for many, many years. It sent a shockwave through the small community of friends who'd been married just as long as we'd been. If it could happen to the Bochcos, it could happen to us!

In addition, I think our friends, all our age or older, were afraid I was going to end up with some young bimbo, which would only have exacerbated everyone's anxiety. But that was never a consideration for me, anyway. I've always been attracted to age appropriate partners, because let's face it – once the pheromones dissipate, and they always do, you better have something more going on than an erection, or you're sunk.

Six months later, Dayna and her husband Marc separated, as well. The rumor mill now exploded into a hyper frenzy.

Blinders on, left foot-right foot, Dayna and I plowed through our respective domestic life issues, and continued to do our work. We had a company to run.

In 1995, my deal with ABC having finally expired, I had made a four series, four year deal with CBS. Within months, CBS was sold to Westinghouse, and Les Moonves was hired to run the network. Les and Dayna and I were long-time pals, and we were delighted to be in business together. The honeymoon didn't last. By 1997, Les and I were on the outs, and I asked to be released from our deal.

In the midst of my CBS debacle, early August of 1997, Brandon Tartikoff called me to make a lunch date. We were to meet at Toscana, a Brentwood Italian restaurant that those of us on the Westside ate at regularly. (I still do.) Brandon had been ill again. It was his third go-round with Hodgkin's disease, and this time they were having a much tougher time getting him into remission.

Over the years, Brandon and I had become good friends. We had been professional friends when I was making Hill Street Blues and L.A. Law for NBC, and after I made my ABC deal, we remained friends, playing a weekly tennis game at Grant Tinker's house in Bel Air, or at my house in Pacific Palisades.

Brandon had suffered real tragedies in his life. He'd battled (and beat) Hodgkin's disease as a young man, then had a recurrence of the disease in the early eighties and beat it back, again. After he left NBC, Brandon become Chairman of Paramount, but in late summer of that year, he had a terrible car accident in which his young daughter, Calla, suffered a severe brain injury. Brandon left Paramount soon after to spend time with Calla, who was going through extensive rehabilitation. All in all, it was not an easy time.

And then, in early '97, Brandon came down with Hodgkins Disease yet again and wound up getting a stem cell transplant.

When I went to meet him at Toscana, Brandon was sitting at a corner table, a baseball cap pulled low over his eyes. I was shocked to see him. He was sallow, gaunt, and painfully thin. I hugged him and sat down, and for two hours, we talked. Brandon had never been a particularly introspective man, at least so far as I could tell. He never really seemed comfortable talking about personal issues. But at lunch, he was more open and emotionally communicative than he'd ever been, and we shared a lot of intimacies that day. I had separated from Barbara, so we spoke of that, and he spoke of Calla and what that ordeal had been like and still was, but he never spoke about his own illness. There was not an ounce of self-pity that I could discern.

When we took leave of each other, he gave me a big hug and promised we'd talk again soon. When I got back to work, I was truly shaken, and walked into Dayna's office. "My God," she said. "You look like you've seen a ghost."

"I did," I said. "Brandon Tartikoff. I think he's going to die very soon."

Brandon died on August 27th, 1997, about two weeks after we'd had lunch together. He was 48 years old. I still miss him. Together, we had done amazing work.

Brandon's disease profoundly altered his life (and mine, many years later).

As a happy, successful, healthy and active man of 70, I had no sense of impending mortality. I had a wonderful life, a wife I loved deeply, I had terrific children who had all in their own way found success in life, and in short, I felt as if I finally had it all. The last thing in the world I could have imagined is getting hit by lightning: leukemia. In the immediate rush of the diagnosis, I was terrified I was going to die. My world was upended. I didn't want to die, obviously. I felt I had so much to live for. But life is an equal opportunity offender. And as I went through the process of terror, acceptance, and then resolve to fight as hard as I could for my life, pretty much all my expectations (fantasies?) about how the rest of my life would unfold went out the window.

Now imagine for a moment that you're not seventy. You're twenty, twenty-one. And you get the same basic diagnosis I got. Except you haven't had the luxury of seventy years of life; of a great and well-recognized career; of having the pleasure of seeing your children grow up, struggle through their adolescent angst, and come out the other side as successful young adults. That was Brandon, when he was diagnosed with Hodgkins lymphoma, a type of blood cancer. I didn't know him then. But even at such a young age, he must have dug deep and found a strength, a resolve, a courage that he probably didn't even know he had. Who on God's earth at twenty years of age imagines he might die? At twenty, you're immortal. The secret of mankind – hell, the secret of war – is that young men and women of that age don't really believe they're ever going to die. (I've always thought that if the rules of engagement were such that only men over the age of fifty could fight wars, war would no longer exist. Men over fifty know better. Twenty year olds don't. That's why we send them off to fight our battles.) But here was young Brandon, fighting to save his life while the rest of us were plotting to create our lives. And Brandon beat the devil. That said, as I found out years later fighting my own potentially fatal disease, even if you win the battle, it puts a crease in your brain. Some part of you is always waiting for the other shoe to drop. And drop it did for Brandon, in his thirties, as he was diagnosed with a recurrence of Hodgkins. And by then we were friends. We had already hatched Hill Street Blues. Grant Tinker had just gone over to NBC as Chairman, and Brandon was elevated to president of the entertainment division at the network. All through Brandon's treatment, which must have been brutal – he lost all his hair, he lost weight, he had to have lost strength and stamina – he never missed a day of work. He wore a wig. He wore false eyebrows. He was determined to beat back this killer for a second time. And he did. What incredible courage. And yet, only half a dozen years older than Brandon, I couldn't imagine the psychic toll (good and bad) this struggle must have imposed on him. I say bad, because at any age, staring down death is a daunting challenge. But there's also the good, which I also was too young to imagine. Having cheated death of its due twice, I think Brandon was irrevocably changed. And I think the change is actually what made him the extraordinary man and executive that he was. At an age when most of us were oblivious to the concept of dying, and were striving endlessly to climb the ladder of success, Brandon had already experienced the most intense and profound success: he had beaten death. Twice. And it gave him a different kind of perspective than the rest of us had. He was dry, witty, fatalistic. He loved our business, but I think he knew it didn't define him. At an age when the rest of us were struggling to make it, Brandon knew that it wasn't that important. We were literally not curing cancer. He had already succeeded in the most fundamental way. And that inner knowledge gave him a kind of freedom. He didn't need to control everything. He had learned, up close and personal, the limits of control. He embraced the fullness of life in a way that none of his contemporaries – including me – could possibly comprehend. I also believe that Brandon, having battled Hodgkins Disease twice, knew somewhere in the atavistic part of his brain that at some point the disease would return and take him, sooner rather than later. And instead of living his life in a panic, I think it actually fostered an inner peace. I believe that Brandon, long before any of us could even imagine dying, had already made peace with the notion – the reality – of it. And so there was always this little semi-grin on Brandon's face. He never took the work, or life itself, quite as seriously as the rest of us did. And I think when this terrible disease visited him for the third time, notwithstanding his courage, his will to live, and his commitment to the fight, he had come to some deep understanding of what the rest of us only knew theoretically: that nobody gets out alive. It was only much later in life, when I myself was diagnosed with leukemia that I thought about what Brandon had gone through with a deeper understanding of the battle he had fought throughout his young adult life.

As I write this, I'm eighteen months removed from my bone marrow transplant. I have every reason to believe I've beaten this terrible disease. But as I channel my old friend Brandon, I also know that cancer is an insidious foe, and that when you least expect it, it can pound its fist on your door. And, like the police, if you don't open it, it'll bust the door down and come in anyway.

Brandon, in his quiet and humorous way, was fearless. . His multiple brushes with mortality had profoundly altered his perspective on life. I have thought of him many times during the last eighteen months, and though I may not have realized it when he died, he became a role model for me, not so much in terms of the dignity with which he died, but in the courage with which he lived his life.

23

Hill Street Blues redefined TV in the eighties, much as All In The Family had in the seventies. In success (which in itself was amazingly fortunate) it expanded the palette of what was possible in terms of story telling, diversity, characterization and sheer density. Hill Street Blues put more information on a single frame of film than any show before it ever had. It had depth. Things would go on in the background that were often as interesting as those in the foreground, and were likely at any moment to erupt into the foreground. There had never been anything like it on TV before.

There's a sweet commercial currently running on TV, from General Electric. Like any good story, it has a theme: ideas are born messy and mistrusted. New ideas are treated rudely. As the voice over intones, "ideas are the natural born enemy of the way things are." That's a perfect description of Hill Street Blues when it premiered on NBC in January of 1981. The audience didn't know how to watch it. There were too many stories; too many characters; it was too noisy, and there was too much background activity. It was chaos, barely contained. But once the audience got it – and it took a season – Hill Street changed the game. The show became appointment viewing; something to talk about around the water cooler the next morning. The year after we debuted, St. Elsewhere came on the air, created by Josh Brand and John Falsey and produced by my dear friend Bruce Paltrow. It was Hill Street Blues in a hospital. I don't think it's a stretch to say that Hill Street changed television, and with it, our culture. (I will always remember walking down a street in London in 1982 and hearing Mike Post's hauntingly beautiful theme for Hill Street Blues wafting from an open window above me. The show had become a sensation in the U.K. as well.)

In 1986, Brandon programmed L.A. Law, and it was virtually an instant hit, particularly with college-aged students. Law School enrollment skyrocketed during the years L.A. Law ran on Thursday nights on NBC. It replaced Hill Street Blues and continued to define NBC as the network to watch on Thursday nights. Over the years I've had dozens of lawyers tell me that their study groups would break for L.A. Law, discuss what they'd seen, then go back to work. For fifteen years, between Hill Street Blues and L.A. Law, I "owned" Thursday night at ten o'clock before John Welles took over the time slot with his smash hit E.R., which ran for almost fifteen years. Imagine: NBC dominated that timeslot for almost thirty years, from 1981 to 2009. I doubt we'll see a phenomenon like that ever again.

Before I accepted the ABC deal in 1988, Brandon and I were up at Grant Tinker's house in Bel-Air for our weekly doubles match: Peter Grad and I versus Grant and Brandon. After the match, and Peter had left, Grant left Brandon and me alone to talk. I told him about the ABC deal. I also told him that I loved our working relationship and that it had yielded two of the great shows of the decade. I told him he didn't have to match ABC's offer, but if he wanted me to stay at NBC he'd have to at least come close. Brandon was totally candid with me. NBC was riding high, and there were only so many series slots available on a network with so many hits already. Brandon was afraid a multiple series deal with me would essentially freeze out most of the dramatic talent trying to sell their pilots. I couldn't argue the point. If ABC had been doing as well as NBC, they wouldn't have made a ten series deal with me, either.

24

Barbara and I had separated in the spring of 1997. Our kids were long gone from the house, and I was acutely aware of the ticking clock in my head and in my heart. Unraveling a twenty-seven year marriage isn't easy under any circumstances, but our marriage was particularly complex in that we'd worked together for so long, and that would unravel as well. Plus, there was a lot of money involved. I had never had an issue with taking a saw and just cutting everything in half. We had started with nothing, now I was a rich man, and it was simply the right thing to do. It was also the law. I didn't grow up with a lot of money, and money was never my primary motivation in life, anyway. Half of what I had was ten times more than I needed, and I knew that, at the end of the day, our kids were going to get it all, anyway.

Though the division of assets went smoothly enough, there was, inevitably, a lot of residual anger and resentment. Barbara was supposed to jet off to London to accept an award on behalf of Murder One, and she was taking Jesse and Jake Paltrow with her. Part of the deal was that after they left, I would call all our friends and tell them what was going on. The other part of the deal was that in her absence, I would move out of the house.

Several days before they left for Europe, Barbara and I were talking about our situation, and I said, "It would have been easier for you if I'd died." She didn't disagree, and I realized that as concerned as she was about losing a marriage, she was equally concerned with losing her identity as Mrs. Steven Bochco.

When I had safely seen them onto the plane, I returned to my office and made calls to all our friends, telling them of Barbara's and my separation. I can't say it came as a shock to any of them. They knew we'd struggled for years, but I think most of them thought we'd settled into a peaceful co-existence. That may have been true, but one has a right to wish that marriage might be more than that.

After I'd called all our friends, I called my mother. I wasn't going to give her the news over the phone, so I told her I'd come by for a visit after work. When I arrived, over a glass of wine, I told her that Barbara and were separating. Tears started to well up in her eyes. I said, "Come on, Mom, no tears, please. I need you to be here for me." She instantly shut down the waterworks, saying, "Well, I never like her anyway." Personally, I didn't believe that, though they'd had their rocky moments, particularly in the early years of our marriage. I like to think she was just trying to demonstrate a mother's solidarity with her son.

I'm happy to report that, as emotionally difficult as our breakup was, Barbara and I are good friends today, and Dayna and I share holidays together with her, Dayna's ex-husband Marc, and all of our children.

In late winter of 1998, I was invited by CBS to the Winter Olympics in Nagano, Japan. I called my friend Kimiko Rudolph, born and raised in Japan, and she told me that Nagano was no great shakes. With no good hotels, no decent restaurants, I'd be spending my time on buses going from event to event, eating out of cardboard boxes.

I consulted with Dayna, who'd received her own invitation. We decided to turn it down. Several days later, another invitation came to me. It was the "consolation" prize: a one-week, all expenses paid trip to Aspen, Colorado, with all the CBS affiliates, where we'd be able to access all the Olympic events via live feed from Japan.

I went into Dayna's office. "Did you get this invitation to Aspen?" She had.

"Well, listen," I said. "We've been accused of the crime for years. Do you want to come to Aspen with me and finally commit it?"

There was a long moment of silence. A lot was suddenly at stake. What if she said no? More to the point, what if she said yes, and it was a bad match? We had a thirteen-year personal and professional relationship on the line.

She said yes.

It was the most romantic week of my life. Winter in Aspen. Skiing all day. Walking through the village at night, holding hands. Incredible.

When we got home, we were a couple, and neither of us wanted to sneak around. Dayna was going to tell her husband what was going on, and I was to tell Barbara and the kids.

I knew if I told Barbara face to face, we'd wind up in a brawl, so discretion being the better part of valor, which is a fancy way of saying I took the coward's way out, I wrote her a letter. Then I invited my kids – Melissa, then twenty-six, and Jesse, twenty-one – to dinner.

About five minutes after we were seated, I broke the news. Melissa screamed, burst into tears, and fled the restaurant. Jesse went after her.

"Uh, check please?"

It was a disaster. But I wrote them a letter that night. I said I loved them both and understood their pain as well as their loyalty to their mom, but that they couldn't expect me to live like a monk for the rest of my life. Their mom and I had separated so that we could have happier lives apart. Dayna and I had found each other romantically after thirteen years of friendship, and we were going to explore our romantic possibilities now, in public and without guilt.

It didn't take long for Melissa and Jesse to come around. In their heart of hearts, they wanted me – and their mom – to find happiness.

Dayna and I were married in our backyard on August 12, 2000, with our closest friends and family present. What a way to start the millennium. We've been happily married ever since. My kids, who were by then thirty and twenty-five, are now forty-six and forty-one.

Tick tock, folks.

25

Over the course of our ten-series, seven-year deal with ABC, there were two shows that ABC didn't want to make. I can't even remember what they were. And, per the deal, whenever ABC chose not to program one of my series ideas, they had to pay a penalty. And through the years, they had paid that penalty on two separate occasions. So, the eight shows we produced for ABC between 1988 and 1995 were 1) Doogie Howser, M.D., 2) Cop Rock, 3) Civil Wars, 4) Capitol Critters, 5) NYPD Blue, 6) Byrds Of Paradise, 7) Murder One, and 8) Total Security.

Of all of them, Total Security – and I say this with some level of embarrassment, if not shame – was the only show I ever – *ever* – phoned in. It wasn't a bad idea. No one had done a modern take on the private eye show, probably since Rockford Files. My idea was to do a modern-era, realistic version of the genre. The show starred James Remar, Jim Belushi, and Debrah Farentino. The idea was that Remar ran a high-tech private investigation firm that specialized in everything from sophisticated industrial spying to car repos, as well as domestic spying for clients trying to catch their spouses en flagrante, etc. I was intrigued by the non-glamorous reality of that work, as opposed to the cliché of the private eye who's always getting involved in a complicated murder mystery where everyone is lying about everything. So far, so good.

But my heart wasn't in it. I was going through a tumultuous time in my personal life, my relationship with ABC had become frayed around the edges, and I think all of us were tired of having to deal with each other.

I had been fighting with Bob Iger and Alex Wallaugh, who was one of Bob's closest friends, and was now a highly placed ABC executive. Alex was a pugnacious guy with a volatile temper. He and I had gotten into some nasty squabble over scheduling NYPD Blue. ABC wanted to push the show's eighth (or maybe ninth) season debut several months, and I was deeply opposed to the idea. I felt that if we didn't start our season in September, as usual, it would disrupt – and perhaps destroy – our viewership. And I didn't trust their promise that they wouldn't move us to another time slot regardless of how well the show they were going to replace us with did. Years earlier, after the third very successful season of Doogie Howser, Bob moved the show from Wednesday at nine p.m., where we had been beating our competition like a drum, to Monday at eight p.m. Of course, I squawked like a duck, first because on Mondays at eight we had no lead in, whereas on Wednesdays, our lead in was Coach, a big hit for ABC. Bob assured me that the network wouldn't have the same expectations of Doogie on Monday that it had for us on Wednesdays. They understood the problems of the switch and would make accommodations accordingly. Needless to say, we didn't do nearly as well on Monday as we had on Wednesday, and at the end of the season Bob cancelled Doogie. I was furious about it then, and it still upsets me today, twenty-three years later. So I had my reasons for not taking their word for it when they made promises based on scheduling.

So Alex and I had a terrible row over the phone, and I remember he was yelling so loudly that I was able to hold the phone's receiver at arm's length and hear every word he was shouting. Of course, I lost the battle. You never win those disputes with a network. Not ever. If they want to move you, they move you. If they want to cancel you, they cancel you. It comes with the territory. My position usually was, if you don't tell me how to run my shows, I won't tell you how to run your network. But I always fought the battle, nevertheless. You always fight for your children, even if – in network terms – they're getting long in the tooth.

So, regarding Total Security: eighteen years later, I want to apologize to all the principals. They were a terrific group of people, but we didn't deliver the goods for them. The show lasted, as I recall, a mere thirteen episodes, before ABC cancelled it.

Officially, we were done with the deal. But since NYPD Blue was still on the air, and would remain so for another seven years, I continued to have dealings with ABC, even though we had now made a new deal with CBS.

Our first show for CBS was a half-hour, three-camera comedy called Public Morals. It was the first time I'd ever done a classic half-hour, joke-oriented show, so I hired a half-hour comedy veteran by the name of Jay Tarses, to run the show. After we shot the pilot episode, Les Moonves told Dayna and me that he liked it a lot. Personally, I had some issues with the pilot, but I was pleased that Les liked it, and we plowed ahead with additional episodes.

In May, we all went to New York for the up fronts. Les called me one rainy afternoon and asked if he could come over and talk to me in my hotel room. I said sure, and called Dayna to tell her that Les was coming over. Her first words were, "Uh oh." I said what do you mean, "Uh oh." Dayna said that the head of the network doesn't come over to your hotel on a rainy afternoon during up fronts unless he's the bearer of bad tidings. She said she was coming down to my room, and when Les arrived, Dayna proved to be right on the money. Les said that his bosses in New York weren't happy with Public Morals, and that Broadcast Standards, in particular, had issues with the show, so he wasn't going to put the show on the fall schedule, but would air the series sometime later. "Some time later, when?" I asked. Les didn't know, and wouldn't – or couldn't – commit to an air date.

I was furious. Why had we bothered to come all the way to New York, just to be told that CBS was essentially reneging on its agreement to put us on its fall schedule?

As well, I thought – rightly or wrongly – that Les had thrown me, and the show, under the bus and had not fought hard enough on our behalf.

Back in Los Angeles, conversations went back and forth regarding the first episode, which Broadcast Standards deemed too raunchy to air without re-editing. My recollection is that we did some additional editing, but it still didn't satisfy the network, and when we finally went on the air, the network wouldn't air the pilot, and went with a different episode. Without the pilot, the whole set up for the show was lost, and the audience was dropped into the middle of a series with a bunch of characters they'd never been properly introduced to. Add to that all the negative publicity that had surrounded the show, and its premiere was a disaster. Les yanked the show off CBS' schedule after one airing. There were, needless to say, bad feelings all around.

The next show we created for CBS was a uniformed cop-show called Brooklyn South. Mark Tinker, our long time co-executive producer and director on NYPD Blue directed the pilot, and did a terrific job. The opening of the pilot was a harrowing seven or eight--minute sequence where a lone gunman starts shooting people at random in the street near the precinct and the cops are immediately embroiled in a frightening shootout with the perp. The pilot debuted to decent ratings, but then, over the course of the next seven or eight episodes, declined.

Having just separated from my wife, my life was a little upside down, so David Milch volunteered to do the heavy lifting on the show. The creators were David, Bill Clark, Billy Finkelstein and me. Particularly with Bill Clark's involvement, I thought that David and Billy would be able to handle the bulk of the writing chores.

I was wrong. Brooklyn South quickly fell prey to the same issues that were plaguing NYPD Blue. David couldn't deliver scripts in a timely fashion, no one could really control him, and – with a large ensemble to look after – things quickly got out of control. And NYPD Blue was suffering, as well – not to mention that the NYPD Blue cast was more than a little pissed off that another show was diverting David's attention from them.

By the time we'd gotten to our sixth or seventh episode, I basically "fired" David. I told him to concentrate solely on NYPD Blue, and that I'd take control of Brooklyn South. Within a few weeks, I'd begun to turn things around. We started getting scripts written in a more timely fashion, and they were better. Whatever my other deficiencies might have been, I knew how to construct a coherent story. By mid-season, I felt we were finally making a show that I really liked. It had "legs." I felt this was a show I could do for years to come.

Unfortunately, a significant portion of the audience had abandoned us over the course of the first seven or eight episodes, and it was difficult getting them to give us another chance.

Television is a tough business. I had always thought of the audience as sitting in front of their television sets with a gun – the remote controlled channel changer – in hand. Particularly with a new show, I figured I had about two minutes to get them to take their finger off the trigger, because if they pulled it, we were dead.

At the end of the season, we had made twenty-two episodes, and our ratings had begun to inch back up, to the point where I thought we had a chance for a renewal, notwithstanding the fact that the show was a wobbler. I lobbied hard for the show, but Les cancelled it, which really upset me. I thought, I've worked my ass off, we turned the show around, our ratings had begun to climb, and I felt strongly that we deserved a chance. Perhaps it shouldn't have been, but it was personal to me. And, rightly or wrongly, I felt like I didn't want to do any more shows for CBS. So I called Les and asked him to meet me for a drink after work one night. Should I have taken a deep breath, as it were, first? Counted to ten? The answer to both questions is probably yes.

Les and I met at The Peninsula hotel in Beverly Hills and, over a glass of wine, I told him I was unhappy and wanted out of our deal. I told him it wasn't about money – I'd give him the money back. I just didn't feel appreciated, and I felt Les hadn't been loyal to me and that, under the circumstances, I didn't feel I could do my best work for him, and that it would be in both our interests if we could part ways.

Les refused. He said if I wasn't happy, he'd try harder to make things right. I said that, as far as I was concerned,it was too late. But he was adamant that he wouldn't release me. He said – and these were his exact words – "I'd rather see you on the beach for three more years than let you go to another woman." Aside from the fact that I found it odd that he would personalize our relationship in that particular way, I pointed out that there was no "other woman," as he put it. There was nowhere else I wanted to go, and no one had solicited me. It got heated. I said things that I probably shouldn't have, and when we parted company that evening, I felt thoroughly stymied. I had three more years to go on this deal, and I had just, essentially, burned the bridge. Genius.

The next morning, I called The Doberman and told him about my meeting with Les. Frank reminded me that part of our contractual obligation was to pitch concepts to CBS on a regular basis, and that if I didn't do that, I'd be in breach of the agreement. And because I had no desire to do any more shows for Les, every time I went over to CBS to pitch, I exclusively threw them half-hour sitcom ideas. Clearly, Les didn't want half-hour comedies from me. He'd had his belly full with Public Morals. I thought that if I only pitched half-hour ideas at him, eventually he'd weary of me and let me go. But Les was as stubborn as I was. He'd meant it when he said he'd rather see me on the beach for three years than go to another woman. Finally, after close to a year of this nonsense, The Doberman struck an agreement with Les. In exchange for one more hour series, Les would release me from the rest of my obligation. I agreed. It was no fun being on the beach every day.

The idea that I pitched to Les, and that he agreed to, was a medical drama. The catch was, it was set in a hospital not unlike Martin Luther King, Jr. Hospital, in the predominantly African American area of Los Angeles, and the cast was, likewise, predominantly African American. Diversity had been a big issue in television for some time now, and I thought that a show with an all black cast would be a welcome addition to television's generally white landscape.

The show, City of Angels, debuted mid-season, on January 16, 2000, starring Blair Underwood, Viveca Fox, Viola Davis, Hill

Harper, Michael Warren, and Maya Rudolph. Another frequent cast member was Octavia Spencer – Oscar, anyone?

City Of Angels got mixed reviews and low ratings, but Les picked the show up for a second season, ordering thirteen more episodes. In its second season, Gabriel Union joined the cast.

Notwithstanding a spirited letter-writing campaign, Les cancelled the series in December of the same year.

I was a free man.

It took me several years to sort through my feelings about that time of my life. I was in the throes of a divorce, I had a bad marriage with CBS as well, but – in retrospect – I had come to believe I'd behaved badly towards Les. At some point, you have to spend a moment or two in somebody else's skin and ask yourself, "What are *they* feeling about this?" I didn't want to carry a grudge. As my shrink Phil Stutz once said to me, "Do you want to be right or do you want to be happy?" Maybe Les had behaved badly, too, but that didn't mitigate the fact that I was stubborn, and somewhat childish in my handling of a situation that I instigated. I'm not sure, also in retrospect, how I might have handled that situation differently, but I knew in my heart I hadn't handled it with grace and maturity. So I called Les and invited him to lunch. He was gracious enough to accept, and when we got together, I apologized to him. I stressed that I wasn't looking for a job. I'm sure he'd had more than enough of me, as it was. But I wanted to clear my conscience and make my amends, and I didn't want either of us to be in the position of having to look the other way when we'd occasionally meet at some social event or other. Les was appreciative of the gesture, and we had a pleasant lunch. And, in fact, I have run into Les and his wife Julie many times since then, and our chats have always been free of any tension. I'll always be pleased that we were finally able to bury the hatchet somewhere other than in each other's skull.

26

Fortunately, my relative lack of productivity over the last several years hadn't hurt my market value, and in July of 1999, The Doberman negotiated an exclusive deal for me with Paramount TV.

The first show we produced under that deal was Philly, created by Alison Cross and me. Alison was a gifted writer, who some years earlier had won two Emmys: one for writing Roe Vs. Wade in 1989 (directed and produced by none other than Greg Hoblit, who also won the Emmy for producing), and the other for Serving In Silence: The Margarethe Cammermeyer Story, starring Glenn Close, in 1995.

Philly was a legal drama set in – where else? – Philadelphia. We cast Kim Delaney in the lead, and Tom Everett Scott as her young associate. Kim's character, Kathleen Maguire, was a low-end criminal defense attorney, divorced, with a kid. It was an excellent show, in my opinion. In fact, several years ago, I was channel surfing and came across an episode of Philly. Years after the fact, I was struck by how good it was.

Philly was a good example of a show that didn't fail, but just didn't succeed. I don't know if the problem was a surfeit of law shows, or if the audience wasn't that interested in a series built around a single mom representing low-rent clients. Whatever the reason, we were cancelled after one season. The ratings just wouldn't support a second season. But I was, and remain proud of the effort, and am grateful for the lasting professional and personal friendship that Alison and I have shared ever since.

The second show we produced under our Paramount deal was Blind Justice, starring Ron Eldard. It was the story of an NYPD homicide detective who had been blinded in a shootout, and had – against all odds – worked his way back into his job by virtue of sheer determination. Distrusted by his fellow detectives, Eldard's character, Jim Dunbar, had to prove his competency with every new case that came across his desk. It was a challenging show, but I liked the concept enormously. Most critics, and I suppose a significant portion of the audience, were skeptical about the reality of a blind detective, and I certainly couldn't talk people out of their perceptions. But Blind Justice had something to say about heroism, and overcoming obstacles and disabilities. The scripts, primarily written by my co-creators, Nick Wootton and Matt Olmstead, were smart and imaginative, and I was proud of our effort.

Blind Justice was cancelled after one season. Another flop. I've always tried to console myself with the notion that if you're a baseball player, and if over the course of a twenty-year career you fail to get a hit six or seven times out of ten, you're still a sure shot to get elected to The Hall Of Fame. (In fact, in 1996 I *was* inducted into the Television Academy Hall Of Fame.) It's in the nature of our profession that every time you come to the plate to take a swing, the odds are against your succeeding, and it's a measure of your talent if you do succeed three, or three-and-a-half times out of ten. I've created over twenty television series in my career. Four of them were big hits, probably three or four of them were middling successes, by which I mean they ran for a couple of seasons, and only a couple of them were terrible failures in the real sense of the word. I suppose if you did the math, I'd have been a .350 hitter in the Major Leagues.

Every time I made a show that didn't resonate with the audience, I tried to learn something from it. But whatever it is I learned, I always tried to balance it against the notion of being a manufacturer. I say this not as a criticism: I think Dick Wolf is in the business of manufacturing TV. He had an idea many years ago for a show called Law And Order, and he saddled it up and rode it for twenty years, essentially franchising it into three or four shows. Law And

Order became an *enterprise*. He's done it again with his Chicago franchise: Chicago Fire, Chicago PD, and Chicago Med. I admire Dick. I tip my hat to his entrepreneurial genius, but that's not me. I like doing shows that are different and challenging, shows that maybe haven't been done before in ways I wanted to do them. I never had any interest in revisiting the things I'd already done. I've been approached on more than one occasion to do a remake of Hill Street Blues. That holds no appeal to me because I don't think you can duplicate what that show was to the culture of the 1980's. It was a one-off.

27

I've been blessed with an abundant imagination. I've never wanted for ideas and, in 2003, I had an idea for a movie called Hollywood. It was a story about a screenwriter who'd fallen on hard times, his marriage was coming apart, his wife was banging a big-shot Hollywood producer, and he was drinking himself into a stupor every day. It was a good story; a Hollywood insider tale that becomes a cop story. I wrote a twenty-five-page story treatment that I thought was pretty good, and I showed it to David Milch for his opinion. David thought it was great, but he suggested that instead of a movie, I should write it as a novel. "Are you crazy?" I said. "I've never written a novel in my life."

"So what?" David said.

I had given a copy of the story to my old friend Fred Specktor, a long-time agent at CAA. Fred had a client list that would be the envy of any agent in our business. Helen Mirren. Morgan Freeman. Danny DeVito. The list goes on and on. Writers. Directors. Actors. I had known Fred since 1976 – forty years, now – and I respected his professional opinion, particularly as it pertained to film.

Fred thought the story was terrific. I'd never had an agent, but I asked him if he'd represent it. Fred said absolutely, and the first person he sent the material to was Michael Mann, the director. Michael thought the material was excellent, and expressed a desire to be involved with it. Fred arranged a phone meeting for us, and I was very excited.

On the phone, after Michael told me how much he liked the material, he began to cast the project over the phone. "We'll get Will Smith for the cop," he said. We'll get this actor and that actor. And, of course, there were problems with the story, but he'd fix them.

Now, I may not know a lot about a lot, but I sure as hell know a lot about one thing, and that's story. And my story was pretty damned good. I chatted with Michael for about five minutes, and politely signed off, telling him we'd be in touch.

I called Fred and told him I didn't think it would work out with Michael, even though I was a huge admirer of his work. And then I told Fred that I didn't want to pitch the project to anyone else. I was going to write a novel!

I'd never had a writing experience like it. Nobody was looking over my shoulder. I wasn't writing to a deadline. I didn't have a book agent, and I didn't have a publisher. I was doing it for pure fun. I became completely immersed in this world I was inventing. I'd wake up in the middle of the night with an "ah-ha" moment; some plot twist or other. Or I'd be in the shower, and I'd suddenly realize how to solve a particular plot problem, and I'd get out of the shower, soaking wet, to go write it down. I wrote the first 150 pages or so in about three months, and I sent them to Fred, who said they were great, and sent the pages to one of CAA's top literary agents, appropriately named Bob Bookman, who in turn sent the pages to the best book agent in the business, Mort Janklow, in New York.

Mort read the pages and expressed interest in representing the book. He asked me if I wanted him to go to publishers right away, or wait. I suggested we wait. I was in a real zone, and I knew I'd have a draft of the completed book in a couple of more weeks.

Three weeks later, I was finished, and I sent the manuscript to Mort. He paid me one of the greatest compliments I'd ever received. "You know, I've had some bad experiences with screenwriters writing a first novel, because they're very different skills. But when I read your novel, it read as if you'd written ten books."

Within days of Mort sending the manuscript to publishers, we were in a bidding war with five of them. How exciting! We finally closed a deal with Random House. They were going to pay me a significant advance, and wanted to ink me to a three-book deal, which I turned down. Hollywood, which ultimately became Death By Hollywood, had been so much fun for me specifically because it wasn't an assignment. It had been a labor of love. I'd spent my life basically writing on assignment, and I didn't want to write two more books because I was obligated to. What if I never had another idea I thought was uniquely suited to being novelized? I didn't want to jam a square peg into a round hole just to satisfy a commitment.

Mort had warned me: "The book business isn't like your business. If you sell 75,000 books, you're a hit." I don't know how many books Random House ultimately sold, but if you want to read Death By Hollywood, you can still find it on Amazon. Writing it was the most fun I ever had.

28

In 2005, I had a meeting at FX with Peter Ligouri and John Landgraf. I had begun to tire of the broadcast network merry-go--round, and I thought cable TV was doing much more interesting, and challenging, material. Peter and John explained that they wanted to do a show about the war in Iraq. I thought they were crazy. We were in the midst of that horrible conflict, and people were getting more than their fill of it on the six-o'clock news. But they were very committed to the idea, and I was more than a little impressed with their willingness to develop a show like that. I agreed to try and come up with a concept.

When I got back to my office, I called Chris Gerolmo, a gifted writer who'd written Mississippi Burning, and written and directed a wonderful movie for HBO called Citizen X.

As a writer, Chris was the real deal. We'd been trying to find the right project to do together for some time, and I thought this might be the right one.

Chris was very intrigued by the idea, and we started to conceptualize the show not purely as one about soldiers under the stress of combat, but in addition, about the stress on the lives of their loved ones, as well. Wives and children and parents left behind; financial hardships; the way in which separation stresses some marriages to the breaking point; these were all elements of the show, the idea being that we would cut back and forth between our soldiers in Iraq, and their anguished and struggling families left behind.

We titled the series Over There, and Chris directed the pilot. It was very compelling. What we were able to accomplish on a shoestring budget was remarkable. We literally built an Iraqi village in Chatsworth, California, a mere forty-five minute drive from my office. The scripts were first rate, and everyone involved in the production of Over There felt a special devotion to "getting it right." I think we did, even though I never thought the show would last. I wasn't wrong. FX, reluctantly, cancelled us after twelve episodes. Nevertheless, I remained upbeat and energized by the work, its relevance, and the loyalty and support FX showed us. It was one of the best experiences I'd ever had, and it illuminated for me the stark and growing divide between the cable and broadcast TV experience.

I had been somewhat insulated from the changing realities of broadcast television by virtue of the fact that I still enjoyed almost total creative control over NYPD Blue. It wasn't until we finished our run of twelve years that I was exposed to what a creatively stifling environment broadcast television had become.

29

Television is society's mirror. It reflects who we are and what we are, as well as what we aspire to be. My career in TV has spanned six decades, from the Vietnam War to Ferguson, Missouri; from the cultural revolution of the sixties and seventies to the tech revolution of the twenty-first century.

The first great show I worked on was Columbo, in 1971. The first great show I (co-) created was Hill Street Blues, ten years later. In the thirty four years since, I've been blessed with the opportunity to be a part of and contribute to the evolution of arguably the most influential medium in history: television.

The TV industry and I grew up together. For me, first as an impressionable viewer, and then later as an active professional, it was an extraordinary opportunity to achieve success as an artist in a medium that had – and continues to have – outsized influence on the world's culture. In our current age of interconnectivity, there isn't a corner of the earth that isn't touched by the American television industry.

That said, the exponential growth of the television industry has brought incredible change to the industry itself. When I first started at Universal Studios in 1966, notwithstanding its size and influence, the big studios were still privately held enterprises, as were the three major networks. It was a time when, in spite of the studios' power, the TV business supported a vibrant and growing independent production community: MTM, Lorimar, Carsey-Werner, Tandem

(Norman Lear and Bud Yorkin), Aaron Spelling, Quinn Martin, Stephen J. Cannell, and many more.

And because the studios, the so-called independents, and the networks weren't answerable to corporate overlords, these production entities each had a distinctive personality based on the showmen who ran them. But over the years, as networks and studios began to vertically integrate, independent television production, aided by the government's reversal of the financial syndication rules (whereby independent producers were eligible for tremendous tax breaks by virtue of their self-financing, and networks weren't allowed to supply their own programming) practically disappeared from the scene.

Large, publicly held companies started buying up the networks. Westinghouse bought CBS. General Electric bought NBC. Cap Cities bought ABC. NBC merged with Universal. Disney bought ABC from Cap Cities and created Touchstone, which became ABC's primary supplier of programming. Comcast bought NBC/Universal, and so on.

Inevitably, these powerhouses all began producing their own programming, co-opting the independents. Today, all the networks produce or co-produce virtually all their own programming. As well, the major cable networks are also owned by parent companies: Fox owns FX; Comcast owns the USA network; Time-Warner owns HBO; and CBS (Viacom) owns Showtime. And every one of these vertically integrated behemoths is publicly owned, insuring the massive corporatization of the entire entertainment industry. I could go on and on describing the extent to which these entertainment giants control every aspect of our business, from producing the shows to broadcasting them, to controlling the distribution platforms, but I think you get the picture. There simply are no more independent producers who own their own product.

Is this vertical integration bad for the consumer? It's hard to argue that it is, with the majority of U.S. homes receiving somewhere in the neighborhood of 190 television channels. That's a hell of a lot of programming, more than most of us could consume if we watched 24 hours a day, seven days a week, and most of it isn't very good. But the notion of a single network showman, with his or her own personal, idiosyncratic tastes defining the brand, has vanished, probably forever.

I hate sounding like a geezer. I understand that you can't unring a bell. But I miss the days when our business was populated by big personalities; when an entrepreneur/writer/creator could practically handcraft a show to his own personal standard and, in success, not only make a lot of money, but retain ownership of the product. In today's world, where the creative process of television is almost totally micro-managed by men and women whose primary concern is the bottom line for the shareholder, that kind of single-view creativity is a thing of the past. The Steve Cannells, Grant Tinkers, Fred Silvermans, Brandon Tartikoffs and David E. Kelleys of my era won't soon, if ever, be duplicated. I'm blessed that I grew up in that era of television and, in fact, arguably helped create it.

Notwithstanding the enormous changes that I've witnessed in my fifty years in television, one thing has remained constant: Content. Without content, there *is* no TV. Without the writers, producers, directors, editors and the hundreds of crafts people behind the camera, the entire machinery of the entertainment business ceases to exist. Content was, is, and always will be at the heart of the matter, and artists – regardless of the particular medium in which they ply their craft – movies, television, theater, publishing, you name it – will always be the backbone of the entertainment business.

A question I'm often asked is, how do I think television will change over the next ten or twenty years? And the answer is, I have no idea. The technology of the medium has changed drastically in my fifty years in the television industry. The business models have changed profoundly. Vertical integration. The Internet. Cable. Video on demand. Streaming. When I started working in television it was a three-network universe. The networks and studios nitpicked you to death. And then, starting with Hill Street Blues, a new era of creative freedom blew threw our business like a cleansing downpour.

Those days and that business are gone, killed by vertical integration. Today, the broadcast networks (all five of them, not to mention the myriad cable networks) are simply divisions of giant, international, media-related corporations, charged with the responsibility of delivering, at all costs, a profitable bottom line. And in that corporate culture, there is no time for, or interest in, quality. There is only interest in *hits*. And in that equation, AMERICAN IDOL or THE APPRENTICE or THE VOICE is every bit the heavyweight that E.R. or THE SOPRANOS or THE WEST WING was. Maybe more so. Cheaper to produce, they generate greater profits. And in the general downward drift of things, artistry is a casualty. Loyalty to quality is a casualty. Loyalty to the talent is a casualty. Risk-taking is a casualty. The men and women who now run networks don't think in terms of art, good, bad, or indifferent. They think in terms of demographics. 18 to 49. Women. Young men 18 to 34. They ask you if the concept is "noisy enough". That's what they care about, because those are the ratings that generate the greatest advertising revenue. Quality? Irrelevant. Not that there wasn't always a section of the menu for those consumers who couldn't care less about good comedy or quality drama. There were game shows. There was, for some years, a glut of news magazine hours that were anything but newsworthy. They were essentially exploitational, tabloid hours, cheap to manufacture, and catering to an ever-shortening consumer attention span.

So, in this environment, this culture of cash at all costs (saving it as well as making it), don't expect the emergence of an art--conscious, quality-driven executive suite. *Do* expect often disrespectful, uninformed managers who resent the hell out of those of us who've been around long enough to want to hold them to a higher standard.

For the record, as of this writing, I'm seventy-two years old. I'm in the middle of my fiftieth year in the television business. I've had four hit series with a cumulative first-run life span of thirty-one years – HILL STREET BLUES (seven years), L.A. LAW (eight years), DOOGIE HOWSER, M.D. (four years), and NYPD BLUE (twelve years).

Additionally, I've had several shows that ran for one or two years, among the more notable in that group of near misses, MURDER ONE (two seasons), the first single-story, full season series ever attempted. All in all, in those fifty years, I've produced and written or co-written somewhere in the neighborhood of a thousand hours of television. Over the last thirty-five years or so, in particular, I've become known (I like to think) for making quality television shows, responsibly produced.

Thirty-five years ago, if you couldn't sell it to CBS, you tried NBC. If they weren't interested, you went to ABC. If you were desperate, you went to the brand-new Fox network. Today, there are probably four hundred scripted series on what – fifty channels? Surely I'd have a better chance of selling my concept today than I would have thirty years ago in a four-network universe, right?

Wrong. Every network today, from CBS to FX to the SciFi channel, has a specific brand. Let's say you have a concept for a series. Is it procedural? Fantastical? Science fiction? Maybe a vampire motif? Super hero? Cops with issues? Lawyers with issues? Cops or lawyers who are vampires? Cross dressers? Spies? Family drama? Every one of those genres, and probably more that I can't think of at the moment, has a place on some specifically branded network. Maybe two, or even three of them. But the extent to which, in this overcrowded universe, you can pitch a particular concept to more than a few networks is limited because of branding. So you might think, as a writer, that you have a vastly expanded market place in which to pitch your wares, but the truth is, you don't. Networks are so strict about buying concepts that conform to their particular brand, that any idea you have is probably viable at only a couple of places.

If you consult the statistics compiled by the Writers' Guild, you'll undoubtedly find that in TV, the living you're scratching out today is probably less than what you were earning twenty or thirty years ago. Pathetic.

For years I spent a couple of hours annually, speaking to the graduating seniors in the drama department of Cal Arts, in Valencia, California. Most of them were actors, writers and directors. I would spend the time not exactly discouraging their choice of profession, but rather, alerting them to the prohibitive odds of succeeding. I would tell them story after story revealing the pitfalls in finding employment in the film and television industry.

I would tell the actors about the two hours they'd spend waiting to walk into a sweaty, smelly room for a five-minute audition. The director is late for an appointment with the editor. The producer and writer are late for a story meeting. The executive producer/ show runner has already postponed a notes call with the network about the previous episode, and is late for the second one. And, five auditions before yours, another actor read for the role and basically hit the ball out of the park. And so, unbeknownst to you, you've already lost the gig before you ever opened your mouth. Welcome to show business. You may be great. You may have a unique take on the role. You may be the best actor out there in the hallway. But by the time you walk into the room, Elvis has left the building. Sorry, Kids. That's just the way it is.

Over the course of a couple of hours, I'd watch their faces fall. I wasn't trying to be cruel. I was just trying to give them a realistic worldview of the industry they were about to try and enter. But then I'd end my conversation with them by saying this: "Every single day in our business, *someone* succeeds. Why shouldn't it be you?"

It's the same for writers. No matter how the business changes, it always boils down to content. Every day, someone sells a show. Why shouldn't it be you?

30

With the final episode of NYPD Blue airing in the spring of 2005, my formal relationship with 20th Century Fox had come to and end. I'd spent the last twenty years of my life on that storied movie and television lot, and I left it behind with a real sense of melancholy.

I also knew I'd miss NYPD Blue. It had been an integral part of my life for almost fifteen years. And I have to say, in all my years of television, I never worked with a better actor or a finer person than Dennis Franz. He was a consummate pro, and the backbone of that series for twelve years. I would miss him, as well, but I will always be grateful for his talent and his friendship.

We left 20th and moved into a very nice suite of offices in Santa Monica, and our neighbors on either end of the office suite were David Milch and Larry David. Not bad, as neighbors go.

In the late nineteen-sixties, early seventies, when I was a kid writer at Universal Studios, I'd wander over to the kiosk in front of the commissary every afternoon around three-thirty or so for a smoke. (Everybody smoked in those days.) It was an informal afternoon break attended by all the great writer/producers in television who were under contract to Universal, working on shows like Columbo, McMillan and Wife, McCloud, and the dozens of other shows that were being churned out by Universal for the three broadcast networks (NBC, ABC, and CBS). Among these elite of television were Dick Levinson and Bill Link, who created Columbo. There was Bill

Sackheim, Jack Laird, Herm Saunders, Harve Bennett, Leonard Stern, Roy Huggins. The list was long and illustrious. For me, it was an opportunity to suck in not only their second hand smoke, but their first hand experience. I would generally keep my mouth shut and listen, and this is the sort of stuff I'd hear: "This fucking business stinks . . . " accompanied by a shake of the head.

"Used to be fun."

"Not any more."

"Cutthroat pricks."

"That noise you just heard was the sound of your option being dropped."

"I hate this fucking business."

And I used to think to myself, *if you hate it so much, why don't you get out and make room for me. I'm having all kinds of fun.* And I promised myself I'd never be one of those guys; that if it ever got to the point where I hated the business and wasn't having fun anymore, I'd just quit and go do something else. What happened to me forty years later almost turned me into one of those chronic whiners.

Notwithstanding my terrific experience at FX producing Over There, I was still very much a creature of broadcast TV, and when Mark Pedowitz, the head of ABC/Touchstone (the producing arm of ABC) called and offered a three-year deal, it seemed like a right fit. I'd been in business with ABC for many years, and I'd known Mark Pedowitz, for years, as he'd been head of Business Affairs at ABC for most of the years I produced shows for them. But that was then, and this was now.

At one of our first meetings at Touchstone, held in their conference room, there must have been six or seven young Touchstone execs around the table in addition to Mark and I, and every single one of them had their cell phone out, just below desk level, scanning their emails during the entire meeting.

Following my exit from Twentieth, I had developed five pilots (two for FOX, one for FX, one for the now defunct WB, and one for ABC). I'd scheduled some minor surgery for mid-October, figuring the three or four days I'd need to recuperate would fall neatly into the lull before I had to deliver our pilot scripts. My wife Dayna (then President of Steven Bochco Productions) and I were in Martha's Vineyard for a wedding the first weekend of October when Mark called. We had barely finalized our agreement. He said he knew I'd never taken over someone else's show before, and that it was probably a long shot, but would I be interested in taking over Cmmander In Chief? I asked him to send me all the scripts and whatever episodes they'd already shot, and we'd get together as soon as I got back to L.A.

I spent the next several days reading scripts and watching episodes, trying to decide if this was a challenge I'd enjoy taking on. My personal sense of the show was that the first half dozen episodes were too freighted with Presidential heroism. It seemed that every episode was an exercise in saving the world, with virtually no attention paid to the reality that even the most powerful person on earth – the President of the United States – is faced daily with the frustrating limits of that awesome power. Their were other issues as well, including overly melodramatic "B" stories involving the President's children – an eight year old daughter and twin teenage siblings (brother and sister), as well as a whole bunch of satellite characters who were truly under characterized and under served. Nevertheless, as fantasized as the show was, and as much as there were elements in it I didn't much care for, there was something fundamentally appealing about the show. It had a good heart. It wanted to be a hit, in spite of itself. It had real stars in Geena Davis, and the remarkable Donald Sutherland, as her antagonist. And so, after some deliberation, and a hurried secret meeting over at Touchstone the day after we got back from Martha's Vineyard, I agreed to take over the show. I felt that if I could turn the ship around and help it become a hit, it would instantly validate Touchstone's faith in me and make me something of a hero to ABC. The worst-case scenario, I thought, was that if I failed, at least I'd get an A for Effort. Fat fucking chance. Taking over Commander In Chief was probably the worst decision I ever made in my life.

Created by Rod Lurie, and starring Geena Davis as the first female President of the United States, the show had debuted to strong ratings. The novelty and appeal of the premise as well as the star power of Ms. Davis and Donald Sutherland, gave the show immediate hit potential. Unfortunately, that potential was being undermined by a degree of production chaos that was threatening to derail the show before it could establish itself. By the time the company had begun work on its sixth episode, there had been three production shut downs, partly as a function of not having scripts ready to shoot, and partly because the network executives at ABC were unhappy with the scripts that had been shot. In that chaotic environment, it was impossible to identify one clear creative vision. Network executives were dictating scenes by phone to staff writers who'd then transcribe the dialogue and "publish" the pages – only to be told the next day by those same executives that the scenes were no good. And then the whole process would start all over again, like musical chairs, with the last pages still standing on the day they were needed being the ones that got filmed.

Like it or not, in series television, someone has to be the Boss. Someone has to say, this is the story I'm telling, and this is how I want to tell it. And while certainly the studio and the network and the stars may all have opinions worth listening to, at the end of the day it's not a democracy. Either because he was ill-equipped by temperament, or hamstrung by inexperience, Rod Lurie lost control of his show pretty early on in the game. By the time production had commenced on the sixth episode, there was no complete script for show seven, and no script at all for show eight and beyond. The studio and the network saw a tremendous asset rapidly slipping through its fingers and decided they had to act quickly and decisively if things were to be turned around.

The show had been on the air for about four weeks, and I'd already heard rumblings that the show was struggling badly. The scripts were late to nonexistent, they weren't very good, production had fallen behind, and costs were skyrocketing. In short, it was an expensive disaster in the making.

Don't ask me why – maybe it was because I was a brand new team member and I wanted to be thought well of by my new teammates – or maybe it was simply a matter of ego; of believing that I could save this show and be a hero – but I called Mark and said I'd consider taking over the show, but before I committed, I wanted to have a meeting with Steve McPherson, the head of ABC. Mark said he'd arrange it the moment I returned from Martha's Vineyard.

I returned home on Sunday, and I went over to ABC for my first official meeting since signing the deal with Touchstone. I didn't know Steve McPherson at all. But I'd heard around town that he was a pretty erratic guy: unpredictably volatile, moody, abusive, or charming and supportive. I was prepared for whatever version might show up. McPherson turned out to be a bright, personable guy, but I had to assume it was like going out on a first date. As Chris Rock says, when you go out with someone the first time, you're not going out with *them*, you're going out with their representative.

Nevertheless, he struck me as being very present, and more than a little concerned about the situation roiling Commander In Chief. It's no small thing to replace the creator and show runner in mid-production, but Steve's willingness to do so was an index of his deep concern. All of them – Touchstone and ABC – had held high hopes for the show, and it was coming apart at the seams.

I told Steve I'd take the show over, but I needed his blessing on two counts: the first was that I was going to shut the show down for two weeks to get the script process re-organized, and that was going to involve my firing most of the writers currently on staff, with the exception of Stuart Stevens, who was a political operative who'd turned to writing, and was also functioning as a technical advisor by virtue of his insider's knowledge of Washington. (Stuart wound up running Mitt Romney's losing campaign for the presidency in 2012.) McPherson readily agreed. Then I told him that I was going to fundamentally alter the creative direction of the show. As it was, Commander In Chief had the president essentially saving the world from one devastating crisis or another, every week. Not only boring, but totally unrealistic. They were trying to make Geena Davis, as the first woman president, an unrealistically heroic figure. My instinct, dramatically, was to take a more honest look at the *limits* of power, even that belonging to the president of The United States. To me, that's where the good stories were. Here's the first female president in our history, and she's constantly running into the fact that world crises won't necessarily yield to her power or her charm. Plus, she's still a wife and mother to her husband and children, president or not.

Steve signed off on where I wanted to go with the show creatively, and then I brought up my final condition. I told him I'd heard that the network was micro-managing the show to death, and that if I were to take over, I'd need his promise that I would be left alone to do my job. He agreed to everything, and so I said I'd do it. You could feel the relief in the room.

As the meeting was breaking up, Steve asked me a favor: would I keep his good friend, Rod Lurie, on staff, but reporting to me now, as show-runner? I was stunned. I said I thought that would be disastrous. Here's the guy who created the show; had a very specific vision of the show; and I was going to come in, change the creative course of the series, and fire most of his writers. And to add insult to injury, he was going to be demoted. I said it was a recipe for disaster. There's no way we wouldn't be at each other's throats. McPherson reluctantly saw my point, but I could tell he was disappointed. Maybe he'd promised Rod that he wouldn't be replaced. I don't know. But I did know that if there was any chance of turning the show around, Rod Lurie looking over my shoulder and/or dividing the loyalties of cast and crew, wasn't going to contribute to the solution of the show's myriad problems. If our roles had been reversed, I'm sure Rod would have said the same thing.

My first order of business was to meet Geena Davis and apprise her of the new direction I wanted to take the show in. We met for coffee, and she was lovely – reserved, but friendly – and she seemed to understand the depth of the problems facing the show, and seemed on board with what I had in mind.

When I arrived on scene at the production facilities at Raleigh Studios in Hollywood, the environment was a hornet's nest of rumors. I quickly got down to the grim business of firing people. I brought in new producers and a new group of writers, including Alison Cross and Joel Fields, two terrific, reliable and good-spirited friends. (Joel is now the executive producer of The Americans. I kept the aforementioned Stuart Stevens, along with one other writer, Dee Johnson.)

I then went to introduce myself to Donald Sutherland. I'd always been an enormous fan of Donald's, and was very excited to work with him. He was a charming, bright and witty man, with a vicious dog who wouldn't stop snarling at me the whole time I met with Donald in his trailer. The dog couldn't have been testier if he'd been Rod Lurie, himself. But, in spite of the dog, Donald and I hit it off quite nicely. What I hadn't yet discovered, but would in the ensuing days, was that Donald had strong opinions and feelings about every single word of every single script we wrote.

My computer would be awash in emails from Donald about his scenes and everyone else's as well. He would email me at great length, wanting to re-write his own scenes. We had too many lengthy conversations to count, in person and via email, about his endless need for revisions. It was grueling. And yet, because of his keen intelligence, even though I often disagreed with Donald, we got along extremely well. He was a delightful man, erudite and intelligent, and we often found ourselves engaged in deep conversations about world affairs, politics, and our personal lives.

Geena was altogether another story. I would get long, detailed critiques of our scripts, and copious notes and questions about every scene she was in. Okay, I get it. She's the star of the show. She's being protective of her character. Fair enough. But I would almost always get these tomes about particular scenes on the morning of the day we were to shoot them. It was virtually impossible to carry on a dialogue since a) she was on the stage already doing the work, and b) there simply wasn't time to intelligently debate and/or alter the scenes without stopping production. Would I have been able to accommodate her if she'd communicated her needs in a more timely fashion? Absolutely. And I'd gotten us to the point where we were knocking out our scripts in a very timely fashion. But, consciously or otherwise, Geena was severely undermining our efforts on her behalf, and it was clear that while she wouldn't out-right say it, she was definitely not on board with the direction in which I was steering the show. It was inevitable then, that the net-work started hectoring me about the scripts, in eerie lockstep with Geena's objections.

One afternoon, as I was driving from my office in Santa Monica to the studio in Hollywood, my cell phone started quacking. On the line were two young Touchstone executives, and two young ABC executives. They started giving me a cascade of notes, large and small, about the current script, emphasizing the fact that these notes came directly from Steve McPherson. This went on for a cou-ple of minutes, before I stopped them. "Guys," I said. "First of all, this isn't what I agreed to. Steve promised me I'd be left alone. I didn't sign on for this. Second, do you guys know *anything* about politics? Do you even read the newspaper? Do you read anything other than your fucking emails? These notes are just plain stupid, and I'm not going to execute them." There was a long pause, until one of the ABC weasels said, "Well, Steve's going to have a hard time swallowing that."

I said, "Well then, tell Steve to open his mouth a little wider."

Talk about a big mouth. They fired me the next week. All Mark Pedowitz said to me was, "I'll do whatever I have to do to protect the asset." Well what about me, I thought. *I'm* an asset, too.

They put Dee Johnson in charge of the show after me, but that only accelerated its downfall.

No good deed goes unpunished, right? Here I'd tried to be a good team player, and I got my ass handed to me. At a mini-mum, with two-and-a-half years to go on my three-year deal with Touchstone, I sure as hell wasn't going to be invited to do any more shows for ABC.

31

Around the time Death By Hollywood (the formerly titled Hollywood) was being published, and through the good auspices of Fred Specktor, I met with Joe Cohen, a senior television agent at CAA. At Dayna's urging, I was considering representation for the first time in my career. Up until that point, I had always had long-term contractual commitments: Universal for twelve years, MTM for seven years, between ABC and Fox, twenty years, and then the CBS and Paramount deals. I never needed anyone to represent my employment interests. Once Hill Street Blues really put me on the map, all The Doberman would have to do is wait for the phone to ring. But as I got older, the business changed, and I was no longer dealing with my contemporaries. I'd walk into a network president's office, and I was always treated deferentially, which was often not in my best interests in terms of pitching ideas or having a free flowing back-and-forth. And let's face it: it's harder to say no to a man who's old enough to be your father than it is to one of your contemporaries. So Dayna thought, and I agreed, that having an agent more or less clearing the way for us, and ascertaining the lay of the land *before* I went in for a meeting, was a good idea.

Joe Cohen is a terrific guy. He's a CAA lifer, now in his fifties, but as plugged into what's happening in TV as anyone I've ever known. And, over the years, he's developed a client list that's a virtual Who's Who in the television business.

After the Commander In Chief debacle, one of the first meetings Joe set up for me was with Michael Wright, the president and head of programming for TNT. It was supposed to be a get-acquainted meeting, as we had never met each other before. Michael was delightful, as was his development executive, Lillah McCarthy, daughter of the late actor Kevin McCarthy. The chain of command at TNT was simple: you dealt with Michael and Lillah. That was it. No big hierarchy. No long lines. No waiting for decisions. No gaggle of junior executives checking their cell phones and sharpening their stilettos.

Several weeks earlier, through a mutual friend, I had a phone meeting with a writer and lawyer by the name of David Feige. He had written a book called Indefensible: One Lawyer's Journey Into The Inferno Of American Justice (a hell of a long title). David wanted to develop the book for television, and I politely told him that as a general rule, I only developed my own projects, but that I'd be happy to read the book. He promised to send it to me right away, and when I got it and read it, I was mesmerized. David had been a Public Defender in the Bronx for something like fifteen years, and the experience had genuinely radicalized him. I thought my politics were significantly left of center, but compared with David's, I was Atila The Hun. His fifteen years of representing the indigent in the New York City Criminal Justice System had given him a unique perspective on the fundamental *in*justice of the system. As far as David was concerned, it was a rigged game, and the defendants didn't have a chance. Many of the stories David wrote about were truly heartbreaking, and I could see how his time with the public defender's office had caused him to burn out.

David, as I would come to realize later, had a heart the size and consistency of an overripe cantaloupe: big, and soft. But he was passionate, and brilliant, and – like a great many lawyers I'd worked with over the years (David Kelley, Billy Finkelstein, even Terry Louise Fisher), he had all the right equipment to become an excellent television writer.

Anyway, I had yet to meet David when I went over to TNT, but I'd read the book, and in our general conversation about the kinds of shows Michael Wright was looking for, I mentioned Indefensible. Michael sparked to the idea of that kind of law show, and we both agreed that it would be a smarter idea if we endeavored to drama-tize, with equal fervor, both the public defender's point of view, as well as the prosecutor's point of view.

I'd always been a big believer, dramatically, in asking the ques-tion rather than providing the answer, and I thought that an honest portrayal of the system, without prejudice, would nevertheless be extremely thought provoking for the audience. And, just like that, I left Michael Wright's office with a pilot script commitment.

When I returned to my office, I called David Feige and proposed that we co-create a series about the Bronx Public Defender's office, cer-tainly using his book as inspiration, but creatively starting from scratch. David readily agreed, and made plans to come to Los Angeles, where we would spend a week or two seeing what we could come up with.

David was as delightful in person as he had been over the phone. He was big – a bear of a man, somewhere in the 6'3" range and about 270 pounds, with a big brain to match. He was strong-willed and opinionated, not much into the world of gray when it came to the justice system. I could see my job wasn't going to be easy in terms of getting David to moderate his point of view sufficiently to portray the prosecutorial side of the system with the same honesty and passion he portrayed the defense side.

Additionally, already in his forties, David had never written a script before. But as I said earlier, mastering the form of the televi-sion script isn't rocket science. Pretty much anyone can learn it. The *art* of the television script, now that's another issue altogether.

Throughout the process, Michael Wright only had one concern: that we make sure we were not tipping the scales too far in either direction. As I said earlier, nobody wakes up in the morning think-ing they're a badass. Everyone wakes up feeling righteous. And it was important that we portray our prosecutors – who David instinc-tively didn't like – with the same even-handedness as our defenders.

I made David write about nine drafts of the pilot script. I could have easily, and far more quickly, taken it and done it myself, but I wanted David to do the work, because every note session was like a lesson, and every written draft was like practicing the craft. And as if with anything that you practice a lot, you get better at it. And David did. It took a while, but we finally had a script worthy of submission.

I don't recall exactly what TNT's notes were, but Michael Wright was always terrific about boiling his thoughts down to a few conceptual headlines. He never told us what to do or how to do it; he'd merely voice a conceptual concern or two and assume we'd figure how to accommodate him ourselves. And Michael always made it clear that if we disagreed, we weren't bound by his comments. It doesn't get better than that, network-wise.

We got a quick green light from Michael, and we began to cast, hire producers, and build sets. Being the shameless supporter of nepotism that I am, I invited my son Jesse to be the co-executive producer on the show and direct the pilot, his first.

One of the real pleasures of working on NYPD Blue over the course of its twelve-year run was working with and getting to know Mark-Paul Gosselaar. Mark-Paul was an excellent young actor who I'd first run across when Alison Cross and I were casting our Philly pilot. Mark-Paul actually gave the best reading of anyone that came in for the role, but he was simply too young to be a credible potential romantic partner for Kim Delaney. She was thirteen years older than Mark-Paul and, as beautiful as she was, he looked like a kid next to her. But when Ricky Schroeder dropped out of NYPD Blue, I leapt at the chance to hire Mark-Paul, and he was on the show for its last five years. Unlike Rick, who was always an awkward fit as a cop – he was too small physically, and never really projected the kind of intensity and strength we wanted in Sipowicz's partner – Mark-Paul, young as he was, had a strength and authority that made him completely credible as a cop. Sipowicz took to calling him Junior, and the two of them, over time, became a terrific duo: the old bull and the young bull. (You know the joke? The old bull and the young bull are standing on a hilltop looking at half-a-dozen heifers grazing below. The young bull says, "Hey, let's run down there and fuck a couple of them." The old bull says, "Let's *walk* down, and fuck 'em all.")

We cast Mark-Paul as the lead in our ensemble. In all honesty, the pilot wasn't the best I ever produced. The script had its flaws, and Jesse, I felt, made an error in his choice of a DP (director of photography). I never really cared for the look of the film. It was washed out with light, which I was assured could be adjusted for in post production (and never really was, at least to my satisfaction), and I thought the framing was, by and large, ordinary. But we had a fine ensemble cast. In addition to Mark-Paul, we cast Jane Kaczmarek, Gloria Reuben, Melissa Sagemiller, Currie Graham, one of my favorite actors, Natalia Cigliuti, Teddy Sears, J. August Richards, another find, and the gifted Jonathan Scarfe. On balance, I'd grade the pilot a B+, and whatever my reservations were, they were more than compensated for by the fact that the pilot really showed the potential range of the series.

We weren't trying to re-invent the wheel with Raising The Bar, which is fine. Even given the title, the bar was a little too high for that goal. Raising The Bar was a fairly standard law show, but it also – and this is what, for me, made it special – was about something. I won't start quoting statistics here, but African Americans and the indigent in general, comprise an overwhelming percentage of our prison population. And Raising The Bar shined a bright light on those social inequities, while also exploring the personal commitment to serving the underclasses that characterized our defense attorneys. That said, we worked hard to also characterize the other side: hard-working prosecutors charged with representing the people's interests and doing all – David would argue too much – in their power to protect the citizenry.

Raising The Bar lasted for two seasons before being cancelled, and by the end of its' twenty-five episode run, I'd become quite proud of it. It was well produced, Jesse had, over the course of directing seven or eight of the episodes, considerably lifted his game, and the scripts were progressively better and better. Running a writers' room on a show like ours was like having a spirited six-hour argument every day for two years. It was rigorous and mentally stimulating. I'd happily do some version of it all over again.

32

In 2011, Joe Cohen introduced me to a young writer he represented named Eric Lodal. Eric had an interesting background.
He grew up in the Washington, D.C. area, and his father worked in
government. Eric played football in high school before going on to
Yale, where he sang with the Yale Whiffenpoofs before going on to
Julliard School of Music to study opera. By the time Joe set up our
meeting, Eric was probably thirty-five or six.

I immediately liked him. He was bright and energetic and he'd
lived long enough to have an interesting life with its share of bumps
in the road, including, but not limited to earlier bouts with alcohol. But when we met, Eric had been sober for some time, and was
very focused on his writing. We decided to see if we could come up
with something together, and for the next two years, off and on, we
developed several ideas, none of which came to fruition, but all of
which were interesting and well executed. Eric was a good writer
with a good mind, and he worked hard – all qualities to be admired
and, hopefully, exploited to our mutual benefit.

At the tail end of 2012, Mike Robin, who was making The Closer
for TNT, its biggest hit at the time, contacted me about an idea
he and Michael Wright had been talking about. The notion was to
dramatize all the different elements that comprise a city's judicial
system: street cops, detectives, lawyers, and judges. They had both
agreed that they wanted me to develop the concept, and for Mike
to direct it.

After speaking with Mike, I had further conversations with Michael Wright, and promised him I'd slap on my thinking cap, which I proceeded to do, noodling the idea around on my morning walks until I'd come up with a comprehensive approach to the idea. I thought San Francisco would be the ideal setting for the series. It hadn't been seen for some time, it was an exciting and diverse city with a real sense of class warfare, the tech industry had bifurcated the economy, and – best of all – their entire judicial system was contained in one, giant building at 850 Bryant Street. The structure, which looked like some Soviet-era concrete monolith, housed the jails, the police department, the D.A. and the prosecutors' offices, and the courtrooms. It was a soup to nuts beehive of legal activity – the sausage factory of the judicial system, if you will.

My idea was to take one case, preferably a murder, and play it all the way through the system: the crime, the investigation, the arrest, the criminal proceedings in all their complexity (from both sides' point of view, a la Raising The Bar), and the trial and verdict. As a window into the legal system, it was ideal. As a murder mystery, it worked all day long, not unlike Murder One, but with fewer episodes and, hopefully, a more sophisticated audience that was more appreciative of long, single-story arcs.

I worked out pretty much all of the details of the story on my morning walks – I came up with two murders, seemingly unrelated – which in the course of the episodes we realize are in fact related, and then I wrote a twenty-some-odd page document laying the whole thing out: Who, what, where, when, how and why. I thought Eric would be an ideal candidate to write the teleplay, and at a lunch with Michael, I broached the topic, assuring Michael that Eric was a first rate writer. By way of example, I told him I'd send him an outline of a western Eric and I had developed, set in Colorado in the 1880's. Michael fell in love with the idea, and by the time lunch was over, he'd bought both premises: Murder In The First, and Lawless, so named because the story took place in a town of the same name. As a young writer looking for a break in the business, Eric had suddenly fallen into a jackpot, with two pilot teleplays to write.

Eric and I commenced work on both projects. We delivered the Lawless script in October of 2012, and Murder In The First at the end of November. It was clear from the start that Murder In The First was the script Michael wanted to go forward with. He liked Lawless tremendously, but admitted to me that he doubted his bosses in Atlanta would approve it. They apparently weren't into westerns. And since Michael had promised us that if TNT passed on Lawless we could shop it elsewhere, I wasn't disappointed. Essentially, TNT had paid us to develop a script we were now free to take to market.

Murder In The First was given the go-ahead to pilot, and we began what became the most laborious casting process I've ever been through. We argued constantly over casting. It was clear to me that TNT's head of casting, Lisa Frieberger, and I had completely different tastes when it came to actors. I think we also had different objectives. She was coming to the process in terms of marquee value, and price point. I also think she saw casting as her private little fiefdom at TNT, and that I and my casting director, Junie Lowry-Johnson were a threat to her autonomy, which was not true at all. Junie's and my sole interest was who was best for the role? It has always been my belief that, especially in television, stars don't make shows a hit. Hit shows make stars.

I honestly don't remember how Taye Diggs' name came into the mix, or who suggested it. But both Eric and I thought it was a really interesting idea. San Francisco is as diverse a city as there is in America, and Taye Diggs qualified for us on every level: talent, ethnicity, marquee value, tremendous presence, and enormous likeability. After we met with Taye, we all agreed he was the right actor for the role of Terry English, Homicide Inspector. We had also met with Kathleen Robertson, a Canadian actress who completely sold herself to us as a beautiful, tough, blue-collar cop from a family of cops.

We now had our two leads, and the rest of the cast finally fell into place, as well. And it was a good cast: Ian Anthony Dale, Raphael Sbarge, Currie Graham, Richard Schiff, Nicole Ari Parker, Lombardo Boyar, James Cromwell, Tom Felton, Bess Rous, Steven Weber, and little Mimi Kirkland, who played Kathleen's daughter.

As bad luck would have it, Warner Brothers TV wouldn't release Mike Robin to direct our pilot, and so we hired Antoine Fuqua to direct. Antoine is a well-known feature film director, and we thought we were lucky to get him, but his involvement was short lived. Antoine had a feature being released in a month to six weeks, and bowed out of our project in order to devote himself to promoting his feature. We got lucky and wound up hiring one of the most successful TV pilot directors in television, Tommy Schlamme, who had directed, among other things the pilot of The West Wing. Tommy was a high-energy bolt of lightning who brought great energy and focus to the pilot. He also brought a reputation for being something of a budget buster. As Tommy himself admitted, "As a producer, I'm all about the budget. But once I begin to direct, I couldn't care less." Well, at least he was frank about it.

Predictably, the shoot was over budget and overly long. By a lot. And so was Tommy's first cut, by about seventeen minutes. Shades of Hill Street Blues. Except this time, I wasn't able to take complete control of the process, nor was I sure I wanted to. Tommy had demanded, and we (TNT and I) agreed, to give him an executive producer credit, and so he had legitimate authority. Eric had written the teleplay, and I believed that earned him a say in the proceedings, as well. I figured that, at the end of the day, if I had to, I would simply make whatever decisions we couldn't come to by consensus. It was a long and arduous process shaving seventeen minutes from the first cut of the pilot. We took things out. We put them back in. We rearranged sequences. We un-rearranged them. We trimmed. We pruned. And, eventually, a forty-two minute pilot emerged that, by and large, was to our mutual liking.

I doubt I would have had the patience to let the process play out as it did, twenty-five years ago. But Tommy's almost as old a pro as I am, and Eric wasn't going to learn anything by being deprived of participation. Besides, I remember, as a young writer, what it was like not having a say in the way my words were edited. It wasn't fun, and I always promised myself I'd be more generous to young writers than Harve Bennett was to me.

The pilot of Murder In The First aired on June 9, 2014, to generally good reviews and fair ratings, though the ratings dropped considerably over the course of the next three or four episodes. But it's an index of how technology has changed our business that, slowly, as the single story unfolded week after week, viewership began to build. Clearly, what was happening is that people were recording the earlier episodes and then binge watching them. And, as with any good show, we as writers became more sure-footed as we progressed, tweaking the story, letting it take us in unexpected directions, and finally concluding the ten-episode-long mystery on August 11th with a resolution that I believe satisfied the audience greatly. It certainly pleased us, and TNT as well, at least creatively.

33

Other than a few predictable bumps along the way as I eased into my sixties – a couple of back surgeries, a couple of shoulder surgeries, the result of a continuously athletic life of tennis, golf, skiing, hiking and weight training – I'd always been blessed with terrific health until I'd suffered the heart attack at age sixty-six. And even then, I was back to normal so quickly, that I never really thought about the possibility of dying. I'd been healthy and active ever since, with no issues to speak of at all, often told by many that I didn't look anywhere near my age. Thank you very much.

When my friends heard that I had leukemia, they were uniformly shocked, loving, and supportive, ready to do whatever they could to help me. (Got any spare marrow?) My son and daughter took the news as well as could be expected, and when they realized I wasn't freaked out, they pretty quickly calmed down.

Except I *was* freaked out. So were they, probably. I was a healthy, successful, active man suddenly told I had a rare cancer that, to me, sounded like a death sentence. So I did what any well adjusted, healthy seventy year old man would do: I called my good friend and former shrink, Phil Stutz, and told him I needed to see him, professionally, as soon as possible.

Through Dayna, I had met Phil in 1997. I was 54, unhappily married, and with my children gone (Melissa was 26, and Jesse had just turned 21), there was an incessant clock ticking away in my head, constantly reminding me that life was too short to remain miserable.

I went to see him and spilled my guts, always an uncomfortable process, more so with a stranger. Phil listened patiently as I laid it out. "I'm fifty-four," I said, "I've had great success, and my wife and children are financially taken care of. But I've spent my whole life taking care of them at the expense of my own happiness." I'm not sure that's altogether true in hindsight, but as Nietzsche said, "Life can only be understood backwards. Unfortunately, it must be lived forwards." Or something like that. I finished my spiel by saying, "I want to be happy, and life is short." Phil said to me, "If life were short, you wouldn't be here. You're here because life is long."

Seventeen years later, sitting in his office, it suddenly didn't seem long enough. Phil heard me out as I shared with him my fear of what lay ahead, then said, "I'm going to give you some rules for the road: Rule number one – embrace uncertainty. If you chase certainty, the only thing you'll find is terror."

It was as if a switch had been thrown in my brain. Maybe it was because of all the years I'd spent with him previously, as I made, with his help, tremendous changes in my life. Or maybe it was the fact that no one can live and function in a perpetual state of terror. Whatever the reason, his words resonated for me profoundly and, with his rules written on a card I kept with me for the next six months of my life, I left his office feeling genuinely at peace. I was no longer afraid.

Phil's Rules For The Road:

1) Embrace uncertainty. Looking for certainty will only result in terror.
2) Stay in the present.
3) Continue to function meaningfully.
4) Stay connected to people.
5) Be grateful for all I have. (Phil calls it Grateful Flow.)
6) Continue to be a leader for others.
7) Everyone is in the Hallway to Death. *No one* knows how long the hallway is.

I spent the next week having tests of all kinds, and by the time I checked into City of Hope under the extraordinary care of Doctor Forman, I was ready for whatever they were going to throw at me, which turned out to be the kitchen sink, and then some.

My dear friend, actress and producer Roma Downey, wife of famed reality television producer Mark Burnett, is a deeply religious person. Me, not so much. Nevertheless, when I was going into the hospital, Roma gave me a rosary that she said was blessed by three Popes. I kept it by my side for the next eight months. I may not believe in God, but under the circumstances, I figured what the hell – I'd take all the help I could get.

A few nights before I went into the hospital, we had dinner with Dana Walden and her husband, Matt. Dana is the co-chairman of both Twenty First Century Fox Television and the Fox network. She and my Dayna had known each other ever since Dana Walden had been a young publicist at Fox. And through the years, she and Matt had been great and loyal friends, not an easy thing to be, particularly for Dana, when I was embroiled in that messy law suit with Fox. The Fox executives, by and large, hated me, and every time Dana was in a staff meeting, they would give her a hard time about being friends with me. And she would always defend me: "Do not talk shit about Steven Bochco in my presence. He's one of my closest friends." That took guts. But then, Dana has guts to spare.

At dinner, Dana said she wanted to hire me to consult on her mid-season pilots so that I'd have meaningful work to do while in the hospital. I said great, except for the hiring part. I was happy to do it for nothing. No, she insisted. She was going to pay me. Bullshit, I said. I don't need the money. She insisted. So the next day, I called my attorney, Don Walerstein, and I instructed him that if someone called from Twentieth wanting to make a deal for my services, he was to accept whatever offer they made. It wasn't a negotiation. I'd take a buck, if that were what they were offering.

What was important to me – and so moving – was that Dana Walden understood that at this most vulnerable time in my life, an activity that made me feel relevant was critical to my recovery. I will be grateful to her for the rest of my life.

In the days before entering City Of Hope, I'd bought a small computer to keep with me in the hospital, and I decided to share my day-to-day experiences with my family, along with a select group of close friends and loved ones. I figured being dead is easy. It's the dying part that's hard. And there was no way I was going to go through this alone.

I entered City Of Hope on July 7, 2014. I was scared, but tried not to show it. I wanted to be as upbeat as all the hospital nurses and personnel were. One woman in particular, Lupe Santana, who was essentially Dayna's and my personal concierge, had been extraordinarily helpful. She had the hospital room next to mine tricked out like a hotel room so that Dayna could stay with me. I had urged Dayna to stay at a nearby hotel, The Huntington, in Pasadena, where she could have a better bed, access to a spa, a real restaurant and bar with a decent wine list, but she insisted on being with me through the whole ordeal. I could have cried. I probably did.

34

Why does a dog lick his balls? Because he can.
Why does a writer write? Because he has to. (Not to imply that all writers are men – but whatever your gender, it takes balls to be a writer.)

I've been writing all my life. Short stories. Stupid poems. Limericks. Letters. Plays. Television scripts. Screenplays. Novels. This book. It's what I do and, to a significant degree, it's who I am. It defines me.

And so, when I was diagnosed with leukemia and realized that I was not only going to spend months in the hospital, but that most of that time would be spent in isolation, resolving to stay in contact with friends and family led me to the only logical conclusion: I would send an email blast to everyone on pretty much a daily basis. Writers write.

One of the things I love about emails is their spontaneity. Normally, when writing, I'm obsessive about neatness. Spelling, grammar, punctuation all have to be "just so." One of the reasons I do most of my writing in long hand is that on a computer, my need for correctness overwhelms my spontaneity. I'm always editing as I write, and I lose my rhythm – my zone, if you will. But emails, to me, are like writing long hand. They're not for public consumption, as most of my writing is, and so their personal nature liberates me from the need for everything to be perfect.

My sense was that, having cancer, I might be dying. But I'd be a writer to my last, dying breath, and writing down my thoughts and daily experiences wrestling this monster might just cut it down to size and make it a less formidable foe. And so, however sick I might become, writing it all down and sharing it with my friends and family empowered me. Plus, the emails invited response, and the daily back and forth lifted my spirits and kept me engaged. Rule number two of Phil's Rules For The Road: Stay in the present. And there is nothing more present than an email.

And so, for whatever they're worth, here, in their entirety, are all the emails – the writings – that catalogued my seventy days and nights at City Of Hope, in Duarte, California.

Sent: July 8th, 2014

Dear Friends,
Day one is in the books! (Remember the old drinking song? Ninety none bottles of beer on the wall, ninety-nine bottles of beer . . . ?) Had my first full chemo blast through the night, slept reasonably well despite it (thank God for Ambien and Xanax), and feel pretty good today. I have another three-hour blast at around ten a.m., and we shall see how the cumulative effect starts to pile on. But in the meantime, under the rubric one day at a time, this first one is under my belt and I ain't puking, I ain't lost my appetite, my exquisite silver fox wig (which you all thought was real all these years) hasn't fallen off yet, and I'm ready to face day two.

As Mahatma J. Rachins once wrote in her incredibly trenchant pamphlet entitled TWO WEEKS IN THE CATSKILLS WITH MAHATMA J.RACHINS WILL CHANGE YOUR LIFE FOR THE PALTRY SUM OF FIVE THOUSAND RUPES A DAY," "Alech Salam alechem, may you find your peace elsewhere since you ain't getting' a piece of me; and a journey OF A HUNDRED DAYS up the mountain of enlightenment takes oh, a hundred and twelve days MAYBE — ain't sure because I only go for the first three days or so and then you're on your own, my acolytes, 'cause no one touches the sacred turd vessel which surrounds the precious and enlightened marrow of my chakra essence, uh uh and no way." In other words, Alech Salam Alechem , Pal — which loosely translated means, your bone marrow is my bone marrow, and my bone marrow is also my bone marrow, and that's how the spirit guides always meant it to be, because marrow by the pound is more expensive than chopped liver."

Enlightenment, Dear Ones. A state to aspire to.

Much love,
Look Who Think He's Worthy

Sent: Wed, Jul 9, 2014 9:59 am
Subject: starting my third full day

Dear Loved Ones,
Still here in glorious downtown Duarte. Eat your hearts out. Feeling surprisingly well as they prep me for chemo treatment number four of six. No horrendous side effects yet, appetite still good, they're hydrating me so much I'm pissing like a race horse. My new name around here is Sea Pisscuit. Probably the last chemo, which is a full 24-hour cycle, will loosen the fibers of my being for a while, but hey . . . I don't have to clean it up. Took a two mile hike around he halls yesterday, will do so again today, so staying ambulatory. When they let you out in the halls, you have to wear a mask. It looked like we wandered into a convention of hairless bank robbers, except for me. If my sister had been there, she probably would have turned me in: It's him! The one with the hair! Get him! The Nazis would have loved her. But I digress. Because I still feel pretty strong, I've been doing lots of reading and stuff (yay, Dana Walden), and eating often. Last night I had a delicious dinner of filet de shoe, with a side of laces. While you Philistines are wandering the world drinking fine wines and eating great pastas, local fresh catches and such, Dayna is drinking cheap wine, I am drinking NO GODDAMN WINE but am enjoying the occasional Xanax, Ambien and Attavan with my twice daily application of

chemo. I think she's jealous, except for the chemo part. She sleeps in the adjoining room so she can be near the Old Jew. I think she wants to make sure I make no sudden changes in my will, though she says it's because she wants to be there by my side to advocate on my behalf. She is great. I keep trying to get her to go the Huntington instead where they have better food, nicer rooms, a real bar, and Puerto Rican cabana boys, but she is so far resistant to these blandishments.

Anyway, folks, I'm doing well, and so feeling your love and good vibes. Candles burning, incense wafting (is it that, or are you just forgetting to turn on the fan in the bathroom?). Please don't feel the need to respond every day. As the young people say, I feel your love. Will let you know how I'm doing periodically, and keep in mind that you are not simply enjoying summer vacations for yourself, but for me as well. I like sleeping, reading, shtupping, paddling around in the pool, eating, drinking, laughing, telling jokes, and spending money on needless tchochkes. And shtupping. Did I mention that? They've told me that in very rare cases with chemo, a side effect is your dick falls off. There was a half-sour on my plate yesterday at lunch, and I hadn't ordered pickles, so I'm a little concerned, but they tell me, like hair, it usually grows back.

Much love to all from Cancer Central!

Steven

On THURSDAY, Jul 10, 2014, at 1:27 PM, Steven Bochco wrote:

Dearly Beloveds,
Starting my sixth of six chemo treatments before the big 24 hour blaster that starts tonight.

Can't wait to see what it does to me. And the sheets. Whatever, I'm up for it. Otherwise, things are pretty much as they have been all week. Good appetite, good energy, no side effects, lots of work and writing and stuff to do, so all in all, not so bad. People here are really nice.

So not a lot to bore you with until tomorrow, when who the hell knows
what'll be going on? All I know is, after this twenty-four hours, they're going to keep me around so I can "recover". Recover? For two
weeks? Oi vey. Couldn't be worse then a hemorrhoid, could it?

Thank you all for your loving responses. I love you all, I know you're with me, and we will congregate on the other end of this adventure for a love fest.
Bochco

Sent: Fiday, July 11, 2014

DEADLINE HOLLYWOOD
STEVEN BOCHCO REVEALS WHAT IT'S REALLY LIKE TO BE DEAD IN HOLLYWOOD
By MIKE FLEMING JR | Friday July 11, 2014 @ 8:59am PDT

SO STEVE, TELL OUR AUDIENCE WHAT IT'S REALLY LIKE TO BE DEAD IN HOLLYWOOD?
Well, Mike, it's not as bad as I thought it would be. No one lets you make pilots down here, too expensive, but on the flip side, there's no such thing as Broadcast Standards.
MIKE: SO, HOW'S THE WEATHER?
A little warm, but not so bad. I have a wide array of banana slings that keep me breathing comfortably in the nether regions.
MIKE: SO, TELL US WHAT REALLY HAPPENED?
I was feeling a little fatigued, and wound up getting diagnosed with a fairly rare form of leukemia. At first I thought it was carbuncles,

but alas, no. So, they sent me to City Of Hope, where I've been undergoing treatment. I'm on my fifth day of chemo, just started some heavy duty shit, but so far I feel pretty good. No fever yet, no terrible fatigue, no nausea, just this sort of . . . I don't know . . . dead feeling? Or maybe it's just this sense of being interviewed prematurely by DEADLINE HOLLYWOOD.

Maybe, just for a day, in homage to an old TV guy, you could call the column *LIFELINE* HOLLYWOOD . . .

MIKE: STEVE, TELL US WHAT IT'S LIKE TO LIE AROUND IN A HOSPITAL SETTING, BIG MACHER LIKE YOURSELF, BEING HANDLED BY DOCTORS, NURSES, ETC. LIKE AN OLD DECAYING PIECE OF FLUNKEN?

Good question, Mike. Not so bad. It's a nice break from always being the Big Guy in the room.

MIKE: DO THEY TELL YOU THE TRUTH ABOUT YOUR CONDITION?

Oh, no. They're not allowed to. Every day they tell me I look great. Doing great. Everything's great. Then some little old Jew comes in with a sewing kit and starts measuring me for a new suit. What's up with that?

MIKE: LAST QUESTION, STEVE. WHILE YOU'RE LYING THERE LIKE A LUMP CONTEMPLATING WHAT IT'S GOING TO BE LIKE TO BE DEAD FOREVER, WHICH AFTER A HUNDRED MILLION YEARS MEANS YOU'LL ONLY JUST HAVE BEGUN TO BE DEAD, WHAT DO YOU THINK ABOUT? COP ROCK? BAY CITY BLUES? WHAT WAS THAT OTHER STINKER OF YOURS, TOTAL SECURITY WITH JIM BELUSHI?

I don't really think about that, Mike. I think about forty eight years of great fun, great shows, great friends, great family, great life and much more to come because I'm going TO BEAT THIS FUCKIN' CANCER THING INTO THE GROUND!!!

MIKE: WELL, GOOD LUCK WITH THAT, STEVE. I'M SURE THAT IF YOU DO, NIKKI FINKE WILL FIND A WAY TO BURY YOU AGAIN.

Such is life, Mike. Such is life.

THANKS FOR TAKING WHAT LITTLE'S LEFT OF YOUR TIME, STEVE, TO TALK TO DEADLINE HOLLYWOOD. Thanks, yourself, Mike. And Mike? Drop dead before I do.

Sat, Jul 12, 2014 at 12:56 PM, Steven Bochco wrote:

Dear Friends,
Led by the infamous pole dancer, Dayna (The Flame Thrower) Bochco, I have been walked around by the pole this morning for the first of my two one-mile walks through the vibrant hallways and bi-ways of City Of Hope. Very adventurous. By night, it's another story: constant interruptions, checking of blood, vitals, machines malfunctioning, etc. All in all, though, I'm doing well. My spirits remain higher than piss on a plate. That may not seem very high to you, but the way they've got me hydrated in this joint, the plate looks more like the Stanley cup (which I always thought was a jock strap). Nevertheless, I am left with plenty of time to contemplate. Sometimes a good thing, sometimes not. For instance:

A GREAT DAY IN THE LIFE OF OUR CHIHUAHUA, SENOR PICO DE GALLO

1. He humps his reindeer toy (he – Pico – is neutered, so that's a dry situation. I haven't checked the reindeer. Would you?).
2. He eats. He begs for more.
3. He crawls under the covers and snoozes.
4. He goes outside and barks at the gardeners, and takes a shit in their general direction.
5. He plays with his toys.
6. He has another snooze in his bed.
7. If she's nowhere in sight, he eats Apple's left over food. (Apple is Dayna's rescue Chihuahua. Senor Pico De Gallo hates her. The feeling seems to be mutual.)
8. At dinnertime, he watches Dayna pole dance around the kitchen cooking dinner, begging for scraps. (Not Dayna, Pico.)

9. Dayna gives him a little medicine for his cough, or eye infection, or whatever.
10. He watches TV with us.
11. He gets his belly scratched.
12. Finally, it's time for bed, and Pico crawls under the covers like a nine-pound hot water bottle and goes to sleep. He breathes like a steam engine.
13. During the night, he wakes up three or four times, coughing, needing to pee and shit, and requiring any of several medications required to keep him from coughing, spitting, or puking. This is, of course, compounded by the other dog, Apple, who at only half Pico's weight, nevertheless costs me ten times as much to keep alive. The rate is about five thousand bucks a pound per year . . . .

So, this by and large is a great day in the life of Pico Bochco. By contrast, here is –

A *LOUSY* DAY IN THE LIFE OF STEVEN BOCHCO

1. Pole dancing around the corridors of City of Hope wearing a mask and occasionally squeezing off a fart. I look accusingly at some slumped over geeze in a wheel chair.
2. I eat.
3. I crawl under the covers of my custom, ten thousand dollar hospital bed that is too narrow to turn around in and snooze until some nurse's assistant comes into my room wanting to weigh me.
4. I go into the hallway, bark at the nurses, then go back to my room – pole in hand – and take a shit.
5. I play with my toys, when I can find the wires to plug them in.
6. I snooze some more.
7. Then I eat lunch.
8. Throughout the day, I take medicine. And more medicine. And more medicine. Chemo. Saline. Insulin. Other stuff.

9. I watch a little TV.
10. No belly scratching, but occasionally a nurse will stick a needle in my mid section.
11. I wake up three or four times during the night, needing to pee. Really pee. They hydrate me like The Hoover Dam.
12. I'm awakened another three or four times during the night by more Third World Individuals wanting my blood, my vitals, my weight – my weight? It's four o'clock in the fucking morning! Who cares what the fuck I weigh??

Alls I can say is, I'm glad I'm not a Chihuahua.

Lastly . . .

I have another ten hours or so of this current chemo regimen to go, and then two weeks of recovery from what it's supposed to do to me, which, basically, is to poison my cancer into remission. So the next several weeks do not promise to be a walk on the beach. Not even Brighton, let alone Mauna Kea.

The walk I did do today was with the afore-mentioned Pole Dancer Dayna (The Flame Thrower), along the corridors of City Of Hope. An amusing amble past people like me with masks, walkers, IV poles, wheelchairs, etc. I keep thinking to myself: what am I doing here? I feel fine.

Anyway, thanks to Phillip for lunch yesterday, and Suzie and Rich for dinner. I ate well, I did some work, and basically stayed with my mantra: embrace uncertainty, do meaningful work, and stay in the moment. You have all been so kind to me. Your words and your love and your spirit have lifted me above my fear. I want to beat this thing for all of you almost as much as for me, because the thought of not having you all in my life tears at my heart. I am in the care of wonderful doctors and nurses. It is also clear to me that I will need some luck. There's a reason there are statistics in life, and I am now one of them. The luck I'll require is that I become one of the good statistics. That's the uncertainty part. But until that picture becomes clearer, I will continue to stay with the program, both medically and emotionally, and hope to catch a fat, lucky break here and there.

I think I will, and if I do, it will in no small part be because of all of you. I don't understand that part of it very much. You know I'm not religious. You've read my previous updates. (Bad) humor is my default position. But I'm not afraid. At least not yet. Maybe because I just don't believe this is happening to me, or can happen to me, or that it will actually kill me.

Come tomorrow morning, I will try to have a little more fun with it and with you all. Because, honestly, doesn't this shit scare us all just a little? Maybe even more than a little? That shiver of mortality that pierces our bubble and makes us realize we're all going to be at the cliff's edge one of these days? So a collective laugh – a group recognition that we're all in this together – may make it easier for all of us. It sure makes it easier for me.

Love you all. Talk tomorrow.

Cancer Boy

On Jul 13, 2014, at 8:29 AM, Steven Bochco wrote:

Variety

BOCHCO'S TRUE BLOOD
LOS ANGELES – JULY 13, 2014

Steven Bochco, who used to be famous as the uber co-creator and Executive Producer of such seminal series as Griff, Cop Rock, Bay City Blues, Total Security, and other well known stiffs, and who, today, would much rather simply be known as the creator of Uber, has taken up short term residence at City Of Hope, consulting with the world famous medical facility about ways to economically increase its supply of blood products (particularly marrow) to an increasingly blood thirsty television audience who seems not to be able to get enough of the stuff. Including, apparently, Bochco himself, who recently discovered he is in need of a bone marrow replacement. Urgent calls were placed to Art's Deli in Studio City, Izzie's in Santa Monica, and Nate and Al's in Beverly Hills, but all potential bone marrow donors had already been consumed by the legions of ravenous Jews who roam the Sunday corridors of Los Angeles' gourmet delis like ghouls at a bar mitzvah. And so, as a last resort, Bochco finds himself, attached to his chemo bag, wandering the halls of City Of Hope whose deli, while, sincere, leaves much to be desired and, even more so than the other more renowned establishments, finds itself under-stocked with a sufficiency of said marrow.

Bochco, long known as a blood sucking writer producer himself, is no stranger to the ghouls and vampires that inhabit our industry. Mr. Bochco will be in residence at City of Hope for two more weeks, before taking a brief hiatus in West Los Angeles, at which point he will return to City Of Hope in consultation with the world famous Dr. B. Stoker, and they will once again commence additional treatment. Should that treatment have its desired result, a search will commence for an anonymous sucker (er, excuse me, donor) who will contribute some portion of his/her marrow to the cause of furthering middling television production. Should this transplant work, Mr. Bochco will expand his oeuvre toward such good works as a remake of Blood Simple, How Red Is My Valley, and Red Is The Color of My True Love's Hair.

Then, of course, there is the great old Negro spiritual Reginald Hudlin taught him many years ago:
White Cells
Red Cells
Black Cells, too,
Let de chemo kill the bad ones,
Let the good ones through.

Amen!!

Love to you all on this Sunday Bloody Sunday!
Cancer Boy

On July 14, 2014, Steven Bochco wrote:

Nothing much else to report, loved ones. Have started on my new chemo regimen that'll last forty-eight hours, so we'll see how that all goes. Then two weeks of recovery, back for more, etc. etc. The search commences for a donor. They say they want a twenty-five year old male with a perfect match. I'll take a broken down old ersatz spiritualist sister with — oh, wait, that train has rattled out of the station already. In that case, if I can't get my wife, or some twenty five year old stud, I'll go with anything that has a pulse, a healthy marrow, and — what the hell — a nice pair of tits.
Love you all, from the Vacation Spa formerly known as Duarte,
Stevie Bee

From: Steven Bochco
Sent: Tuesday, July 15, 2014 11:00 AM
Subject: Chemo

The first week I kind of skated through this chemo shit. I thought, piece of cake. Then they hit me with the second blast. Still. Pretty good. Sort of feeling like Super Jew. Then, yesterday, the Chemo Monster sidled up behind me and hit me with a two by four. Then last night, the two by four became a four by six. Fever, chills, aches, etc. I've been weak as a kitten, sleeping all day, achy and out of sorts. I'm told this is a function of my white cells being almost down to zero. At some point, those white cells will begin to regenerate, and my count will climb back up. When that happens, I'll feel stronger. In the meantime, the thought of food is pretty yukky. The thought of anything other than sleeping is pretty yukky. Even vanilla ice cream and a little pound cake isn't enough to lift my spirits. But this is temporary, and I'm sure I'll go through several more bouts like this before this adventure of mine comes to its successful conclusion. Point being, if you don't hear from me for a few days, don't worry. I'm just a little low on energy. Well, okay. A lot low on energy. But I'll pop back up.

Anyway, dear friends, this is the first report I haven't been up to amusing you with some sort of stupid Deadline Hollywood or Variety mock up, but you gotta take the good with the bad. It ain't a sprint. It's a marathon.

Love you all and will keep you posted.

Chemo boy

On July 16, 2014, Steven Bochco wrote:

More musings from City Of Hope, Duarte California . . .

When my doctors told me I had leukemia, and would need a bone marrow transplant in order to survive, one of the first questions to arise was whether I had any siblings. Yes, I said, an older sister. Well, Dr. Forman said, we'll get her tested, because there's a one in four chance she could be a perfect match. When I passed this information along to her in hopes she might consider being tested (a simple blood test, which many of my friends had alrady submitted to), I heard nothing. When I asked her, days later, if she'd gotten my email, or if it had somehow fallen through the cracks, here was her reply:

"Of all the ways I could be there for you, all the parts of myself I could offer, I cannot offer you what you ask. I have spent many years healing my body from the toxic effects of emotional and physical abuse. I must now honor this body that I've worked so hard to heal, in the way that is the most beneficial for me and my family." – Joanna Rachins.

Hmmm. "Toxic effects of emotional and physical abuse."

Wow. Almost seventy years later, that's a mouthful. Having grown up in the same family, I can certainly attest to the fact that the Bochco clan wasn't exactly the Jewish upper West Side version of the Beaver Cleaver family. Nevertheless . . . "The toxic effects of emotional and physical abuse."

Well, dear friends, I have to address this, finally and once and for all, so I can truly put it behind me. After all, no matter how complicated and twisted a relationship one has with an only sibling, there are times one has to open the windows, air out the linens, and clean out the closets. I have been in this hospital bed now for eleven days, fighting a potentially fatal disease – as in, I might die – and that paragraph up there has continued to take up more of my chemo-addled attention than it deserves. And so, with this writing, the hope is I will banish it forever.

First: Abuse and toxicity.

When I was in Junior High School, I was walking a girl home from school and got mugged. Had the crap kicked out of me by five other kids. Don't know why they picked me, maybe because I was with a girl, but it was humiliating. Black eye, bloody nose, etc. Anyway, I got the girl home, then ran all the way back to my apartment, holding back tears, waiting for a little TLC from dear old Mom, whose first words upon seeing my face where, "Where the hell were you?" "Walking a girl home," I sniffled. And then she did the oddest thing. She whacked me hard across the face. "Why were you walking a girl home when you should've been doing your homework?"

So much for Tender Loving Care. So much for showering affection on the younger brother. I recollect locking myself in my room and not coming out for damn near a day. And dear old Mom, whose vocabulary never included the words "I'm sorry," never quite managed to understand why I was so upset. Was that physical abuse? I guess. Certainly it was emotional abuse. But here's the thing: at a certain point in life, we get to decide who we are. Victims? Or winners? Doers or Whiners? Passives or aggressives? We get to build a new identity. We're stuck with some of our genes. We can't escape all of them, and we should be glad we can't. Some of them hold us in good stead over the years. But there's all kinds of work we can do on our own behalf that redefines us as something more than just our parents' kids.

The world is full of inconceivable abuse. African girls raped and sold. Children fleeing violence and risking violence to come to America with no hope other than the ineffable confidence of youthful ambition that somehow, their lives will be bettered if they just don't lie down and give in. Sometimes, desperation translates to courage translates to hope.

Countless children are being abused, beaten and tortured every day by horrendous parents with no proper values, no maturity, and no role models to help them be any better than what they themselves have become. We have become consumers of casual outrage. We kill people. We shoot them. We bludgeon them. We tear off their limbs. We behead them. We execute them in front of their familiies. Can you imagine? This takes the notion of abuse to a new level of consciousness. Thank you, CNN. Thank you Fox News. Thank you MSNBC. Thank you You Tube and Google. You have given us access to the most incredible, moment-to-moment, 24/7 documentation of violence and mayhem the world has ever seen.

Now, THAT, ladies and gentlemen, is abuse. Toxic and otherwise.

Now let's talk Toxicity for a moment. Toxicity is poisonous. Anything toxic is not so good. Though candidly, the disease I'm being treated for wouldn't have the cure rate it has unless we were willing to submit to a level of toxicity that damn near kills us before it makes us better. So even toxicity is a complicated notion. But let's just stick to the uncomplicated notion of it: Tobacco smoke. Toxic. Pesticides. Toxic. Fracking. Toxic. Stuff we throw in the oceans that choke and kill our marine life. Toxic. How about toxic air? There's plenty of toxic to go around. I bring this up because of these words:

"Of all the ways I could be there for you, all the parts of myself I could offer, I cannot offer you what you ask. I have spent many years healing my body from the toxic effects of emotional and physical abuse. I must now honor this body that I've worked so hard to heal, in the way that is the most beneficial for me and my family." – Joanna Rachins.

Okay, I don't think I have to belabor the point. Every. Single. One. Of. Us. Has had our ration of toxicity and abuse. Ask Nelson Mandella. He had a few stories to tell. Ask any black man or woman about toxicity and abuse. Oh, you'll get an earful. And I'm not talking about a hundred years ago. I'm talking about yesterday. Profiling. Police brutality. Cops lying to cover up the daily atrocities they perform or witness. Beatings. Broken bones. Broken psyches. Have you ever had your very identity stripped from you, to the point that you suddenly realized you were less than human and that your human tormentor could absolutely do with you what they wanted? Nazi Germany, anyone? Send In The Kleins? Talk about toxicity and abuse.

Or check out the current mess in the Middle East. Toxic and Abusive don't quite do justice to what they're doing to each other over there.

Which would you rather be? A spider in Dayna Bochco's shower, or some poor fifteen year old shmuck in a Conga line of Arab prisoners being marched off to a beheading (your own?) 'Cause either way, you're about to meet your Maker. (Personally, I'd rather be the spider, but that's another story . . .)

But here's the good news, and it is good. In all the history of mankind, men and women have OVERCOME this mindless, grinding abuse and toxicity because of something called the Human Spirit. Don't exactly know what that means, but I think we all know it – and bow down to it – when we see it – the man or woman who overcomes inconceivable odds in order to achieve something worthy. Something groundbreaking. I've said before, and said it often, I am not religious. I don't believe in God. But there's something, yes? Maybe it's just – ha! Just – the cumulative energy and love that we all bring to the party. Not that we throw it around thoughtlessly, but we have it in us – like a secret bank account – that we can reach into when necessary and make a little withdrawal to give to someone who in the moment needs it more than we do. And I think most of us know, at the end of the day, it'll come back to us with interest. Compounded, as it were. Think of it as the Bit Coin Theory of Love. Doesn't really exist to where you can touch it, maybe, and maybe you're not even sure you believe it, because you can't see it. But somehow we know it's out there. It has to be. How could we be here for each other if it wasn't?

All right, I could go on. Hospital days and nights are lengthy, and the brain tends to meander. I'll try to get to the point, here.

I have a sister. My only sibling. We go back over seventy years. Used to steal comic books together and read 'em in bed Sunday morning. Like all siblings, we fought. I was three years younger, enthralled with her older friends, always wanting to be part of their mysterious rights and passages. Good luck with that. What I usually wound up with was a finger in the eye, a smack under the table, some other subtle form of – abuse? Toxicity? Nah. Just usual brother-sister shit.

You don't get to choose your siblings. They just come as part of the package you're handed. But they're yours, like 'em or not. Sometimes you're lucky and you really really like 'em. Sometimes it's a mixed bag. Like 'em sometimes, sometimes not so much. But we grow up with them, we are raised to believe blood is thicker than water, and every once in a while, it turns out it's actually true.

So, this sister of mine. That would be you, Joanna. You total fucking phony who has spent her whole life talking the talk and NEVER ONCE REALLY WALKING THE WALK when it counted for a damn thing. Joanna Bochco Frank Rachins. Lot of different identities there, not to mention the self-selected ones. Spiritualist. Healer. Transcendental meditator. Teacher. Giver of Wisdom. Many years spent in study. Trips to India. Lots of spirituality. (Look it up on Face Book, kids.) Me, personally, I never quite got it myself. Seemed way too complicated. I never really felt the need to fill a void. I had what I had, I knew what I knew, believed what I believed. Frightened as I always was of death, I always figured when the time came, I'd reach down somewhere deep and come up with whatever I needed to get me through it with a modicum of dignity and strength. Dying is, after all, the last great act of parenting we engage in. And who wants to be a lousy role model? How hard could it be, really. Did you actually have to do all that studying, and narcissistic obsessing, and self-realizing to know that the spider dies; the beautiful sparrow dies. As Phil Stutz (who's probably gonna smack me for even writing this screed) says, we're all of us – ALL – in the Hallway to Death. Straight Shot. Door at the end. "Uh, Bochco, Steven? We believe it's your turn, Dude. Step up. Walk Through. Don't let the door hit you on the ass on your way out."

How hard could it be? A lot harder thinking about it, apparently, than actually doing it. Has anyone ever gotten out alive yet? Call me if you know someone. I want to talk to him/her.

Or, in the alternative, if anyone knows a good Fortune Teller in Duarte, get me their name.

Anyway, in the fullness of life, as is often the way of these things, one sibling gets lucky; catches the brass ring, as it were, and finds himself in a position to do things in the temporal world, like support his parents, bring them to live in L.A., pay some of their bills, and – inevitably – when our Dad passes (remember that last great act of parenting?) buy Mom a home and a guarantee of security it is my great gift to be able to give.

And in the meantime, I was also able to give my brother-in-law a career – we tried writing first (not so good); we tried directing (also not so good, as I recall); but acting – LA LAW – came around, and Alan found his niche. And Joanna, though convinced that her little brother didn't trust her (as she revealed to the world in a People Magazine article in 1988- look it up for laughs), and that our parents had showered all their attention on her younger brother, also got a nice bit of a career out of the show. All in all, not so bad.

Toxic?
Abusive?
Or just a plain old garden variety version of Envy?

And then, inevitably, when bad times reared and LA LAW ended its eight year run, and the money train of a hit series got derailed, there were the loans, a college education to help out with, and much, much more. Not to mention half of our mom's estate that I also gave to her. This stuff may sound petty, but hey – add it all up, and it came to MILLIONS of dollars of aid, sibling to sibling, because where I came from (like it or not) blood actually was thicker than water. And no good deed EVER went unpunished.

So I've rambled on too long with these Musings From Duarte . . . But if these are my last days on the planet, I'm simply not going to pass up the luxury of finally saying what I think of my older, passive-aggressive, endlessly envious, pseudo-spiritual pathetic loser of a sister.

Have to flat out say it, Joanna. You weren't worth the effort. It turns out, after all that shared life, shared resources, the countless ways I gave you guys a life and then bailed you out when you couldn't even figure out how to make that work, that when push came to shove, you threw me the spiritual finger. I didn't even know there was a middle finger in transcendental meditation. How naïve of me. Why would God have given us a middle finger without the manual on how best to use it?

Be that as it may, turns out my blood actually WAS thinner than your water.

Okay, dear friends. Sorry to have taken so much of you time today. I'll shoot for pithy and amusing or downright filthy tomorrow. And with each day, I know I am closer to seeing you all again, which keeps me going. But today . . . today was the day to get a lot of dark shit off my chest, stuff that could only hold me back. I haven't lost my temper much in life. (Don't tell that to the networks, they'll call you — and me — a liar!) Hell, doesn't even feel like I lost it today. But I unraveled some old smelly lies today, and absolutely burned a bridge that needed burning a long time ago. They say fire is cleansing. And if I'm going out of the picture any time soon, I want to be blazing as I go.

More tomorrow. And lots shorter, I promise.
Cancer Boy

On Jul 19, 2014, at 3:54 PM, Steven Bochco wrote:

After the dramatics of chemo, and blood letting of the emotional type as well, things have quieted down. Fatigue has settled in like the early morning marine layer over the Palisades. Coastal Eddie, as it were. I force myself to eat three meagers a day,(a baked potato and a protein shake as we speak) which I wouldn¹t even do if not for the intrepid Dayna and her stinging whip. I never knew I liked that kind of discipline that much. Must be why I married her. Oh, no, not the whip. (Please, the whip. The whip. Maybe a little spanking first? Dayna: Beg, you worthless Jew, beg. And so, helplessly, adoringly, I obey. Please, may I have some more whip, I whimper to the Goddess?)

I've received a platelet transfusion and a regular blood transfusion, which gave me a shot of energy today. I almost look my normal self, or so the intrepid Dominatrix Dayna tells me. Showering is a big event. Brunhilda comes in with a soft brush and cleans me up real good while Dayna stands back flicking the switch. Brunhilda shivers. Quite a sight. There's a lot of Brunhilda to shiver. Sort of like a slow motion break up of an ice flow. Impressive.

Napping is big on my list of activities. I've recently (last two days) added small walks back into my itinerary. I am monitored all day and all night by lovely hospital workers who gently poke, prod, and steal a little blood here and a little blood there at all hours of the day and night. My white count is virtually at zero, where the chemo wants it to be, hence the blood transfusion. The hope is my body will start to manufacture some of the little buggers on its own to the point where they can send me home for a little while. We'll see. I'm taking it day by day. In the meantime, they're extremely conscientious monitoring for every little infection, hence the IV bags of antibiotics, anti-fungals, and anti-siblings. (Oops, who said that? Not me. I'm over that. Really? Almost.)

So that's pretty much it, folks. Not much more to report except that early this morning, not asleep but sleepy-lazy, I was seeing you all in a private dining room, with me thanking you all for the collective effort which saved my life. I believe that day will come soon, and it will be the best day of my wonderful life.

Enjoy your weekend. Far as I'm concerned, you've more than earned it.

Much love to all,
Cancer Boy

On Jul 21, 2014, at 10:12 AM, Steven Bochco wrote:

Well, folks, the follicles are finally catching up with the program. Got up today, brushed my tooth, washed my face, put a little water in my hair, dried off with a towel, and my black t-shirt suddenly went white. With hair! My hair! WTF! I'm in it now, kids. No turning back.
Early morning results on white cell count are in, and they're still in the basement, so another bag of Gogetemtiger is on the schedule, along with a blood transfusion. They said it should take about a week for those numbers to really spike back up, so hopefully by week's end I'll have something resembling an immune system that they can send me home with for a few days so you can all laugh at me close up and personal.

Yesterday was travel day. Jesse Bee headed down to Las Ventanas for three days for some quick R&R, Rick and Paula and Dana and Matt and Fred and Nancy all returned from their various exhausting trips to Italy, so I figure our Industry will be more or less up and running in the next 24 to 48 hours as these revelers pretend like it was okay to miss two weeks of work. (It was. Trust me).

Mine is now a waiting game. How do you spell boredom? N-A-P. N-E-W-S-P-A-P-E-R. H-O-S-P-I-T-A-L F-O-O-D. M-E-D-S. But no pain, no nausea, just rest and wait for those numbers to come up. And when they do, Cancer Boy is out the door, sprinting (Ha!) for the car to whisk him back to the high rent district from whence he came. (83rd Street?) I'll check with the docs, but I suspect, you'll be pleased to know, that with my white cells so low, visitations will be commensurately low as well. The scenic drive to Duarte can be as long as 90 minutes if you catch bad traffic (an oxymoron, I understand), and I would only wish that on any of you if I was going out of the picture which, so far as I can tell, is not happening yet. So, unless you're dying to visit my hair as a separate event from my corporeal (corporeal: that took an hour by itself to write; more on that later) self, it's probably smarter to wait a week and check me out in my natural habitat.

Later in the day, I am looking forward to about thirty bathroom visits, almost all of the standing up squirting into a plastic bottle variety. The bucket brigade is forming as we speak. Hazmat suits abound. Generally speaking, I can handle the sit down event on my own. They have a BIG POLICY here at COH about preventing falls. I guess the patients around here get blinded by hair falling into their eyes, or too much Attavan or morphine, and knees go a-buckling. And when you don't have white cells, I guess it can get a little messy. At the first sound of those knobby knees chunking the floor, every vampire from the second floor is up here in a bat's breath, singing Fangs For The Memories. (Sorry. My only excuse for that one being I still have chemo brain.) So, every other day they want you to watch a video about falling, or sign a piece of paper saying you watched it. I fell down watching it the last time, and I still have so many puncture marks on my throat that I think this time I'll just sign.

Speaking of chemo brain. I guess it's a real thing, but since I normally drink so much wine it's hard to notice the difference. But now that I'm on enforced sobriety, which sucks the wet one, I might add, I notice that it takes me probably an hour to write one of these little missives. Every single word (not kidding) has multiple errors of spelling; my fingers just don't seem to work right; so I go back after every word and correct it. Then, I realize I fucked up the correction. Ah well. Just another way to kill some time here in Duarte. It sure ain't Margaritaville. (I just respelled *that* word four times!)

Okay, I admit it. It wasn't very funny today. You read it just because you had to, and it's early, and you're having a cup of coffee and so what the hell. My excuse is, it's early a.m., (or it was when I started), not a lot has happened to far, and I have a hunch there won't be much in the way of melodramatics until Act Two of this Three Act Play. And, as Dana Walden always cautions, if you don't have lines in the play, SHUT UP!!

So, SHUTTING UP FOR NOW (but you know me — not for long — and loving you all more than you care to know,
I remain, temporarily,
Cancer Boy

On Tuesday, July 22, 2014, Steven Bochco wrote:

Well, folks, after shedding like an Afghan for two days, I went for the Lex Luther look! My hair hasn't been this short since I was eight months old!
Love you all. The picture says it all.

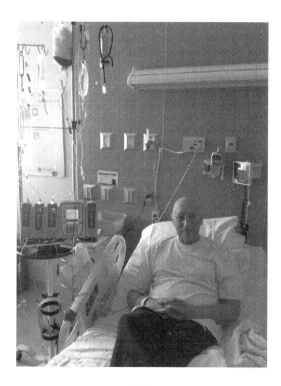

From: Steven Bochco **Sent:** Wednesday, July 23, 2014 2:39 PM
Subject: The Borders of Boredom and Beyond

Dear Friends,
I realize I've fallen down on the job somewhat. I think it's because True Boredom and Fatigue have settled in. And there's not much interesting to write about either one of those topics. Here's my typical day, halfway into my third week of this adventure. Wake up. Pee. Get back into bed. Doze. Pee again. (Usually I get out of bed first.) Negotiate breakfast with Dayna, who insists I eat. I have no appetite. She always wins. How does that happen? Then, after a little breakfast, I climb back into bed to read The NY Times. By the time my ass hits the sheets, I can't keep my eyes open. So what the fuck? Where am I going? I sleep. Then the docs come by in their white coats. Any pain? Any swelling? They listen to my chest. They listen to my back. They listen to my stomach. Why? It's not like there's Books On Tape in there. Then they tell me that, basically, nothing is going on. My white cell count is still pretty much zeroed out. But not to worry. They'll come roaring back. And when they do, I can go home for a few days before coming back and starting the same routine all over again. Oh Happy Day! Okay. Now, it's about nine thirty am. Let's give the NY Times another shot. ZZZzzzzzzzzzzzz . . . . . . Then the nurse's assistant comes in. Time for vital signs. I have been here for seventeen days. I have had my vital signs checked one thousand four hundred and sixty three times. They're the same every time. Temperature normal, BP 105 over 65 thereabouts, and blood oxygen level around 97. I randomly wonder what's filling up that other three percent. Maybe that's where my white cells are hiding. Now begins lunch negotiation, in earnest. She Who Must Be Obeyed will not take no for an answer. I consider it a win when I can get away with a frozen vanilla protein shake.

Afternoon: Rinse my teeth for the fifth time. Suck on an anti-fungal. Perform ritual ablutions of an internal nature. Take a shower. Change into a fresh set of sweats and a T. Then I stare at this strange bald man in the mirror. He looks familiar, but not really. Something's off. Maybe it's the hair. Yeah, that's it. The hair is off. As in gone.

Anyway, you get it . . . This is worse than one of those Xmas letters you get from Cousin Lorene. We went pumpkin shopping! We chopped down a Xmas tree! We had all the cousins up to the cabin for a reunion dinner. Uncle Barney fell in the lake! Cousin Earl got soused on likker, decided to chop some firewood, and cut his big toe off with a hatchet. What a sketch!!

So I guess here's the deal: You're lying in the hospital, you have a potentially fatal disease, and you're so fucking bored you can't even muster up a good scare about it. But through this gauze of boredom, you get these wonderful emails from your friends and family telling you how cute you look like a shaved rat; and you realize that there's a world of love and friendship out there hammocking your body and your spirit, and suddenly you feel like a nine year old kid about to bust out crying.

Or maybe it's just the drugs. Which, for some of you, may actually be of interest. I know they are for me. Xanax. Vicodin. Attavan. Ambien. In fact, I was in sufficient discomfort the other morning around three am, that they gave me 2mg of morphine. Holy Shit! It took me out of the game for over twenty-four hours. So, when all else fails, I whine a little, they give me drugs, and I slide down the rabbit hole for a while. But honestly, you can keep the morphine. That's a little rich for my feeble blood. I still miss my vino.

Okay, dearests. I hope something a little more interesting pops up in the next couple of days I can report about. I have to hold up my end out here in Duarte, you know.

Much love to all,
Cancer Boy

Sent: Thursday, July 24, 2014

Dearest Friends,
Leukemia Limbo means you're waiting around with your thumb up your ass for your white cells to make a move. Right now, they're bunkered down somewhere near zero land, kind of like Hezbollah in the tunnels, with no particular inclination to come out and start doing the Hora. Must be very cozy in there. *Why should I come out? They're just gonna kick the shit out of me again, when I do.*

The docs are giving me a daily bag of medication called neupogen designed to kick-start the little fuckers, but so far they've been wise to the ruse and are lying low. So I lie here, watching my water drip and my antibiotics drop.

Thursday of the third week, and I have to admit, it is getting old. Thank God for Dayna Bochco, who sits in the next room reading and watching movies, and periodically comes in to berate me for not eating enough. I did avail myself of a bowl of matzoh ball soup at lunch. Basically tasted like boiled cardboard. I'm holding out some hope that by Saturday/Sunday, these pesky white cells will start to make their guest appearance so that perhaps by mid next week I'll be home for a few days. We shall see.

Here's something straight out of the Noel Coward playbook. You get a little diarrhea (who can even spell it, much less look at it?). So the nurse leaves you a little plastic hat inside the bowl so next time you poop they can analyze it for infection, bacteria, all that good stuff. So you go to the bathroom and leave your charming little specimen behind. Nurse comes and collects it. Compliments you on the way out. Oh, nice little dump. (Or words to that effect.) Good job, Mr. Bochco. Who's Mr. Bochco, I say. That specimen there belongs to someone who snuck in here when I wasn't looking and left that humiliating and pungent dump with my name on it. Find that man and have him flogged. Yes, Mr. Bochco, she says, and scurries out with my specimen firmly in her grasp, tendrils of vague odor trailing in her wake. Is there no shame? Apparently, here at City Of Hope, none.

Any moral to this particular story? I wish there was, but alas, no. You are simply a specimen, to be poked, prodded, examined and moved to the next medical activity. I'm actually getting used to it. It builds character. (Theirs, not mine.)

Not sure I have much else to report on this Thursday afternoon from Duarte where, from what I'm told, it's a hundred degrees outside. I've been in 72 degrees Fahrenheit for eighteen days, so I have nothing to converse with the locals about. Should anything anywhere near reasonably exciting occur in the next six hours, I promise to pass it along. But, as I said to the nurse who went to collect my specimen, don't hold your breath.

Love you all, and thanks to those of you who schlepped to City Of Hope to give of your bodily fluids on my behalf. Needless to say, I am touched and grateful. The check is in the mail.

Cancer Boy

Actually, Rene Auberjonois suggests CANCER MAN, and his faithful sidekick CHEMO BOY. I think I may go with that for a while. Sounds more aggressive.

Sent July 25th, 2014

Well, today was basically a pretty shitty day in glorious Duarte. Lots of fever, body aches and pains, and mostly sleeping. I must have slept eighteen hours today. Of course, drugs help. Vicodin. Xanax. Attavan. Ambien. The bad news is, you feel like a shitsicle. The good news is, you don't give a shit. Excuse me, you got another Vicodin down there? How about one of those nifty little Xanax. And, hey,

Attavan is no slouch either, particularly when you mix it up with a small amount of Ambien. That's why they call this place City Of Hope. Not because you're hoping they're going to save your life, but because you're hoping they'll give you so much drugs YOU WON'T GIVE A SHIT!! The only drug they haven't figured out for me yet is the one that makes my teeth stop chattering. That's no fun. I feel like I've escaped from a Stephen King novel.

Today I kept postponing phone calls. Tell him I'll call back in half an hour. Did I say half an hour? I meant forty-five minutes. Did I say I'd take a little walk around the halls in thirty minutes? I actually meant an hour. That said, the good news is that this fever is stimulating my white blood count, which is the whole concept here: Nuke these guys into submission, then let them start spontaneously regenerating. So, hopefully, the body is beginning to respond the way it's supposed to.

Think of this: Who is your worst enemy? The person you least like in the whole world? Someone you wouldn't mind see going through a little bout of this humbling, scary disease? I don't know about you, but there's a few names on my list over the years that, at least twenty or twenty five years ago, I might've signed up for this particular tour. But the new me says no more. The new me (Mahatma Fuckin Ghandi) doesn't wish this on anyone. Putin? I'm thinking. Scalia? I might make an exception. But honestly, fuck those guys anyway. They have to live in their own skin, and that's punishment enough.

I have no room in my heart for such nasty wishes. And that is because I am a fucking saint. I move among the people in my mask, pushing my pole, offering prunes to the weary and constipated. May I wash your feet today, Sir? Okay, don't get snarky. Any chance you might wash MY feet?

Haven't eaten much today. The Bitch Goddess of Nutrition (aka Dayna) has been very annoyed with me. But hey. I have fuckin' cancer. I gotta take a stand somewhere, right? Otherwise, I'm just another old henpecked Jew. Which I guess I am, anyway. Now that she's gone to bed, maybe I'll eat a nutrition bar or something.

Obviously, not much to report today. It was still 72 degrees inside City Of Hope. If I'm lucky (?) I will continue to be a little feverish, and my white count will rise and maybe I can come home next week for a few days. I'll keep you posted, obviously.

Much love to all.
Cancer Man and His Faithful Sidekick Chemo Boy

Sent Saturday, July 26, 2014:

I guess this chemo works as advertised. They've been giving me a daily bag of this drug called Nupogen (don't know how spell it, but I can tell you it kicks the shit out of you: fever, shakes, chattering teeth, the works.) Yesterday was the worst. Nurses were all over me with compresses, hot blankets, you name it.

Then, last night I busted a sustained fever of 103 degrees. The nurses earned their pay last night. But the good news is, when I woke up this morning, the fever was pretty much gone, and my white blood cell count had gone from 2 (it'd been at one the previous day) to SEVEN! That's good news, folks. And all the other numbers were up, as well. Platelets over 30, hbg over 9 . . . in short, a good report card. A hopeful start to the day. Now if I don't fall down and break my crown, I may get out of here next week.

Under the category of six degrees of separation, how many people do you think you know who have or have had cancer? I'll bet it's a staggeringly high number. And I'll bet equally high is the number of folks you know who have cancer who have survived it. I bring this up because all of you have been so encouraging to me in telling me stories about multiple friends who are cancer survivors. 'Course, we're not going to dwell on those who didn't survive. That's not positive. I haven't done the math, but I'm betting we all know more survivors than not. I think every single one of you has shared a story with me that has a happy ending. And every time I get a little blue, I think about all those survivors out there living happy, normal lives, and I think to myself, "I can do this. I can."

So as this is Saturday (weekend) I won't check in with you unless I have something really interesting to report, such as my toes have fallen off; or my hair has grown back green. But these new numbers are very encouraging, and if I keep it up, I could be home soon for a few days.

Much love,
Cancer man and his faithful sidekick, Chemo Boy!

On Jul 27, 2014, at 6:47 PM, "Steven Bochco" wrote:

Well, just when I didn't think it could get any weirder . . . it got weirder . . . I spent the craziest forty-eight hours yet here at glorious City Of Hope, and it turns out the joke's on me. It was only 24. When I wrote about my fever-driven night of the day before, the fever had finally broken and I felt strong enough — and lucid enough — to write my little MacBook Air prose ball and lob it out there. Not exactly the next edition of a Dicken's Penny Novel, I grant you, but hey — you gotta go with what you got. So, then, because a fever is kind of like a crazy woman you can't get out of your system, the fever came back. Steve, want to take another ride on the whirly bird? No, please. One ride was enough. Well hang on tight, Slugger, because here we go again. And the fever came back with a vengeance: same stuff, 103 fever, terrible shakes, teeth chattering, bones feeling like they were being expertly worked over by Guido The Knucklebuster. Nurses in and out. Whisper whisper whisper. Would you like some drugs. Uh, let me think about that for a second. Oh, okay . . .

So now (I think) in rapid succession, I had a vicodin and two tylenol to knock down the fever. Lots of luck. This bitch had me by the throat. Now more teeth chattering. More bone aching. Nurses in and out. Vital signs. Blood pressure down somewhere around my socks. Course, in the meantime, because the idea of eating food made me vomit, they put me on an IV line to pump delicioso food into my system. Yippee. Except this bag they hung up there: Big ugly sucker, filled with what looked like a mix of urine and lemonade. Okay. Not going to look up there anymore.

Dayna had wisely chosen to take a day off and went home to do some chores, have dinner out, take a break from a whining husband who refuses to eat, and just generally check in with this other life we supposedly have outside City Of Hope. So now I am in full--blown drug-fever hell, I've passed uneasily between consciousness and unconsciousness maybe twenty times, and finally, I am so weak I don't know which end is up. Some hours earlier my cell phone had signaled me: Steve, open me up, I got a nice picture of your wife having dinner out WITH OTHER PEOPLE, AND NONE OF 'EM ARE YOU, HOTSHOT! So okay, yeah, I opened it up and, as advertised, the pictures were very nice. Then I passed out again. Next think I know the nurses are in my room. Whisper whisper whisper. Hot blankets? Cold compress? More drugs? I say look guys, this has been a grueling night. What I'd really like to do is change my clothes and wipe myself down. Imagine the level of humility I have achieved in just a couple of weeks that my sister hasn't even come close to in forty years. There's gotta be some very high altitude Himalayan chakra obeisance thing going on here, because she's out there teaching this ridiculous shit, and I GOT IT!! Irony of ironies. I'm really the Guru in the family, and she's just the one who shleps along behind selling the snake oil.

But seriously. I digress. So here's lowly humble me being ministered to by these lovely Phillipino nurses who are changing my clothes, wiping me down, making my bed, etc. And I am so exhausted and whipped, I don't care. Sure, you want to touch my ball sack? Be my guest. What are you gonna do with it. You say you wanna run a wash cloth through my breezeway? Sure, no problem. You want to hold my hand so I don't fall down and piss myself while I'm pissing myself? Come on down, room for everyone. Who's that old crone in the hallway with the babushka shuffling around the perimeter OF MY FUCKIN SPACE?! It's a visitor. She says she's your sister. Tell her to go down to the fourth floor and wash everyone's feet. NOW!

Okay, so none of that is true, I grant you. But it was pretty weird, anyway.

So, finally, they get me cleaned up, clothes changed, and back in bed. Great. I'm just snuggling into some Attavan-induced fog when the cell rings. Its Dayna. Hi Honey. How're you feeling. So so. Where are you. At the restaurant with the Sikkings and Woottons. What? Can't be. It's nine in the morning. No. It's nine o'clock at night. No. I went to bed nine at night, then the nice ladies cleaned me up when they came to do their five a.m thing . . . I'm missing like a big chunk of time here. Yes, you are, Honey Bun. Go back to sleep. So that was yesterday. And I will swear to you it was also the day before. But obviously, I'm the least reliant source here.

The good news is, they're taking my off this horrendous drug Neupogen, which is what causes all that bone chattering fever in the first place, because my white cell count is now over the line where it needs to be. It's another trick. I know it. Just around the corner some other ghoul awaits. When I meet it I will kill it.

Love you all. Happy Sunday. Yes, by now I'm convinced it really is Sunday.

Cancer Man, and Faithful Sidekick Chemo Boy.

On July 28th, 2014, Steven Bochco wrote:

I have to desperately try and organize this shit in my brain that right now doesn't seem of have an on-off switch.

Last night. Three a.m. I wake up. There's something very strange about my room. My IV pole with all the computers lit up looks like a space ship, looming over me. I look around. It doesn't feel as if anyone's at home. But I have to take care of some pressing bowel business. So I get out of the bed, forgetting, of course, that I am tethered to Apollo 15, and halfway into the bathroom, which sorta looks like the bathroom here (but honestly? not really), and I think I started to try to get my pants off — good luck — I was tangled in more wires than Kukla Fran and Ollie and then a familiar woman's voice out of nowhere, somewhere — Dayna. Steven, you okay? Oh sure, Steven said, knowing the jig was up, I'd been found out — but don't come in. Really got it all covered. Really? Now there are other voices. Where the fuck where they all hiding out? Everything all right? I think this is an approximation of what happened. I was half in half out of my sweat pants, helplessly tangled in wires and pissing all over my tee shirt, and squirting streams of high quality shit all over my pants. I say high quality because there hadda be a lotta good drugs left in that doodoo. I'll leave the imagery at that. Except for this: you'd think by the time you got to be a seventy year old man you'd have figured out your bathroom routines such that 1. It's your own bathroom, so on the rare occasion you do make a slight miscalculation, or you feel like taking a quick ride down Wilshire driving the porcelain bus, you got it covered. Who's going to know? 2. You're seventy years old, you have the worst flu of your life, and what the fuck. You camp out in your snazzy bathroom, do all your dark doodies, and the next day a wonderful maid makes it all go away. Ah, but one never thinks about the hospital — the total care — in return for which they demand your total lack of privacy. They want the four-digit code to your asshole. The three-digit code to whatever's going on in your bladder at all times. Anyway, you get my drift. I was not ready for a high-grade hallucinatory experience of that magnitude fueled by lack of sleep, 103 degree fever, lots of hospital grade drugs that, all wrapped in a package, turned into what? Three minutes in a Ryan Murphy movie? (Dana, tell him if he wants me to do it, I'm available, but it'll cost him.) Anyway, I think what happened after was, they somehow got me cleaned up, but I knew it would do me no good. I was in another universe of rocket ships, rooms that could change into whatever they wanted, and people who looked like they cared about me but were only interested in my bodily fluids. And then I guess while they were debating what drugs to give me to get me to sleep, I simply passed out. Again. So here's what's happening. My body has broken out in a nasty rash all over the place. Code 3 alert. No visitors. Anyone want to come near me practically has to wear a Hazmat suit. This infection brought to you courtesy of some antibiotic or other. It seems the stage we're in now is trying to unravel the Gordian knot of drugs that either individually or in combination have caused these wonderful adventures. They say they should have it under control in a few days. We're going to hugely simplify the sleep time meds. No point in a Louisville Slugger when a tap on the cranium with a #2 pencil will do the trick. I'm going into as much disgusting description here as I can, because I think it's more fun when it's not you streaking the walls.

Okay. it's a good sign I got through this. Didn't know if I could. Chemo brain, sad to say, as you can see, is the real deal.
Love you, appreciate your patience, and will check in soon.
xoxo
Cancer Man! And his Faithful Sidekick Chemo Boy!

On Jul 29, 2014, at 8:10 AM, Steven Bochco wrote:

Every day at City of Hope starts out with a lie. Some woman barges in pushing a vital signs cart. Good morning! How are you? Good, thanks. (First lie.) It's four o'clock in the morning. How good can it

ever be? Then you spend the rest of the day backing into the truth, which is basically this:
WHAT THE FUCK AM I DOING HERE? WHY AM I MORE TIRED WHEN I WAKE UP THAN WHEN I WENT TO BED? WHY AM I SO FUCKING CRANKY JUST TRYING TO ANSWER THE SAME QUESTION FOR THE NINE HUNDRED AND FIFTY SEVENTH TIME? "ANY PAIN RIGHT NOW?"
NO.
I COULD WRITE A PAPER ON THAT WORD. NO. A TWO LETTER WORD FOUND IN ALMOST EVERY DICTIONARY IN THE WORLD; THE OPPOSITE OF YES; USED TO GIVE A NEGATIVE RESPONSE, AS IN NO!

Is that a little cranky? Okay, yes.

But the truth is, I've get an upper body rash caused by one of these drugs or another that makes my torso look like an overcooked Domino's pizza. Oh, it's looking so much better, Mr. Bochco. Really? How would you like to go to the prom in a backless two strap look-ing like me? Even forgetting about the hair for a moment? Or the fact that you don't have tits.

So, all this is actually good news, because if I'm bellyaching about this shit it means:

1. My fever is gone.
2. I'm not hallucinating anymore (my torso really does look like an overcooked pizza. I'd take a picture and show you, but I don't think that's part of the deal you signed on for).
3. My white cells are on the move without that horrible drug helping them along.

The bad news is, I have one of those hospital infections. Very common, I'm told. They happen in hospitals, apparently. Which means now I have to take ANOTHER antibiotic. And no one can come in the room without gowns and gloves and masks. And I'm so toxic I can't leave my room. And then this lovely Indian doctor comes in surrounded by his pair of young proteges. I don't think together they're eleven years old. Oh, Mr. Bochco, my great grandparents used to watch Hill Street Blues. Thank you, doctors. I'm so pleased. Then the Indian doctor commences a dialogue not totally easy to understand when there's a mask between him and me, but the upshot being that I'm doing so well I may never go home. They're feeding me intravenously because the thought of food makes me want to puke, so that's an issue that's keeping me tethered to the pole. I'm halfway tempted to ask him what he thinks about the concept of changing the name of the Washington Redskins to the Washington Hebes. But I know that would be rude in the extremis and totally out of his area of expertise, so of course I don't do it, and before I know it, they've flapped out of the room leaving my nurses to clear up anything I may not have totally understood.

Later, the Big Boss, Dr. Steve Forman, swings by and I get the up to the moment news in English I can understand. I know I can understand him because who doesn't understand ANOTHER BONE MARROW TEST? MAYBE TOMORROW, MAYBE THE DAY AFTER?

Home by the weekend? Let's see: Pizza body? Gut infection? Not eating on his own? Bone marrow test? Nah.

So that's today, and I'm not lying when I tell you I feel better today than I did yesterday.

Stay tuned.

Love you all.

On Aug 5, 2014, at 7:34 PM, "Steven Bochco" wrote:

Dear Friends, All

I'm in full remission!! Home for these next two weeks before the next round.

Love to all,
Steven

35

The ride home from City Of Hope was overwhelmingly emotional. Being outside the confines of my small room after thirty
days was thrilling. The drive from Duarte to our home in Pacific
Palisades takes about an hour, and I loved every minute of it. I'd
been imprisoned in my hospital room for a month, and I felt like
a guy who'd just gotten a reprieve from the governor. An hour of
freeway time, usually a drag in Los Angeles, was like a drive in the
country. I was out of jail.

When we got home, I walked into the kitchen and out the door
to the back yard, and for the first time since I'd been diagnosed, I
broke into tears. I was so happy to be home. Shit, I was so happy to
be *alive*!

For the two weeks I was home, Dayna had to carefully police visitations. All our friends wanted to come by to say hello, and I wanted
to see them all. But I would get exhausted so quickly, that often I
could only socialize for half an hour before I had to get back into
bed. But day by day, I gained strength, put on some weight and, by
the time I was due to check back into City Of Hope, I was feeling a
lot better than when I'd left.

On the business side of things, we had yet to hear anything from
TNT regarding a pick-up for a second season. On the other hand,
priority wise, it wasn't that high on my list.

When I checked back into the hospital for what they called
a consolidation round of chemotherapy, my spirits – for the first

time, really – sagged. Being home for two weeks was like having a two-week summer vacation before having to go back to school. It wasn't enough. The good news was, I was only due to be in the hospital one week for this second round, and I cheered myself with the notion that I could do a week standing on my head. Which reminded me of the joke about the guy who dies and goes to hell, and he's met by the Devil himself, who tells him he has three options, one behind each door, for the rest of eternity. He opens the first door, and as far as the eye can see, there are people in loin clothes, shivering in the terrible cold, their skin blistered and blue, unable to find warmth. "No, no," the man says. "Close the door. I can't be in there. I hate the cold. I could never spend eternity in there." The devil opens the second door. Within, again as far as the eye can see, are men and women in impossibly hot weather, sweat dripping down over their blistered skin, screaming in agony as flames lick at their feet. "Shut the door," the man cries. "I can't spend eternity in there. It's worse than Florida in the summer." The devil says, "Okay, but this is the last option, and you're going to have to pick one." He opens the door, revealing a vast sea of humanity standing in shit up to their waists, drinking coffee. "Hmm," the guy says. "This isn't so bad. I could do this." "Are you sure?" the devil asks. "We're talking eternity, here." The guy nods and wades in, someone hands him a cup of coffee, and he's just about to take a sip when a booming voice comes over the P.A. system: "All right, People, coffee break's over. Back on your heads."

Sent by Steven Bochco on August 18, 2014

Dear Friends,

I'm baaaaack . . .

Checked into City of Hope for Round Two. Chemo starts tonight for six days, then I remain here for probably another couple of weeks of recovery, which means giving my white cells, platelets, hemoglobin, etc. a chance to regenerate. Hopefully, it won't take as long as it did last time, since my marrow is in much better shape (the joys of remission). Everyone wants to know why, if I'm in remission, they have to put me through another whole round of chemo. The answer is, I have no fucking idea.

The last two weeks at home were wonderful. You don't think about how much you love being home til you're gone for a month cooped up in a hospital room with tubes hanging out of your arm. (Although I have to admit, it's probably better than being on Death Row.) Everyone's emails and visits meant the world to me – I only wish I'd had the stamina to see more of you – and during the next several weeks (which I hope will be a little easier than the first go round), your collective good wishes and spirit will strengthen me daily – that, and the occasional vanilla ice cream enema.

For now, I have to watch a very exciting and informative video on the perils of falling. Falling is a big deal here at City of Hope. There are signs all over the room: "Call, Don't Fall. Llame No Se Caiga." (Which I assume means the same thing in a foreign language). They're very strict about the video. If you don't watch it, you don't get your tv privileges. So, gotta go now. The video awaits.

Love to all, more to come.

Steven

August 19, 2014

BACK ON THE BAG!

Dear Friends,
Well, I've been hooked up to the chemo bag for the last twelve hours or so, and will remain so for about another eighty-four. It's a ninety six-hour drip trip, followed by a different bag of chemo for

two last hours, and then I'm done with the chemo phase. The rest is observation and recovery. So far, I have not grown hair all over my body. My skin color has not turned green. I haven't grown a foot. And so far as I can tell, what's left of my muscles don't appear to have grown prodigiously, or at all, for that matter. In other words, I'm still me, I haven't turned into an outsized crime buster (Oh my God, it's him! HEBROID!!), and I'm not feeling too out of sorts. I guess this is a good start. I wouldn't be surprised, however, if over the next three days, this changes somewhat. Since most, or hopefully all of you, have never been through chemotherapy, here's a brief rundown on the cocktail of drugs they're continuously running through my body:

1) An all purpose goody called Etoposide, which is used to treat (take your pick) testicular, bladder, prostate, lung, stomach, and uterine cancers. Hodgkin's and non-Hodgkin's lymphoma, mycosis fungoides, Kaposi's sarcoma, Wilm's tumor (never even heard of that guy), rhabdomyosarcoma, Ewing's sarcoma, neuroblastoma, brain tumors.

2) Prednisone. An anti-inflammatory used to treat certain kinds of autoimmune diseases, skin conditions, a variety of cancers such as leukemia and multiple myeloma. Treats nausea and vomiting associated with some chemo drugs.

3) Vincristine. Used to treat acute leukemia, Hodgkin's, blah blah blah.

4) Cyclophosphamide. Used to treat about eighteen different types of cancers and, specifically in my case, as a conditioning regimen for bone marrow transplant.

5) Doxorubicin. Used for bladder, breast, head and neck, leukemia, liver, lung, lymphomamesothelioma, multiple myeloma, neuroblastoma, ovary (I lost mine years ago), pancreas prostate, sarcomas, stomach, testis (still have those), thyroid and uterus.

6) Plus a few more I won't bore you with, all designed to do some version of the same thing: KILL EVERYTHING IN SIGHT!!

Possible side effects (this is the fun part): You may bleed more easily. You may have more chance of getting an infection. Allergic reactions include rash; hives; itching; red, swollen blistered, or peeling skin with or without fever; wheezing; tightness in the chest or throat; trouble breathing or talking; unusual hoarseness (I GOT THAT!!); swelling of the mouth, face, lips, etc. (WOMEN PAY HUNDREDS OF THOUSANDS OF DOLLARS FOR THAT!!) throwing up blood that looks like coffee grounds; blood in urine; black, red, or tarry, tarry stools (to be sung); bleeding from the gums, etc.; headache, trouble focusing, memory problems (HA!); loss of appetite, loose stool, hair loss, and the ever popular vomiting.

How's breakfast so far?

The good news, twelve hours in, is I have no side effects. None. Though my friendly nurses tell me somewhere in the next three days, something might pop us. It's kind of like a grab bag. Stick your hand in there, you're gonna come out with something. Maybe I'll lose my uterus. That damn thing has been a pain in my ass for years, and what's it doing down there, anyway?

In conclusion, I wish for ALL of you, NONE of this. The good news is, I can do anything for three days, so I'm just focused on next Saturday morning, when the bags come off. Of course, there's aftermath, but I'll deal with after, after.

Love you all, I raise my glass to your health, and I'll be in touch soon.
Much love,
Remission Boy

August 21, 2014

Dear Friends,
I wish I could do better today. Diarrhea. High fever. Aches and pains. Fluctuating blood counts. Gut infections. Body rashes.

Hallucinations. Unfortunately, all I have to report today is boredom. For me, at least, this is a good thing. My biggest event of the day so far has been my morning dump. The chemo hasn't overly taxed me. My blood pressure is a tad high, my heart rate is quite low (must be all those marathons I'm running), my blood count numbers are dropping appropriately due to the chemo. I'm still bald. I don't have diarrhea. I can still spell diarrhea. I'm on my third bag of four bags of chemo, with a booster bag for a couple of hours behind that. Then a couple of days to recover, and if there are no surprises, I might be home earlier than originally thought. Fingers crossed. I'm told that the third round, the transplant round, has a lot more potential for drama, so hopefully these missives will get a lot more interesting. For now, however, at the risk of boring you all to death, I'm enjoying the lack of surprise day to day. Will keep you all posted, but for now, I may be forced to take a nap, then walk the halls, then read the New York Times, then have lunch, then read some more, take another walk with Ms. Dayna around the halls, then think about dinner, various drugs, a little TV, and another day at City of Hope slides by.

Love to all, have a great day, and don't give me a second thought right now. I'm not,
either.
Steven

From: Steven Bochco
Date: Friday, August 22, 2014
Subject: Pissing Race Horses

Dear Friends,

I checked into the City of Hope on Monday August 18th. Today is Friday the 22nd, my fifth day. In the five days I've been here, I have gained twenty pounds, primarily fluid, probably from the 160 mg of prednisone (steroids) daily. That much prednisone has made me look like Rosalind Russell before she exploded. (I hope she was

standing next to a burning building.) In addition to the fluid retention, my blood pressure shot up from a nice, leisurely 105/68 to this
morning's 150/137.

By this morning, I looked like Rosalind Russell without hair. Not a
pretty picture. Rosalind Russell WITH hair was probably not such
a pretty picture toward the end, as I recall. So anyway, I finally pre-
vailed upon the crack medical team here to insert a diuretic into
my hydration line, which they did. You remember the expression
"pissing like a race horse?" Well, no horse could've finished the race
if he was pissing like I'm now pissing. I literally am pissing every
four to five minutes. I can't stop laughing. I piss. I climb back into
bed. Two minutes later, I have to piss again. I'm getting my exercise
today just running back and forth to the can. By tonight, I will probably have lost at least ten pounds. I don't even want to think about
trying to sleep tonight. Maybe they should wrap me in a wet suit, or
give me a motorman's helper.

On a lighter note (Ha!) – I may be home Monday or Tuesday. I
have, miraculously, tolerated this round extremely well. No infections, no pain, no fatigue to speak of, just the afore mentioned fluid
retention, which is un-retenting as we speak. I have received my
transplant schedule, which will be a hell of a lot more rigorous than
this past week has been. But I'm beginning to see light at the end
of the tunnel, and if the light isn't a train, I'm going to get a good
result out of all of this.

(Excuse me. Gotta go pee again.)

I'm back. Lying around here these past five days and nights, I've been
struck by how our routines defines our lives. We expect to do certain
things at certain times. Daily, weekly, monthly, yearly. These things
we do are our unconscious clocks. Work. Exercise. Kids' birthdays.
Our birthdays. Vacations. Physicals. Weekend activities we take for
granted. Dinner dates with our pals. The sum and substance of our

lives. We don't really think about them, we just do them. And then something like this happens: an illness. Routines go out the window. Now it's doctors, needles, anxiety. Am I going to die from this (the ultimate disruption of my routine)? And while I don't think I'm going to – at least not yet, and not from this – I am struck by certain temporary disruptions to my routines that I will miss in the coming weeks and months. I suspect, for instance, that the annual Christmas party may have to be postponed. I'm guessing my docs won't want me standing around hugging and kissing two hundred people during flu and cold season while I'm still developing the immune system of a new baby (which, actually, is kind of what it is. With a brand new bone marrow and DNA, I'm going to have to get all those childhood shots all over again: measles, mumps, polio, all that shit). I'm guessing as well that our holiday trip to Hawaii may have to be postponed. It's scheduled immediately during the time they're supposed to be monitoring me two or three times a week during those first hundred days. I'm going to miss these routine and wonderful events this year (probably). On the other hand, I know how much more I'll enjoy them the next time around, not only as a reminder of what might have been, but as a reminder of the miracle of what is.

It's twelve-fifteen pm. I've pissed into a bottle about eight times in the last hour.
How's your morning been?

Love you all, hope to speak to all from home next week.

Remission AND Retention Boy.

From: Steven Bochco
Date: August 23, 2014

Hi Folks,
I'm done with the chemo for this round. Feel pretty good. Bored. Ready to get out of here. Will be home Monday, so they tell me, for

roughly four weeks, and then we start the last part of this journey on or about Sept. 28th, with the actual transplant On October 7th. Can't wait to be home and talk to you all. Have a great weekend, and much love to all and — again — my heartfelt thanks for all your good wishes.
Steven

From: Steven Bochco
Date: August 24, 2014

The Great Houdini has escaped a day early and is back at home! Love ya all!
Steven

36

After that second round, I came home for about five weeks before going back to the hospital for the grand finale, which would include intensive chemo – a carpet bombing, if you will – designed to completely eradicate (as in kill) my immune system prior to having my bone marrow transplant. The cumulative effect of the first two rounds of chemo was pretty debilitating, and while I was home gathering strength for the final leg of the journey, my TNT show, MURDER IN THE FIRST, was renewed for a second season. Candidly, I hadn't really given it much thought one way or the other, and to the extent that I thought about it at all, I was pretty resigned to the fact that we'd probably be cancelled. The news that we were renewed came as a pleasant surprise.

On an almost daily basis, friends came over to visit with me, and toward the end of my five-week hiatus, I actually went out to dinner a couple of times. I had put back a lot of the weight I'd lost, and other than the fact that I was bald as an egg – not a hair on my body – I was feeling more and more like my old self.

I knew that in a couple of weeks I'd be back at City Of Hope for another month, and that I would be in no shape to be involved in the second season's production for many months after that. And so I had my co-creator, Eric Lodal, who'd never run a show before, come to my house every day for over a week, during which time we talked about stories and character arcs for the coming season, as well as the myriad responsibilities that came along with running a show. I wasn't sure Eric was up to the task, but he was more than anxious to prove he could do it, and I had no choice but to hand over the reins to him and hope for the best.

Over the course of the next ten days or so, we got a lot of work done, and shortly after that I returned to City Of Hope on a three-day outpatient regimen of chemotherapy. I then checked into City Of Hope full time on October 3rd, 2014, for what would be the most difficult and scary thirty days of my life. My actual transplant was scheduled for October 7th, and for the four days leading up to it, I was chemoed to within an inch of my life. After the transplant, and for the next ten days, I was in virtual isolation, and with no immune system (my white cell count was zero), an infection could have killed me. The last thing on my mind was MURDER IN THE FIRST.

I was now in the last act of this drama and, candidly, I was scared as hell. Most of our lives are spent thinking about the future in big, giant hunks. Where do I want to be in five years? Ten years? How many children do I want to have? What kind of life can I afford to live? What are the things I need to accomplish to accommodate those goals? This is all long-term thinking. But as I approached my transplant, I was living my life on a day-to-day basis. I was acutely aware of how little long-term might be left to me. The feeling reminded me of a roll of toilet paper: the closer it gets to the end, the faster the paper spools out.

I was very lucky. I came through the first hundred days. I came through the first year.

I'm well into the second year of being cancer free. Most days I genuinely believe I've beaten this enemy. Occasionally, when I go back to City Of Hope every few months for a blood draw and a checkup, I get a little nervous. What if those little motherfuckers have crept back into my marrow?

I now maintain a full schedule of work. I'm never fatigued, Dayna and I travel and we enjoy life immensely. I'm not looking over my shoulder as much as I once might have. If you had known me before I was ill, and not seen me for a couple of years, I doubt you could tell anything had ever been amiss. But my bout with leukemia changed me, in many ways for the better and, I suppose, a few for the worse. The headline is I'm not really afraid of death anymore. I certainly don't want to die, but I don't live in fear of it. That in its self is liberating. The flip side is the crease in my brain that reminds me daily that I had a long, slow encounter with death and that death, as the old saying goes, remains undefeated.

I can't say I'm glad I got cancer. I'd rather have not. It probably would've been lots easier to just sail into my seventies and beyond, blissfully unaware that a safe might fall on my head. But you can't get the toothpaste back in the tube. It happened. I survived. All things considered, I'm the luckiest guy in the world.

From: Steven Bochco
Date: Oct 3, 2014

Dear Friends,
Checked into City of Hope a couple of hours ago. I'm all hooked up and being hydrated as we speak. In about four hours they'll have me suck on ice chips for an hour (apparently it helps prevent mouth sores from the chemo), then they'll blast me with a twenty-minute dose of chemo that will probably knock my socks off. We shall see. Then tomorrow, they start infusing me with anti-rejection drugs for two days. Then for two days after that I lie here with my thumb up my ass while my body adjusts to the meds, and my blood cell counts go to zero. (I keep asking about side effects and I keep getting the same answer. They don't know. Everyone's different. Maybe nothing, maybe mild, maybe deathly ill. I vote for maybe nothing.) Then, on Tuesday, I get the transplant.

I want to tell you all how grateful I am, and have been, for all your support. Your visits, your calls, and your emails have really made me feel loved and supported. I will keep you all apprised as to how it goes. I hope it's a piece of cake. I'll settle for surviving.

Love to you all, and more tomorrow.

Steven

From: Steven Bochco
Date: October 4, 2014

Dear Musees,
I've sailed past the chemo part of the program. Didn't finish til around midnight, but the actual process was quick and painless. Twenty minutes. By then they'd junked me up with Attivan, Xanax and Ambien, so I was, if not a happy camper, certainly a goofy one. Notwithstanding the half dozen interruptions during the night, I rested comfortably. Right after the chemo, they began the first of several anti-rejection infusions that will continue for today and, I think, tomorrow. I made the mistake of reading the literature they provided me about the drugs. Among the known (but not common) side effects is a rapid brain infection or virus that causes deteriorating vision, confusion, and (gulp) death. I suspect I will not be in the tiny subset of poor schmucks who suffer this consequence. All the obvious side effects (nausea, bone and muscle pain, stuff like that) they can anticipate and medicate for. It's that pesky death side effect that gets my attention. Most of the side effects, so I'm told, are kind of delayed. Anywhere from a couple of days to a week or more, as they load all this shit into my system. But the transplant itself is Tuesday, and that's the next goal. I'll deal with whatever comes my way after that. The docs here are quite pleased that my donor is such a young male. Apparently, young people have what are called telomeres, that are like tails at the end of their DNA strands (or something like that) and when you're young, the tails are long, and they get shorter with age. There's a body of thought that these telomeres are the secret to aging. So here I am, an old goat, but I'm going to have long telomeres. Watch out, ladies! Speaking of young ladies, Dayna the Dominatrix is in attendance, whip at the ready, urging

me to "eat something, dahling," and so far I've been compliant. This will change.

Anyway, I'm glad to report there have been no terrible surprises, so far. The only weird part is coming back. The first time in, I didn't know what to expect, and then I had complications, and the four weeks seemed to fly by. The second time I was in, it was only six days and it felt like four weeks. This time, I know I'm going to be in for that long, and that's kind of depressing. I'm working on ratcheting down my conscious boundaries to one nurse's shift at a time: twelve hours. And every twelve hours has specific chores; meds, vitals, blood draws, meals, corridor walks, sleep, reading, etc. And of course, once I get my new telomeres, who the hell knows what. The docs tell me that once the new marrow is in, it'll take anywhere from nine to fifteen days to start manufacturing cells, but that once it does, they'll come fast and furious. Sounds like a plan.

Anyway, I think that's about it for this report. Everything seems to be under control. Should that change, some guy in a black suit and a lugubrious manner will give you a call.

Much love to all,
Transplant Boy

From: Steven Bochco
Sent: Monday, October 06
Subject: side effects

Dear Friends,
I'm on so many drugs I can't keep track of them. What I can keep track of are the side effects. Dizziness. Nausea. Puking. Headaches. Grogginess. Flushing. Itching. And every time I try to close my eyes for a little snooze, the door opens. It's the physical therapist. The nutritionist. The plumber. The electrician. The nurse. The gal who takes my vitals. My case manager. It's the Grand Central Station of

hospitals. Among the tidbits of info I've collected however, is that my transplant arrives at twelve-thirty tonight (tomorrow morning, technically), and I'll probably get it infused around ten or eleven a.m. tomorrow. It's like a transfusion, about an hour. Very anti-climactic after all these chemo doses and rejection drugs, etc. I'll take a picture to send. Hopefully my silver wig will arrive in time.

I'm glad I got my email off to you all early yesterday, because the afternoon turned into a vomit and headache fest. It's amazing how quickly you can go from feeling good to feeling horrible. But that's the deal. They make you sick to make you well. Right now, I feel okay. No headache, no nausea. Various meds have taken care of those symptoms, leaving me nothing but groggy and a little dopey. Hence the lack of scintillation, email wise. I'm told by the nurses (who are by far the most well-informed of anyone) that my chemo side effects will last about a week, but after that I should start to feel better. The chemo dose was all of twenty minutes the night I got here, so it had to be a moth-erfucker to last this long. The anti-rejection drugs will be a con-stant companion for some time, at least six months, so I guess my body will get used to those. Hopefully, they just work on my new bone marrow. If I start to reject all my friends, something terrible has gone wrong.

Thank you again for all your email responses. They make me laugh, they touch me, and make me feel connected to you all. For those of you who are Jews, I hope you have properly atoned for your sins this past weekend, though fasting doesn't really seem like much of a sac-rifice. At least it wasn't for me. For those of you who are not of the Hebroid persuasion, I hope you have sinned sufficiently to make up for our rectitude. I promise you we'll catch up soon enough.

Much love to all, and more to come.
Transplant Boy (Soon to be Transplanted Boy)

From: Steven Bochco

Date Oct 7, 2014

Hi friends,
It's 12:45 pm, and they should be transplanting me within half an hour or so, so don't be surprised if I wind up in your back yard sticking up out of the ground.

Last night's meds had me hopping to the bathroom a couple of times an hour. Between the diarrhea and the water they're flushing through my kidneys, it was a lost night's sleep. Plus the immodium, the anti-nausea meds, and god knows what else, well you can imagine . . . several changes of underwear were the order of the night. Getting cured is humiliating.

Anyway, I've been pretty much snoozing all morning, but the time seems to finally be upon us. My charming nurse Mindy is prepping me as we speak, and then she'll go get the bag of gunk and we're off to the races. Stay tuned.

Fifteen minutes later. I'm transplanting as I speak. They gave me a bunch of Benadryl as a pre-med, so I'm pretty woozy. The attached picture is self-explanatory. I'll check in later. Love you all.
Steven

Steven

From: Steven Bochco
Date: Oct 8, 2014

Dear Friends and Family,
I was too goofed out on Benadryl while I was getting my transplant earlier today to really reflect on what an extraordinary experience this has been and continues to be. Imagine – twenty years ago this cancer would probably have been a death sentence. And today, while there are obviously no guarantees, there's a pretty good chance that

today's procedure will result in a total cure. I can't even begin to thank everybody who had a hand in this process. There's the 23yr old young man, who ever he is, who first and foremost gave me his healthy marrow. There are all these wonderful doctors and nurses at City Of Hope who collectively made this all happen. And there are all of you – friends and family alike – who have been there with me from day one with love, support, jokes, friendship and company. There is simply no price one can put on that kind of support system. And then there's the previously mentioned Dayna, for whom this had to have been a very difficult ordeal. More so for her in many ways, than for me. I'm sure there'll be some more bumps in the road ahead: infections, setbacks, whatever. But I feel like I'm in the home stretch and the crowd –you all – is urging me on.

So tomorrow, or the day after, I'll be back kvetching about life here at City of Hope, but for this one moment, let me take the opportunity to be a little sappy and thank you all for holding me up when I really needed it. I love you all.

Transplanted Boy

From: Steven Bochco
Date: Saturday, October 11, 2014
Subject: The Ass Tonsil (as my daughter calls it)

Dear Friends,
You didn't hear from me the last day or so because I was in the worst pain I've ever been in my life. Hemorrhoids. They were so big the doctors were selling tickets to see it. I've rolled spares with smaller balls. They were so painful I couldn't answer emails, watch TV, or read. Doctors and nurses would come in and say, "Can I see your hemorrhoids?" "Sure, what the fuck. Take a look." I'd roll over, pull down my pants and this is what I'd hear: "Oh. Wow. Geez. Holy . . . " Needless to say, in addition to being the worst, most painful day of my life, it was also the most humiliating. Oh well. I guess it beats

dying. Though there were a few hours yesterday when it was a close call. Needless, to say, today is better. I had one team of ass docs come in this morning who wanted to take a look. I said it won't be necessary. I feel much better. Took a shower, put some medication on it, I'd just as soon leave it be for now. They looked so disappointed, I said "Oh, alright, take a look." They were, of course, delighted. No one wants to be left out.

All kidding aside. Pain will fuck you up. It is sometimes so relentless it just saps your spirit. I can't remember the last time I was so depressed. And all these docs were saying, "oh yeah, that's not going away anytime soon. Two weeks, easy." I thought, no way. I cannot deal with this level of pain for two straight weeks. Honestly, I'd rather be dead. And hemorrhoids. Is there anything funnier to make jokes about? Is there anything more painful to be afflicted with? Not in my lifetime. Horrible. So that was my day yesterday, arguably the longest, crankiest day of my life. I didn't exactly bark at the nurses, but I wasn't kind. And they were so sweet. So such is life here at City of Hope. My white blood cell count is 0.1. That's about as low as it can get without me turning into a walking infection. Dayna keeps walking into my room without a mask. Is she trying to kill me? I suspect we share so many bodily fluids and germs and such in common that it doesn't really matter. The good news is, she's here. There was nothing she could do yesterday to ameliorate my pain (oh, what a big word for a nine-year old!) but she hung in there anyway. She reminded me of the joke about the horse sitting at the bar and the bartender says "why the long face?" It was one of those days.

So if yesterday was a ten on the pain scale, today is like a four. Very manageable. And hopefully by tomorrow it'll be down to somewhere around three or even two, and you won't be hearing any more about Stevie's humiliating hemorrhoids. Thanks for your patience, folks. I wish I could have had a more dramatic story to share with you. Fever spiking to 105! My diagnosis was wrong all along — it was really nothing worse that anemia! But, alas, nothing as exciting. Just . . . hemorrhoids. I'll never live it down.

Anyway, I love you all dearly. You're such good friends. Your jokes, your videos, your good wishes. David Kelley sent me a beautiful video of him catching a big ass salmon and releasing it to curry favor with the leukemia gods! Now that is a true sacrifice, for all you salmon fishermen out there.

Take care all, my spirits are higher today, and I'll be in communication with you tomorrow. Have a great weekend!

Love,
Steven

From: Steven Bochco
Date: Thu. Oct 16, 2014

So this is how it is for me: Dayna came in a little while ago and asked me how I'd slept. Good, I said. Me, too, she said. I took half an ambien, she said. Now the nurse comes in. Do you want to take a shower? No, I say. I pretty much just had a nap, everything's nice and neat. How about change your sheets? No, I say. They look ok. So the nurses leave. Dayna comes back into my room. Jesse's coming by today with Kate to give platelets. Cool, I say. But I thought they were coming tomorrow. Today, she says. Their email said tomorrow. Check it out, she says. So I do, and I'm right — the email does say tomorrow. It's dated two days ago. I've slept through — and lost — an entire day. No wonder they wanted to change my sheets. I have no recollection. No wonder I feel so cockeyed. No wonder it's taking me an hour to write this. No wonder it's getting darker and not brighter. They don't need to change my sheets. They oughta change my brain. So if you've been wondering why I haven't kept up (and I haven't), there's your reason: I'm cheating.

Ha!

Love you all. I'm sliding back into dementia. "bye bye . . . "
caiao . . . adios . . . fuggedaboooudit

From: Steven Bochco
Date: Oct 23, 2014, at 5:49 PM

Hi, Friends,

Sorry for not being regular (literally!)

When it came to the choice between involuntary expulsion of
bodily fluids and emails to you all, guess which one won out. I have
been pissing, vomiting (lot of dry heaving — almost as much fun)
and leading from the rear (apologies to the President) for about
three or four days. Very exhausting, time consuming, etc. Basically,
I feel like a hot shit tamale. And with all the drugs and fitful sleeping in between, I literally haven't been able to focus on a coherent
back and forth. So please accept my apology. The good news, at
least accordion to the docs, is that this is all pretty normal and on
track for getting out of here in about five to seven days. I'll believe
it when I see it, but that's the word. So, again, my apologies, but I
just haven't been in shape to snap out those emails. Hopefully, as I
pull outa this joint, I'll hit you with a few final missives. I can't wait
to get home (permanently) and start the process of normalizing my
life (which in English means DRINKING DRINKING DRINKING.)
Love you all for your patience. Cant wait to see you all again.

Caio.
Steven

From: Steven Bochco
Date: Saturday, October 25, 2014
Subject: Have a menu

Dear Friends,
I've had an interesting couple of days here in dear old Duarte. On the menu du jour has been, in no particular order:
Runaway bowel movements
Hemorrhoids
Dry heaves
Queasy stomach
Loss of appetite
Dry mouth in the extreme
Terrible facial flushing and itching
Headache
Fatigue
Aching bones
Flying snot
. . . and a partridge in a pear tree . . . .

I and my anonymous donor's marrow have been host to all of the above in the last couple of days. It's been a delight. But this is the road home, so I'm on it, and hopefully in the home stretch. The culprit in this case is a drug that stimulates white blood cell manufacture. It's called Nupogen, but that's really just its nom de plume. Its real name is Lie Still While I Kick The Shit Out of You. Which I did and it did. But it works. My white cell count went from 0.7 to 5.9 in 24 hours. I paid for every fucking point of it. Retail. That said, I'm feeling somewhat better today, and my personal target is to be home by Halloween. I don't need a costume this year. I AM the costume. As nasty as this process is, I try to keep my eye on the goal: get through it, get home, and never ever come back. As in, cured. Your emails of love and support, even when I didn't have the energy to respond, have meant the world to me, and I thank you all from the heart of my bottom, beat up as it is. Hopefully by late next week you'll be hearing from me out of the airier confines of home. Until then, much love to you all.

Steven

From: Steven Bochco
Date: Oct 27, 2014

It ain't over til it's over, but there's a rumor loose in the land that I'm coming home on Wednesday. Keep all appropriate digits crossed!

Love to all,
(The newly reconstructed) Steven

From: Steven Bochco
Date: Wednesday, October 29, 2014
Subject: Journey's end

I'm home!!

Love you all!

37

If there's a single theme that organizes the narrative of this book, it's survival – physically, and artistically. Life is finite, as are television careers, as new generations of viewers, artists and executives dominate the business. And arguably, that's how it should be, although there's a wonderful story about the great writer and director, Billy Wilder, who went to a meeting with some young film executive who said, "So, Mr. Wilder, tell me about yourself." And Billy Wilder said, "You first."

I've had a remarkable career. Hill Street Blues changed my life, certainly, but it also changed television forever. I like to think Hill Street dragged television, kicking and screaming, into the eighties and nineties and beyond. I, along with a whole generation of writers, came of age, paving the way for St. Elsewhere, L.A. Law, E.R., and a host of other great shows. I thought NYPD Blue might have a similar effect in terms of language, nudity, and adult themes but, alas, it was not to be. NYPD Blue existed in its own separate little niche. The Bochco Niche, if you will, but it never translated, as Hill Street had, into the broader television landscape. I think, however, that NYPD Blue showed the way for cable drama. You could argue that The Sopranos might not have existed if not for NYPD Blue.

In regard to my career, whatever its impact on the culture of our time was, I hope it's not over yet. But I certainly accept that I'm not able to work at the level I did twenty-five years ago, when I was routinely running two, and sometimes three shows, at a time.

When I went into the hospital, I had to face the real possibility that I might die. And facing it squarely altered my world-view in many ways. It simplified things for me. It wasn't just that I couldn't do what I used to do. I no longer wanted to. I didn't have the emotional stamina to fight the battles I used to fight on a daily basis. And things that might have excited me fifteen or twenty years ago didn't anymore. Everything I think about doing in television, I now think about through the prism of time. When I was thirty-five, time was in my budget. At seventy-two, not so much. It's not that it's my enemy, exactly, but if I'm going to commit to doing something for television, I have to think in terms of devoting a minimum of two years of my life to it. And two years of my life today means a hell of a lot more to me than it did thirty years ago. And so, for all those reasons, I make the joke, which is actually not a joke at all, that I *used* to be Steven Bochco. I'm not that person anymore. That person was afraid of death. That person wanted to cram everything in before the clock ran out. Those months in the hospital – my battle with leukemia – helped me come to terms with my mortality.

Here's a fact: If, say, in 1997, when I was running NYPD BLUE, BROOKLYN SOUTH, and MURDER ONE simultaneously, I got hit by a bus, there'd be a short period of boo-hooing, and after a couple of days, someone else would be sitting in my chair.

Life goes on, as it must and should.

38

Somewhere during the second half of October while still in the hospital – I had survived the first critical ten days, and my body was starting to manufacture new blood cells – I received the outline for the first episode of the new season. MURDER IN THE FIRST is essentially a single-story, twelve-episode mystery and, as such, the first episode is absolutely critical in that it sets in motion an entire season's story line.

I read the outline and didn't like it, and wrote Eric a long, very detailed critique with all my notes included. I received an angry, defensive reply. In truth, there wasn't much I could do. I wasn't there (in more ways than one). I wasn't running the show. I hadn't hired the staff. All I could do was register my opinions and hope for the best.

Over the next several weeks, the full impact of my treatment – months of chemo, the destruction of my immune system, the bone marrow transplant, and the myriad side effects of all the drugs they were pumping into me – really took its physical toll. By the time I finally came home, the day before Halloween, I had lost more than thirty pounds, I didn't have a hair on my body, and I was as weak as a kitten. I looked – and felt – like an Auschwitz survivor. I could barely make it up the flight of stairs to my bedroom. It was as close as I ever came, during the entire ordeal, to feeling like I might actually die.

But time is a remarkable medicine.

Over the course of the next four months, I regained more than half my lost weight, I started working out again, I started feeling stronger, and I was even starting to sprout a little hair.

When I was a kid, my parents traditionally held a Christmas Eve open house party every year, which was a legacy I continued into my adult years. It was a blow out event. I loved it. Because we had no money, my mother would wait until Christmas Eve day, then give me five dollars to go down the street to Zingone Brothers' market and negotiate the purchase of a Christmas tree which would otherwise, the next day, be consigned to the trash heap. No one was going to buy a Christmas tree on Christmas day.

One year, I was probably ten or eleven, my mom gave me the five bucks, and I went down to Zingone Brothers, prepared to do business. But every remaining tree in their sparse allotment was totally pathetic. Amongst the few remaining trees, there wasn't a one worth buying. One tree would look great on one side, but the other side would look like it had been run through a thresher. Another tree looked the same: great on one side, nearly bald on the other.

With my five bucks in hand, and only a few hours to go before I could get the tree in our apartment in time to decorate it, I seized upon a great idea: take *two* trees, shave off the bad sides, and wire them together at the trunks, resulting in *one* great looking tree. The Zingone brothers bought into the concept (for five bucks), and within forty-five minutes, for my five-dollar investment, I had a gorgeous, bushy, Christmas tree. It was so thick you couldn't see the trunk, let alone the bailing wire. I dragged that bad boy up the street and wrestled it into our apartment, and we got it fully decorated about five minutes before the first guests arrived. Whew!

Normally, in the tradition I'd been raised with, Dayna and I would throw a huge Christmas party every year. It was a party I looked forward to all year long – a chance to see many friends we didn't socialize with regularly. Along with our really close friends and work colleagues, the guest list was usually around two hundred, and it was always a wonderfully festive event. But this year, my doctor forbade me to have the party. I was still too fragile, and I was supposed to avoid crowds. And particularly, at Christmas time, in the prime of flu season, my doctor didn't want me standing in the doorway hugging two hundred people. He was right. No big party.

But since my birthday is mid-December, and he didn't forbid me to have a *little* party, we invited about thirty people for a catered Christmas dinner. It was a special celebration for me, as I hadn't been sure I'd be alive for my 71st birthday.

Sometime in mid-March, Dayna kicked me out of the house. "Go back to work," she said. "It's time." And she was right. I certainly felt strong enough to contribute, and I had been so out of the loop for so long that I really wanted to go back and get into the swing of things.

Our production offices were at 20th Century Fox, and having spent twenty years of my life there, it felt wonderful to be back on the lot. A second homecoming. But when I found our offices, I immediately knew something was wrong. I grew up in something of a dysfunctional family, and I had learned from the time I was a little kid how to read the mood of a room in a matter of seconds. And the mood in our offices was terrible. People literally were hiding out in their offices, their heads down. Caroline James, our producer, told me that assistants were quitting like rats jumping off a ship.

I found Eric and said I didn't want to rock the boat, but the company was exactly six shows into a twelve-show season and, problematically, there was no story or script for episodes seven, eight, nine, or ten. I suggested we shut the company down for two weeks in order to regroup, catch up on scripts, and think our way to the end of the season. Eric said no. He promised he would write episode seven within the week, and said everything was going to be fine.

I sat in on the writers' meetings for the next several days and realized that things were a total mess. The writers were demoralized, Eric was overriding everyone, and I realized that things couldn't continue this way.

There was an emergent pattern of behavior that was profoundly undermining the morale of the company, both on the stage and in the production offices.

I confronted him in his office and reiterated my belief that we should shut the company down for two weeks. He angrily accused me of plotting to get rid of him. I had to laugh. I said, "I spent the last six months fighting for my life. You think all I wanted to do was lie around thinking of ways to get rid of you in the middle of a desperately dysfunctional season? Are you out of your fucking mind?"

He said, by way of defense, that TNT loved his work. I reminded him that TNT was in business with me, not him, and if I told them we were shutting down for two weeks, they'd back me. He said, "Well, if you're not happy with what I'm doing, I'll quit."

I said, "Never threaten to quit unless you're ready to walk out the door. I've turned shows around before under similar circumstances, and I'll do it again if I have to. And if by some chance I can't" – and here I channeled Grant Tinker – "then I'll call TNT and we'll just bag the whole enterprise. It's only a TV show." I went on to tell him that there's a book on all of us – mine was fifty years old, his was fifty *minutes* old – and I wasn't going to let his little book ruin my big book, of which I was very proud, and which had taken me fifty years to earn. And with that, I walked out of his office.

So much for Welcome Home.

The following week the company was due to be in San Francisco for exterior shooting, and by Monday morning, Eric had cooled his jets considerably. I'm guessing he'd called Joe Cohen, his agent, who'd told him to stop being a baby. Eric said he was driving up to San Francisco to keep an eye on the company, and while there would write the next script. I asked him why, when he only had a week, he was going to waste two days behind the wheel of his car driving up there, but he assured me it would be fine. I shrugged. "Okay," I said. "If you insist."

I spent the next three days in productive meetings with our writers, but on Friday morning I got a bunch of very troubling reports about Eric's behavior in San Francisco. Enough was enough. I called TNT, since technically Eric was under contract to them, and I basically said either fire him or I was going to pull my company out of our co-production arrangement. According to reports, Eric's behavior was sufficiently erratic to put both TNT and my company in legal jeopardy should any number of aggrieved employees decide to sue.

TNT fired him that weekend.

On Monday morning, I drove onto the lot. I was sure word of the firing had already reached the company, as they'd had a six--thirty a.m. work call. As I pulled into our parking area, I had to laugh. The first thing I saw was another producer's car, already parked in Eric's space.

It was a perfect metaphor. Boo hoo. Life goes on.

That same Monday morning, as promised, there was a script for episode seven on everyone's desk, written by Eric Lodal. It was garbage. I suspected, but couldn't prove, that he didn't actually write it, but had essentially farmed it out to a young staff writer he'd taken with him to San Francisco. Nevertheless, I could feel the cloud lifting. People were smiling again. We faced a formidable task in undoing the damage that had been wrought, but I sensed everyone's willingness to get the job done. With Eric gone, our remaining writers, Jonathan Abrahams and Daniele Nathanson, and I, quickly revised the story elements of episode seven, and Jonathan and Daniele set about rewriting the episode. They did a hell of a job. Three days later, what had been a sow's ear had been transformed into a silk purse, and Reggie Hudlin – a close friend and a wonderful director, with an unflappable personality – directed it masterfully.

In the ensuing days, Jonathan and Daniele and I essentially reverse-engineered the rest of the season, by which I mean, we figured out the ending to our several season-long story lines, then worked our way backwards to episode eight. After having done a superb rewrite of episode seven, Jonathan and Daniele wrote episodes eight and nine, and finally, eleven and twelve. I threw up a flare for help, and Alison Cross came to our rescue, coming in and writing a terrific episode ten for us.

All in all, I believe the second half of the season was significantly better than the first half, due primarily to the great talent and good spirit of Jonathan, Daniele, and Alison, and to my skills not just in story construction, but in creating an environment that empowers people to dig deep.

The key to being a good show runner is in understanding that yours is not a solo act. You're the choral master, and it's your job to see that all the voices in the chorus are heard. If you become so big headed that you stifle people's enthusiasm for their work, then you've shot yourself in the foot. And if you shoot yourself in the foot, the entire organism is wounded. If Eric ever gets a chance to run a show again, I hope he's learned some important lessons about being right-sized.

39

After my wrestling match with leukemia, there's not a day that goes by that I don't think of my mortality. One day you're healthy, and the next day you're not. It happens that fast. One moment you're driving the I-5 to Napa, happy as a clam, and the next, you've suddenly suffered a heart attack. Any way you slice it, it's a life-altering event. And then, just when you're congratulating yourself for having dodged a bullet, here comes the howitzer: leukemia.

Now, when I wake up every morning (that in itself is a blessing), I look in the mirror. An old man stares back at me. The stubble on my face is grayish. My hair, which has mostly grown back, though much softer and silkier than it used to be, is sleep-mussed. I have bags under my eyes. (I think they're filled with the wine I drank the night before.)

I have aches and pains. Hell, I had them before I was sick, so why do I feel them differently now? Is it because any given ache or pain could be a recurrence of cancer?

I purposely stayed away from the Internet when I was sick. I didn't want to read about what my odds were. About four months ago, I finally got the courage to ask Dr. Forman what they were when I entered City Of Hope. He said he thought they were around sixty-forty. Slightly better than fifty-fifty. I had been told, by another doctor who'd actually gone through her own bone marrow transplant, that my realistic two-year odds of survival were more like eighty-twenty, against. Whatever the actual odds were, they weren't great. If they were roughly fifty-fifty, we'd be talking about a coin flip. Would you want to gamble your life on a coin flip? I have too vivid an imagination as it is. I know how quickly life can be snatched from you. In fact, Dr. Forman recently said, in a televised interview, that my chances of surviving without a bone marrow transplant were close to zero, a piece of information he didn't bother to pass along to me at the time – and I'm glad he didn't.

I have friends in their late eighties in perfect health. I envy them their genes, their longevity. But I also know that even if you live to be a hundred (not a particular ambition of mine, I might add), old age will marginalize you. I saw it happen to my mother, who lived with us until her death at 92. And I saw it again with my mother-in-law, who lived to be 97. Neither of them, toward the end of their lives, had any particular passion for living.

My mother died in the apartment above our garage eight years ago. Hers had been a quick, violent death. She had an aortic aneurysm that burst, and she was gone in seconds. When my mother was eighty-eight or eighty-nine, Dayna and I had been married about four years. Mom lived alone, after her second husband had died, in a condominium apartment on Wilshire Boulevard, in Westwood. It was a lovely apartment. But one night, an irate son tried to kill his father in an apartment several floors above hers, and the ensuing gunfire punctured a main water line, flooding three floors of apartments below. The building's management had to move every one the tenants out of those apartments in order to repair the water damage. I suggested to my mom that she should stay with us for the month or six weeks the repairs would require, rather than live in the hotel room the building was willing to provide for her.

Mom took us up on the offer and, when she was ready to move back into her apartment, and at Dayna's urging, I suggested to Mom that she might like to move into the apartment above our garage. It was actually a lovely space: a large living room, a kitchenette, a spacious bedroom, and a fully equipped bathroom. It was a hell of a lot nicer than most of the apartments I had lived in as a young man.

To my surprise, my mom jumped at the chance. It wasn't long before she had moved in with us, and we sold her apartment (I had bought it under Jesse's name), for about what I'd originally paid for it.

About a year later, after mom had moved in with us, I convinced her to go to my doctor, Bob Koblin, for a complete checkup. I wasn't in love with her doctor, who I'd known for many years, but my mom was loyal to a fault. Loyalty aside, I didn't think her doctor was doing right by her, and I insisted that she at least go see Bob. She finally did, and the results of myriad testing revealed that she had a significant aortic aneurysm. Bob confided the results in me, and asked me how I wanted to handle it. I had lots of questions, and Bob had answers: her aneurysm was not a candidate for surgery. She'd already had too many for a woman her age. Bob said the operation itself would kill her.

My options were to tell her, and do nothing, or not tell her, and take it day by day. Obviously, at least to me, I chose the latter. If there's nothing you can do to fix the fact that you have a time bomb inside of you, why know about it in the first place?

I asked Bob how long she had. A week? A month? A year? He didn't know the answer. It could be a week, he said, or even a year, maye two.

Every morning, after Dayna and I read the newspaper, I'd bring it up to my mom's apartment, never knowing what I was going to find. About a year and a half later, she grew ill, and we had to put her in the hospital for about ten days. When she came home, she was weak, but anxious for our weekly family dinner on Sundays. I ordered a bunch of pizzas (her favorite food) and salad, all the kids came over, and we had a festive meal. She had her entire family around her. Well, not her *entire* family. My sister, her husband Alan, and nephew Robbie weren't there. Joanna hadn't talked to me, or our mom for quite some time, dating back to when I had refused yet another opportunity to help them out financially and suggested, instead, that they sell their house, which was worth a considerable amount of money. When Joanna, pissed off at me, complained to our mom, mom looked at her and said, "You know, he's not your father." And that was that. Now both of us were in Joanna's doghouse.

After our pizza dinner, mom said goodnight to everyone and retired to her apartment. I had put a baby monitor up there when she came home from the hospital so she could call out to me in the middle of the night if she needed anything.

At three o'clock the next morning, I heard a shout over the baby monitor and rushed from my bedroom up to her apartment. It couldn't have taken more than ten or twelve seconds. She was crosswise on her bed, convulsing, eyes rolled back in her head.

Dayna proceeded to administer CPR while I called 911, but it was obviously too late. Her aortic aneurysm had probably exploded, killing her instantly.

Dayna's mom had lived for many years in an assisted living facility in La Jolla, but as her legs became less and less dependable, both Dayna and I felt we ought to have her close. My mom's apartment waited, empty, replete with elevator chair. She had died a couple of years earlier.

I think the last several years of Helen's life were among her most pleasant. She loved the apartment, considerably larger than the one she'd lived in for years, and its airiness, and she fed the birds and squirrels on her balcony porch every day.

When my mother-in-law started to fail, we put her in hospice care, at home. There was nothing that could be done for her, no further medical interventions. She was simply going out of the picture, old age being the culprit. When it became clear that she was going to die within days, Dayna and I called her brother, who came down for the deathwatch from his home in Berkeley, California. The only thing wrong with the picture was, she wouldn't die. This tough, stubborn old bitch wasn't giving up. We had a nurse for her around the clock care. Our beloved housekeeper, Irma, wouldn't go home. She loved Helen, and wasn't going to abandon her in her final hours.

After about two weeks, Helen was in a morphine-induced semi-coma, but she still wouldn't die. One Friday night, Dayna and I had a dinner date with friends, but she said she wasn't up to going, so I went myself. When I got home, around ten o'clock at night, I went up to Helen's room and asked the nurse and Irma how she was doing. The same, they said. Nothing had changed. I asked where Dayna and her brother David were. Irma said they'd gone to bed.

I sat down on the side of Helen's bed, and I put my hand behind her head and lifted her up to me. I whispered in her ear. "Helen. I love you. We all love you. You can go. It's all right." Helen drew one more breath, and died in my arms. You know the old saying about the hair on the back of your neck standing up? Well, the hair on the back of my neck stood up.

Somehow, she had heard me. I had given her what she needed: permission to die.

Helen had been a Mash nurse in WWII and had liberated the camp at Mounthausen, Germany. It had been a harrowing time in her life that she really never talked about. But when the mortuary guys arrived with their gurney to collect her body several hours later, they saw pictures on her wall of her as a young woman, quite beautiful, in uniform. They asked us if Helen had been in the armed forces, and we told them yes, she had. They asked us if we would like them to drape an American flag over her body bag. We said yes. When they removed her body, draped with that flag, Dayna and I cried. It was one of the most moving moments of my life.

Nearly forty years earlier, my father had died at home, in a coma, gasping his last breaths of air before he finally quit this world. What I learned, and re-learned from both my parents' deaths and from Dayna's mother's death, was that life often hangs by a thread. But it's a remarkably sturdy thread, thin as it may be, and no one dies as quickly as we think they will – or should. The life force in all of us is unbelievably strong. We don't give it up easily. But in the end, as we have earlier noted, no one gets out alive.

And so, as I celebrate my good fortune and my new lease on life, I also appreciate how tenuous it is. I'm not far enough past my recent brush with death to take life for granted. I doubt I ever will again. My dad died at seventy-seven. I used to think I would easily surpass his life span. I always had this belief that I would live to be ninety-three. It was very specific. Ninety-three. Now, at the age of seventy-two, I hope I live as long as he did.

When I was diagnosed with leukemia, I had lunch with David Milch and told him what was going on. From that day forward, I never heard from him again. Not once. Not a note, not a phone call, nothing. Ten months later, I called him. I said, "You mother-fucker – if I didn't call you, I'd be dead by the time you called me." I wasn't angry. I knew David too well. After all these years, I even thought I had come to understand him to a degree. We made a lunch date, and on the appointed day, I walked him through what had been the crucible that was my life for the last ten months. And the good news was, I was now fine. It was probably a little premature from my doctor's point of view, but as far as I was concerned – *am* concerned – I was cured.

David admitted to me that when I told him I had leukemia, he thought I was going to die, and, in his head, he said goodbye to me. And then he said, "I was afraid to talk to you after that." Here was this crazed, brilliant, volatile man I'd been close to and loved for over thirty years, and he was too scared to look at me – at death – in the eye.

When we took leave of each other's company, David embraced me. "We did good work together, didn't we?" he said. I agreed that we certainly had. And then he said, "I love you." I told him I loved him, as well. He turned away then, saying, "I can't look at you. If I look at you I'll cry."

40

As I write this book, or memoir, or whatever you want to call it, I have just passed the one-year anniversary of my bone marrow transplant. There's an anonymous donor out there somewhere, who saved my life. Literally. Saved my life. I'm hoping that, assuming my donor is willing, I'll find out who he is and where he is, so that I may find him and hug him and personally thank him for what he's given me. I don't know why he volunteered to be an anonymous donor. Did he lose someone close to him to leukemia? Was it plain old altruism? Who knows? But I am eternally grateful to him for saving my life.

That said, if I die tomorrow (check the obits, just to see), I will go to my Eternal Nothingness knowing that I've lived a good and generous life, and that I've left my ex-wife, my children, my wife and my step-son in good shape. Barring unforeseen catastrophes, they should all be well taken care of, at least financially.

I have no illusions about, nor interest in, governing from the grave. I don't have an elaborately constructed will that controls every penny doled out to my heirs after my death. I trust them all to look after their own interests. And if they don't, well . . . what the fuck . . . I'm dead and gone, and they're on their own.

Because I'm not religious, and because I believe that when you die you are truly gone, I also believe that your only legacy lies in the memory that your loved ones have of you. And once they pass on, you are, irrevocably, mort.

I don't wish to leave you with a sense that I'm morbid, though in fact, I've always had a somewhat morbid imagination. Actually, I'm a great optimist. I believe in life. I believe in the spirit of community. I believe that love is curative. And in the end, when there is no longer a cure in sight, I believe that love is palliative, and that it makes our end of life as important as the prime of our life has been.

I savor every day, I love my wife a little more intensely, I'm consciously grateful for the bounty life has given me and, all in all, I have to admit that the experience of being ill taught me some incredibly valuable lessons about trust, about selflessness, and about the countless ways in which human beings devote themselves to the care and welfare of others. There is no way I'll ever be able to repay all those people who contributed to my care when I was ill. I hope I can simply pay it forward as life's opportunities allow.

When I was debating whether to write this book, I asked myself several questions. First and foremost, would the book be interesting to a general readership, that is, a non-television industry audience? My experience has been that most industry-centric books have an extremely limited readership. Most people's interest in film and television is cursory. Gossip sells, but it has a limited use-by date. Another consideration, equally as important, was how much would this book mean to me personally? I realized how little of my own father's life I really knew about when he died – how little of it he'd communicated to me in a coherent, chronological way. I was in my early thirties when he died, and I promised myself that when my time came, I'd make sure my kids knew who their dad was, in the most literal sense.

Also, I was worried that the life I've lived wasn't nearly as interesting as the life I've experienced, by which I mean that my career has yielded more interesting anecdotes than my childhood or private life has.

My life has been, relatively speaking, pretty uneventful. I had a more-or-less normal childhood. I went to college. I married young. I divorced young. I had two children with my second wife, to whom I was married twenty-seven years before we finally divorced. I re-married a few years later to the love of my life, and have happily remained so for the last sixteen years. Certainly I feel like I've lived a full and eventful life, but really no more so than most folks. I lived through the cultural revolution of the 60's and 70's, but I can't say I really experienced them. I was married, I was a young father, and I was completely career oriented. I never experienced the creative/ artistic drug-induced "epiphany" that so many of my friends and peers did. In fact, I never did drugs at all. I was, like so many of my generation, deeply opposed to the Vietnam War, and marched in several protest demonstrations. Fortunately, a history of childhood asthma kept me out of the service so that even war didn't really disrupt the orderly progression of my life. I remember – and was amazed and thrilled by – the great technological achievements of my era: from Sputnik and men walking on the moon, to the evolution of mass communication epitomized by the cell phone and the Internet. But the world of personal adventure – not so much.

And so I've come to the conclusion that it's my career that has defined my life rather than the opposite, and to the extent that people are interested in reading about me, an emphasis on my fifty years in the television industry, and the hundreds, if not thousands, of people I've met both in front of, and behind the camera, is of greater interest than the details of my early life – though some of the details of my later life are of significant consequence, and have played an important part in this narrative.

Lastly, I wanted to write a book about my career primarily because of my children, now in their productive middle age, neither of whom gave a shit what I was doing while they were busy growing up.

This would be an appropriate moment to speak of my grown, adult children. I love them very much. They're very different people. Melissa, the oldest, was always complicated. By the time she was seven years old, I knew she had severe problems. We lived in Santa Monica at the time, and I had moved my mother and father to Los Angeles. My dad had been diagnosed with prostate cancer, and in those days, there wasn't much by way of treatment. Besides, by the time he'd been diagnosed, his cancer had probably metastasized. In any event, I wanted my parents in L.A. so we could all be together, and one evening, Melissa said to me, in front of her grandmother, that she hated herself. This was a frightening statement coming from a small child. My mother poo-pooed it. "You don't mean that, Melissa."

"Yes, I do," she said, quite seriously. And I believed her. I also thought that this wasn't a normal way for a child to think of herself. So Barbara and I took Melissa to a well thought of child psychiatrist in Brentwood. He was a kind, empathetic doctor, but in the mid-seventies, there just wasn't much beyond basic play therapy in dealing with troubled kids. It was only years later that Melissa was diagnosed with genuine, clinical conditions such as depression, obsessive-compulsive disorders, and the like. She had drawn a terrible genetic hand of cards to play, and it wasn't until she was much older that she was able to access the kinds of drugs that could successfully deal with her collection of psychological and clinical disorders.

There is no worse feeling in the world, as a parent, than knowing you have an unhappy, disturbed child, and not knowing how to deal with it.

One night when Melissa was thirteen, Barbara and Jesse and I went to my mother's apartment for dinner. (My father had long since died.) Melissa said she wasn't feeling well and didn't want to go. It was an early evening, being Sunday, and when we returned home and pulled into the driveway, the first thing I saw was that Barbara's car – a Jaguar – was missing. In a panic, we ran into the house. Melissa was gone. I told Barbara to call the police, and I would drive around the neighborhood seeing if I could find her. I was terrified.

I pulled my car out of the driveway and sped down our street, my heart racing. Out of the corner of my eye, I spotted a car bumping slowly along in the opposite direction, its headlights off, with two flat tires. It was Melissa, behind the wheel, wide-eyed. She had punctured both right side tires when she backed out of the driveway and ran over the lawn sprinklers.

I made a U-turn and followed her as she bounced over the curb and into our driveway. As she emerged from the driver's side, and her friend Evie exited the passenger side, I started screaming at Melissa. You stole your mother's car! You don't even know how to drive! You scared the shit out of us! You could've killed yourself! She ran into the house, hysterical, screaming at me as if *I* had done something wrong, and in full thirteen-year-old prima donna mode, hollered back at me, "I give and I give and I give, and all you do is take!" before running into her room and slamming the door.

Welcome to parenthood.

To her credit, Melissa, as an adult, has fully taken charge of her life, personally, psychologically, and medically. She is the mother of a wonderful son, Wes, and she and her husband Joel are sensational parents. Whatever lousy genetic traits she inherited from her parents seem to have skipped a generation, and Wes, at the age of twelve, is a terrific, well-adjusted boy.

Jesse was the opposite of Melissa. He was sweet, had a beautiful disposition, and was the most empathetic person I've ever known, a recognizable trait even when he was a little boy. Mothers on our street in Santa Monica would marvel at Jesse's concern for their welfare. It was genuine, and it endeared him to all who met him.

His mother, Barbara, and I would have terrible fights. We always tried to shield our kids from our own conflicts, but children are the most observant little buggers on the planet. They see and hear and intuit everything in regard to their parents.

When I was little, my parents were always fighting. There's nothing more frightening to a little kid than seeing two furious grown--ups going at it. I remember once, my parents had a horrendous fight. It was wintertime, and I couldn't have been more than eight years old. The fight scared the crap out of me, especially when my father, in a rage, threw on his coat and hat and stalked out of our apartment. I thought he was leaving forever. I chased him out into the hallway outside our apartment, where he was waiting for the elevator. When he saw the stricken look on my face, he said to me, "I'll be back. I promise. I'm just going for a walk."

When Jesse was about eight years old, Barbara and I got into a terrible row. We were in the bathroom off our bedroom. I have no recollection what the fight was about, but I was so angry, I threw a soda can against the wall and stormed out of the room. As I passed through the bedroom, I saw Jesse, lying on the floor, pretending to watch TV, big tears streaming down his face. Without even thinking, I said, "I'll be back. I promise. I'm just going for a walk."

It wasn't until I was blocks away, trying to walk off my anger, that I remembered my own exact experience with my father when I was Jesse's age. It chilled me to the bone.

So Jesse grew up perceiving his role in life as the family peacemaker. He was, and is today, a true peacemaker. And don't kid yourself. That's a tough role to play in life.

But in certain regards, the apple doesn't fall far from the tree. In 1983, when Jesse was eight years old, we needed a young actor to play Frank and Fay Furillo's young son in Hill Street Blues. I asked Jesse if he'd like the part. He thought a moment, and shook his head no. I told him he'd get paid for doing it. He perked up. "How much?" he asked. I told him that he'd probably get paid about four hundred and fifty dollars for half a day's work. Suddenly he changed his tune: "I'll do it," he said.

When the day arrived for his scene, his mom took him to work, and he performed a scene in which he's being driven to school by his mom and dad, when Furillo gets into a fender bender with the car in front of him. The trunk of the car Furillo rear-ended flies open, revealing contraband, and suddenly Furillo has to make an arrest right there in front of his ex-wife and son. Jesse's one line was, "Nice bust, Dad!"

When his work was completed, Barbara told Jesse that our Teamster captain, Dave, was going to drive him home. Jesse started to cry. Barbara reassured him. He knew Dave, and our housekeeper would be waiting at home for him. He cried harder. Concerned, Barbara asked him what was the matter. He held out his hand. "Where's my money?" he cried.

In the fall of 1997, about six months after Barbara and I separated, Jesse called me from college. He was attending the San Francisco Art Institute, and he and his long-term girlfriend had just broken up. He was so emotionally distraught that he didn't feel he could stay at the same school they were both attending. I told him to come home, and I would put him to work on Brooklyn South, the CBS police drama we were producing at the time. When he started working, at the lowest rung on the ladder as a P.A. (production assistant), I put him under other people's wings. I didn't want him to feel that, as the boss's son, he had any particular privilege. And, as it had been in childhood, everyone fell in love with him. Jesse learned the business from the ground up. He did everything: getting lunches, learning post production, working his way up to associate producing, and producing. When we made Philly, our last show under our Paramount deal, our supervising producer and director, Rick Wallace, a very special friend ever since our days on Hill Street and L.A. Law, mentored Jesse and was the first producer to give him a chance to direct. By this time, Jesse had been working for me for about five years. He'd always wanted to direct, and Rick Wallace gave him his break, shepherding him through the process. I'd had my own mentors in life, so I knew what Rick meant to Jesse.

When Philly was cancelled, Jesse came to work on NYPD Blue as a producer, and Mark Tinker (Grant Tinker's son, and a long time friend), who was a co-executive producer on the show, became another directing mentor for Jesse, and over the remaining life of the show, Jesse wound up directing about a dozen episodes. Dennis Franz, who played the iconic Sipowicz, came to see me after Jesse directed his first episode, and told me – unsolicited – that Jesse was one of the best directors that had ever worked on the show.

Today, Jesse is a seasoned pro. He's directed over fifty episodes of television, and executive-produced several of my series (Raising The Bar, Murder In The First). He's a talented man and, more importantly, a good man.

In the kid department, I'm batting a thousand. This book is for Mel and Jesse, and Dayna's son, my stepson, Sean Flanagan.

Sean was ten when my wife Dayna and I got married. He was a painfully introverted boy who had a very hard time connecting with adults. He was only happy when he was hanging with his band of compatriots, Huey Rosenberg, Tyler Newell, and Matt Kramer. They were an inseparable quartet all through grade school and high school. By the time Sean was in his late teens, like many boys his age, he was seriously enamored of alcohol and weed. (What else is new? – my son, Jesse, as I would only half-joke, majored in marijuana in college.)

But in spite of those bumps in the road, Sean went to USC, majored in Critical Studies in their Film School, and today works at CAA (Creative Artists Agency, arguably the most powerful talent agency in the world). He's a wonderful young man with a great future ahead of him, and at the risk of embarrassing him, I have to reveal that I also love him very much.

I've probably not even scratched the surface of how I feel about my kids, but I've written this book for them, so that they can know about the events of my life. Maybe my grandchildren will someday be interested, as well. Melissa and Jesse are in their forties now, with lives of their own that I am not a part of. But whether they know it or not, my life has been inspired by them, as their lives will be inspired by their children.

One of these days, I'll go out of the picture, hopefully later rather than sooner. But I will have left a legacy, such as it is. I believe I have contributed something to the world, and I hope that contribution outlasts me. But regardless, as long as my children and grandchildren are alive, I will be, too.

Lastly: For every pain in the ass I've worked with in the course of my fifty years in television, I've also had the pleasure of working with literally hundreds, if not thousands, of great executives, technicians, crafts people, and artists, both in front of, and behind the camera, without whom my career could not have existed. These are dedicated, hard working people with tremendous spirit and creativity, who have made incalculable contributions to the shows I've created over the years.

I am forever in their debt.

I savor every day, I love my wife a little more intensely, I'm consciously grateful for the bounty life has given me and, all in all, I have to admit that the experience of being ill taught me some incredibly valuable lessons about trust, about selflessness, and about the countless ways in which human beings devote themselves to the care and welfare of others. There is no way I'll ever be able to repay all those people who contributed to my care when I was ill. I hope I can simply pay it forward as life's opportunities allow.

THE END

EPILOGUE

Earlier this spring, I was invited to meet my bone marrow donor on the morning of May 6, 2016. Every year, City Of Hope celebrates its donors and recipients with a press conference at which two recipients get to publicly meet their donors for the first time. After the press conference and a few local news interviews, there's an entertainment-filled barbecue for the (literally) thousands of donors and recipients in attendance. (Over the course of the last forty years, City Of Hope has performed over thirteen thousand bone marrow transplants.)

I'd never been to the event before. I knew nothing about my donor other than the fact that at the time of my transplant he was a twenty-three year old American male. I didn't know how the meeting would take place, or whether I would be called upon to say a few words. I decided to simply show up with my wife and let the experience unfold.

On the day of the event, with storm clouds threatening overhead, we arrived at City Of Hope at eight-thirty a.m. and were segregated in a small conference room prior to the event. I'd been urged to invite any friends and family who might like to attend, and so my daughter and son – she with her spouse, he with his significant other – came, along with my stepson and his girlfriend, as well as ten of our closest friends.

After milling about for almost an hour, it was show time. My family and friends were escorted outside where the press conference was to be held, and suddenly my wife and I, along with the other recipient – a fifteen-year old teenager and his parents – were alone. The teenager, Dominick, had written a little speech and actually had a small Lucite trophy engraved with the words, "To my hero." I, on the other hand, like a schmuck, had nothing.

After about ten minutes, our small group was escorted downstairs to the press conference, where we were hidden from view as Dr. Steve Forman welcomed everyone.

Suddenly, I was nervous as well as excited. I had been anticipating this moment for twenty months. Who was he? Where did he live? What motivated his incredible generosity toward a complete stranger?

Dr. Forman first introduced Dominick to his donor and, being hidden behind the screen, I couldn't really make out all the young man's words of thanks. And then, finally, it was my turn. Dr. Forman introduced me, and as I looked out at the audience, I located all of my friends and family. These were the people whose love and support had sustained me during my long illness and recovery, and I felt an enormous wave of gratitude towards them.

Now the moment arrived: Dr. Forman introduced my donor, a young man named Jon Kayne, who appeared from behind a screen on the opposite side of the stage. It's hard to explain the rush of feelings I instantaneously felt for him: kinship, affection, gratitude, and a weird sense of familiarity. He had a broad smile on his face. I instinctively put my arms around him, hugged him tight, and whispered, "Thank you for saving my life."

I said a few words expressing my thanks to City Of Hope, to friends and family, and to my donor, then Jon said a few words that revealed him to be part of a close-knit family who were all in attendance, and the ceremony was done. I knew the day would be long and filled with interviews and celebratory events, and so I'd arranged through City Of Hope to host a dinner the following night for Jon and his family, consisting of his younger brother, his parents, and three living grandparents.

All of Dayna's and my parents were long gone, and I think both of us felt that the Kaynes were like a new, second family for us.

We lingered over our Saturday night dinner for three hours, trading histories, telling stories, and getting to know one another. There wasn't an awkward moment throughout.

Jon is twenty-five, works at a tech start-up in San Francisco, and his family lives in New Jersey. Jon was thirteen when he lost his much-loved grandpa to brain cancer, and one of his two grandmothers was herself dealing with chronic, though treatable, leukemia. Jon had signed up to be a donor when he was twenty-one. His living grandfather was a wonderful gentleman of 85, and his other grandmother was a sharp-witted pistol of a woman, aged 92, who I instantly fell in love with.

I know the Kayne family, and particularly Jon, will be in my heart and in my life for as long as I live, and I will always be there for Jon if he ever needs me.

In the words of another, unrelated, Cain (Herman – remember him?), Jon will be, forever more, my "brother from another mother."

ACKNOWLEDGMENTS

Sometime in mid-March of 2015, I was having dinner with my good friend, the well-known sports broadcaster and personality, Rich Eisen. I mentioned to Rich that I was thinking of writing a book about my illness and recovery, wrapped around a memoir of my fifty years in the television industry. Since I was never a meticulous record keeper, I said I was thinking of hiring a journalist to interview me off and on for several weeks so that the recorded transcript would function as something of a verbal diary that I could then begin to shape into a coherent narrative of my career. Without hesitation, Rich said, "I'll do it." I pointed out to Rich that a) I didn't want to impose on our friendship, and b) he had a day job – in addition to his NFL chores, he hosted a daily three-hour radio/TV show. He wasn't exactly a man of leisure. But he insisted he wanted to do it. "I'm a journalist," he said. "That's what I do." So I said, "Let's sleep on it. And when we're sober tomorrow, let's talk." (We'd had our fair share of vino by then.)

The next morning Rich emailed me that he still wanted to do it, so I agreed. For the next three months or so, he came to my office every Thursday afternoon after he'd finished his show and, with a little recorder running continuously, grilled me about my career from day one. As I started to answer his questions, dozens of anecdotes and memories flooded back, and I realized that there was no way I could have compiled all those recollections without Rich's digging and prodding. And so it's no exaggeration to say that

I couldn't have written this book without his invaluable friendship and assistance.

Thank you, Rich.

I'd also like to thank those friends and colleagues of mine who read early drafts and gave me their input. David Kelley, Billy Finkelstein, Alison Cross, my dear pal and long time agent Fred Specktor, his talented son Matthew, Amazon's David Blum, and CAA's Cait Hoyt all were enormously helpful in sharing their suggestions and insights with me. I actually listened to them all, and I think this book is better for it.

Lastly, and most lovingly, I want to thank my wife, Dayna, always my first and most astute critic, who saw me through the hardest time of my life as my wife, my advocate, and my very best friend. I believe what we went though together was harder on her than on me, but I never saw her cry, or despair, throughout the entire ordeal. I am eternally grateful to her.

Made in the USA
Lexington, KY
16 August 2016